MORE POWER FOR
YOUR CHURCH

By WILLARD A. PLEUTHNER

BUILDING UP YOUR CONGREGATION

MORE POWER FOR YOUR CHURCH

MORE POWER FOR YOUR CHURCH

Proven Plans and Projects

By WILLARD AUGUSTUS PLEUTHNER

With the Assistance of
Several Hundred Clergy and Church Workers
of Different Denominations and Faiths

FARRAR, STRAUS AND YOUNG   NEW YORK

The author's royalties from this book
will be given to
interfaith religious charities.

Limited First Edition

DEDICATION

*This second book is dedicated
to our all-girl Pleuthner family* . . .
KATHARINE, KIT, ANNE *and* LYNNE.
*Each one of them, especially Katharine (Mrs.
Pleuthner) is unusually understanding of the
author. Of them I can paraphrase that old truth,
to read:* "An Understanding Family is more to
be desired than gold . . . yea, much fine gold."

INTRODUCTION

WHILE READING THIS WONDERFUL BOOK by Willard Pleuthner, the thought came to me how excited and disturbed we would be if the Communists should issue such a suggestion manual for their workers. We would be aware that they were employing the highest efficiency in their activities, and as a result would make tremendous gains.

Mr. Pleuthner's book will render such service to the Christian cause. It is the most amazing compilation of practical and workable suggestions that I have ever seen. The author has drawn ideas from churches everywhere. Seemingly every project, idea, or plan that has ever worked anywhere is described in these pages. I firmly believe that, if ministers and laymen study and apply the ideas herein contained, any church (and I mean any church anywhere) can increase attendance, improve its financial position, make a greater impact on the community, and attain the supreme objective of winning people to Jesus Christ.

I am going to give a copy to each of my official associates in the Marble Collegiate Church. I shall ask each man to study the methods of church activities outlined and bring his suggestions for our consideration. We shall use the volume as a source of fresh, new ideas.

I am enthusiastic about the practical value of the book. May I underscore the author's emphasis that this is not merely a "reading" book. Rather, it is a working manual. It is not only to read and meditate on, but it is a direct action, new idea source book.

Efficiency methods work in business and in every other phase of human activity. Why not in the church, as well? The Bible says, "The Kingdom of God is within you," meaning among other things that within us are enough creative capacities to meet all our problems and enter into the richness of God's blessings. This book will stimulate our own creative powers and give a great impetus to the whole Christian movement.

I, for one, want to give thanks that the Church can produce such consecrated, enthusiastic, and efficient laymen as Willard A. Pleuthner. We owe him a great debt of gratitude for his book, *More Power for Your Church*.

Norman Vincent Peale

CONTENTS

*"Do the work of an evangelist, make
full proof of thy ministry"* 2 Ti. 4:5

"Faith Without Works Is Dead"

"All things come of thee, and of thine own have we given thee" 1 Chron. 29:14

"Build thee more temples oh my soul"

"We declare unto you glad tidings" Acts 13:32

HOW THE CLERGY AND LAY
WORKERS PLANNED
THIS BOOK

THE AUTHOR of this book is just one of the hundreds of thousands of laymen who are trying in their individual ways to help the church grow in influence and spiritual life and to bring the ministries of the church to more people. Only in his case "his way" consisted of using and spreading proven plans for greater church attendance . . . support, and church power. After working with clergy and lay groups for years, he put the tested ideas into a book, entitled *Building Up Your Congregation* (now in its third edition). The response was overwhelming and the author is very humble as a result. He was prevailed upon by friends and readers of various church literature to write another book. This book is no substitute for Christian faith, worship and daily consecrated living. "The greatest power of the church is the power of the Holy Spirit. You shall be filled with power after the Holy Spirit is come to you."

As was stated in the opening part of the first book, the author does not consider that all the various plans and activities are in the least way a substitute for one's going to church. They are no substitute for any of the activities of the clergy. These servants of God put in too long hours, do too many things to ever have a substitute.

Also it must be repeated and made clear that the author . . . the collaborators . . . and all who helped write both books do not believe that mere numbers ever take the place of depth of spiritual life. Churches and churchgoers must grow in grace and prayer as well as grow in numbers in order to have more power for their great work.

The interest in and use of *Building Up Your Congregation* continued to grow long after it was published. Clergy and lay workers urged the author to write another book on church activities. Therefore he decided to have the potential readers decide the answer by sending out the following letter and questionnaire.

March, 1952

Dear Friend of *Building Up Your Congregation:*

You have shown such an encouraging interest in *Building Up Your Congregation* that I thought you should have a confidential report on its status and future possibilities. The publishers and book sellers are finishing up the third edition. The publishers have been sent suggested revisions and additions for the fourth edition. These are mostly on the jacket . . . to make it more interesting and more informative.

Because it is still the best seller in its field, fourteen interfaith charities have been enjoying the proceeds from the author's royalties. Best of all, all three faiths are reading and using the book. Press and broadcast support continues and is most sincerely appreciated. In fact, it is the genuine interest of the magazines . . . religious publications . . . and broadcasting people that has resulted in their giving *Building Up Your Congregation* more reviews than any religious "how-to" book in publishing history.

In response to requests, the author has given over 40 talks at churches . . . convocations . . . conventions . . . communion breakfasts . . . schools . . . men's clubs . . . women's clubs . . . broadcasts . . . and, most important of all, theological seminaries. Four of his magazine articles have been accepted. One, published in *Pulpit*

Digest magazine, was the best-read piece of editorial material in spreading the type of tested building ideas contained in *Building Up Your Congregation.*

Mail keeps coming in from all over the United States and even foreign countries. It tells how churches used the ideas and have secured attendance or membership gains from 25 to 50 percent. Some churches have used the direct mail letters and reported that as a result they have been able to pay off their mortgages.

Just last week Colonel Paul Rusch, founder and leader of KEEP, the Christian Community Center in Kiyosato, Japan, asked for permission to arrange for a Japanese edition of *Building Up Your Congregation.* He believes that many of the ideas can be successfully adapted to the growing Christianizing of our friendly ally in Asia.

This news is interesting and encouraging. Yet it carries with it a deep responsibility for the author. He has been asked time and time again, "When are you going to write another book and give us more help in building up our churches? . . . in getting more people exposed to Christ's way of life?" The author, who is not a professional writer, is really embarrassed by all this.

Since *Building Up Your Congregation* was published, he has accumulated and developed a lot of ideas and material on church work, church growth, etc. In fact, it's more than enough for a second book on ways to help church workers and the clergy. Yet the writer does not want to use it just to publish another book for publishing's sake. If a book of additional ideas would be really helpful, he is willing to devote his weekends and spare time to get it out. But if it would be only "another book," he'd rather devote his off-hours to writing religious articles.

To make this decision the author would like the opinion of a few of the leading people in the field; therefore, the attached questionnaire is being sent to you and a small number of other key leaders in church work and in publishing. Your thoughts will be the deciding factor in this situation. To help analyze the feelings of the

"Friends of Building Up Your Congregation," the attached questionnaire has been developed. It will be grand if you would help me by filling it out . . . answering it frankly . . . and mailing it back to me in the enclosed stamped envelope.

The first and key question on the questionnaire read as follows and was answered as follows:

Here is how I really feel about your writing a second book on church promotional ideas:
(Please check one)
( ) Forget about it; there are already enough books on the subject
( ) I don't know whether or not it would be worth while
( ) Yes, I believe a second plan and idea book would be helpful

With this encouragement the author continued to write up the material he had been gathering for his second book. Yet to recheck his sights and make sure *More Power to Your Church* contained only material of most help to the clergy and church worker, he worked with Farrar, Straus and Young to send out a second survey. This second questionnaire is reproduced on the following pages.

What was the list to whom this questionnaire was sent? It consisted of 1600 clergymen plus 1600 lay workers in the following denominations: Methodist, National Baptist, Southern Baptist, Jewish Congregations, Episcopal Church, Presbyterian Church of the USA, United Lutheran, Disciples of Christ, Lutheran Missouri Synod, American Baptist, Congregational, Greek Orthodox Church, Evangelical United Brethren, Evangelical Lutheran Church of America, American Lutheran Church, African Methodist Episcopal, African Methodist Episcopal Zion Church, Presbyterian Church in the US, Church of God in Christ, Evangelican and

HELP WANTED FROM KEY PEOPLE

TO MAKE "MORE POWER FOR YOUR CHURCH" MORE USEFUL

CONFIDENTIAL QUESTIONNAIRE TO FIND OUT WHAT IDEAS, PLANS, PROJECTS, AND INFORMATION

WILL BE MOST HELPFUL TO CLERGY AND LAYMEN WHO WORK FOR THE GOOD LORD

1. I am checking with an "X" those chapters in the following list which I believe
   will be most important and most helpful.

( ) Getting More People Into Church

(X) Greater Inspiration Through More
    Congregation-Participation

(X) Turning Man-Power into Church Power

( ) Programs of--and for--Laymen's Groups

( ) Improving the Services Through
    Every-Member Surveys

(X) Projects for Teen-Age Groups

(X) Projects for Younger Marrieds

(X) Projects for Men's Clubs

( ) Projects for Active Old Timers

(X) Using Your Religion in Economic,
    Social and Political Situations

( ) How You Gave to Your Denomination
    in 1951

( ) New and Different Ways of Raising Money

( ) A Proved Direct Mail Plan for Annual
    Canvass

(X) Detailed training and Plan for Every-
    Member Canvass

( ) Give Your Church a "Garden for God"

(X) Inexpensive Ways to Make Your Church
    More Inspiring

( ) How to Give Your Church a "Lords Day Look"

(X) Let Your Church Grow by Starting Its Own
    Mission

(X) Public Relations for Your Church

( ) Quotations for Church Bulletins

(X) Better Christians Through More and Better
    Reading

2. In my opinion, it would be helpful to have a chapter on the following subject or
   subjects:

   Ways of Interdenominational Community Cooperation

- -

3. RESPONDENT'S HELP TO READERS OF "MORE POWER FOR YOUR CHURCH"

   If you have any tested idea or plan which would come under the above classifications
   or chapter headings, would you do the book's potential readers a great big favor?
   Would you kindly highlight the facts or details of your idea on this questionnaire?
   The writer can't tell you how much this will be appreciated. Naturally, all of
   these contributions of ideas that appear in the book will be identified with your
   work and your church. Just write their description here (continue on next page).

_____
_____
_____
_____

- -

4. To be of most help to the reader (clerical or lay), I believe the book "More Power For Your Church," should include the following information, data, or sources in addition to the above group of ideas:

_____
_____
_____

- -

5. Miscellaneous Comments_____

_____
_____
_____
_____
_____
_____
_____
_____
_____
_____

- -

My Name Is____ Rev. Ernest Tonsing

Title____ Pastor, First Lutheran (ULCA), President Kansas Synod

In Organization_____

At Address____ 434 Harrison St., Topeka, Kansas

Reformed Church, Reformed Church in America, Church of Jesus Christ of Latter-Day Saints.

The names were selected and given to the author by key executives in the various denominational headquarters. For example, Dr. Ralph Stoody, head of the Information Service for the Methodist Church, was the willing cooperator for that great body of Christians.

In addition, questionnaires were sent to: deans of theological seminaries . . . leading women church workers . . . religious writers and broadcasters . . . and members of the Religious Pilgrimage to Washington.

The response to that field survey was overwhelming. It filled the author with humility. For this book is not his book. In reality it should not carry his name as the author. "More Power for Your Church" is actually the "Church Worker's Book." It was planned by and written by hundreds of clergy and lay people. They in their local . . . national . . . and mission activities are bringing More Power to Their Churches. All the author did was to bring you, the reader, the benefit of all the experiences, the proved plans and projects of these co-authors. May God bless every one of you who made this book possible.

ACKNOWLEDGMENTS

THE MOST PLEASANT PART of any book for the author to write is that chapter which publicly acknowledges those grand, cooperative people who have helped him in so many ways. Thus, he counts his blessings *in print*.

If this author mentioned all their names and listed their individual help, it would constitute a separate book of gratitude. Unfortunately, space limitations only permit him to highlight his acknowledgments. If you have helped, and your name is not mentioned here, nor listed under the idea you sent in (and perhaps not used in this volume), will you please forgive the author, who has far from a perfect memory. Remember the good Lord knows you helped, and that's more important than any printed credit.

In giving thanks, the author would like to start with those influences which made this book possible. First, he thanks God for being born of Christian parents and reared in a Christian home. The influence of my Mother and Father is a joy to recall. Yet, I am ashamed that I do not remember it often enough and sometimes fail to give my parents' Christian home life enough credit for influencing my entire life.

This chapter enables me to publicly acknowledge the tremendous influence of several outstanding clergymen.

I have been blessed by being guided and inspired by the following ministers of the Gospel: The late Samuel Van Vranken Holmes, D.D., Bishop Austin Pardue, Dr. Albert G. Butzer, and my present spiritual advisor, the Rev. Walter McNeely. Walter also edits my writings. All these clergymen have helped me more than I can ever say.

During these years of week-end writing, my faithful secretary, Evelyn Strittmatter, has been a "Girl Friday" without whom I could not operate. Her memory of names, places, situations is unequaled. Her devout and constant interest in my church work and religious writing will always be a pleasant memory to recall. No man ever had a better secretary than Evelyn.

Closely associated with me have been two towers of strength, advice, and cooperation . . . Lee Bristol, Jr., and Frederick H. Sontag. Without these two collaborators, this book would never have been as complete or as helpful. Lee worked on several chapters and developed the title, *More Power for Your Church*. A devout churchman, author, hymn writer, and Lay Reader, Lee Bristol, Jr., is a leader in the new generation of younger men who give so much strength and enthusiasm to the church.

Frederick H. Sontag has been my eyes . . . ears . . . critic . . . and my slave driver on this entire project. Frederick has helped me collect the right material and made sure that the best material was included. His knowledge of outstanding leaders, sound and courageous public relations strategy, and varied publications is a blessing enjoyed by few public relations directors. Month after month his guiding hand has touched more phases of this book than space permits listing.

In the professional field, I am deeply indebted to Lester Doniger for publication counsel, to Mrs. Peggy K. Rogers of the Presbyterian Board of Missions for information, to Dorothea Seeber and Eleanor Tomb for typing and collating.

As in the case of *Building Up Your Congregation*,

several of my associates at Batten, Barton, Durstine & Osborn helped on this second book. These include Carl Spier, Walter Tibbals, Tom Bull, Robley Feland, Charles Brower and Bruce Barton.

To Grace Huntley Pugh goes an orchid for her jacket design and the illustrations for chapter headings. A devout church woman, Grace mixed sincere Christianity with her brushes and paints.

The following publications cooperated by allowing the author to reprint in this book chapters he had written previously for their magazines: *Pulpit Digest, Guideposts, Christian Herald, Episcopal Churchnews,* and *This Week* magazine. Other publications from whom the author borrowed much quotable material, reports figures, etc., are: *Time, Newsweek, The Living Church, The City Church, American* magazine, *Pathfinder, Redbook, Presbyterian Life, Lifetime Living, The Witness, New Republic, Coronet, Pulpit Digest* and the *New York Times.*

The author's head bows in thanks to his co-authors: Bishop Wilburn C. Campbell, Bishop Richard S. M. Emrich, Bishop G. Bromley Oxnam, Dr. Albert Butzer, Dr. Louis Finkelstein, Dr. Norman Vincent Peale, Don Bolles, Joseph E. Boyle, Alfred Politz, Walter H. Rockenstein, Charles Schmitz and Roger Whitman.

And last but not least, the author thanks God for the hundreds of men and women who answered the questionnaire, who suggested material, who contributed their proven plans, and projects. Each and every one of you is a true witness for God which inspires others to seek and live a worshipful life.

ONE WAY TO GET *MORE* RESULTS FROM THE CHAPTERS

J UDGED BY ITS SHAPE . . . form . . . and usage, this is just another book, well-printed and promoted by our fine publishers, Farrar, Straus and Young. Yet if you consider it just another book to be read, discussed and put on the shelf, you, the author and publisher have *all* wasted their time. And in addition you have wasted your money, which had better been put in Sunday's collection plate.

This collection of ideas is presented in book form, because that is the established and handiest way to broadcast them to many important people. But *More Power for Your Church* is more than a book! It is a church promotion manual, or ecclesiastical sales tool, or religious advertising plan-book, or guide to tested and proved evangelism. You can call it by any of these descriptions or any one you choose to make up. But it is not just a book to read!

This book was planned and written by hundreds of clergy and church workers for *you to use*. People from *all* faiths, *all* denominations and from *all* parts of the country worked almost two years to bring you proven plans and projects which can be used, adapted and put to work *right away*, in *your* own congregation. Right in your own hands *now* is the cream of the methods other churches and congregations used to increase attendance, increase membership—increase financial support . . . to widen the congregation's usefulness and to deepen the spiritual life of the members. So for God's sake do not finish reading this book and put it on the shelf without doing something about its ideas, plans, projects and suggestions. They are to be tried out, and used by you and your religious associates.

If you are a layman, pass this book on to your clergyman after you have read it and written in your observations and conclusions in the "First Steps to Take" report form found on page xvii. If you are a clergyman, read the book, then write your ideas on a separate sheet of paper, then route the book to five, or all the members of your top or most active official board. Ask each of them to fill out the "First Steps to Take" report.

You may wonder why we suggest the clergyman write his observations on a separate sheet of paper. That is to prevent his conclusions from unduly influencing the thoughts of his board, who will read the book *after* he does. This helps the lay workers to think more independently. This independence can assure their thoughts and conclusions being of more help to the clergyman and the church, than if they were tempted to "yes" or "Amen" the minister because his observations had been already filled out on the "First Steps" report.

After all those requested have read the book and filled out the "First Steps," then the clergyman calls a meeting, tells them of the votes for "First Steps," and *all* votes are tabulated.

Next, plans are developed to carry out those 5 to 10 plans or projects which received the most votes. This automatically assures their receiving the most support. The above proved plan of action was developed for our first book, *Building Up Your Congregation*, by the Reverend Robert Anthony of the North Presbyterian Church in Flushing, Long Island. In fact, he secured three copies of the book for his board members, to speed up the reading, and to hasten the carrying out of the most popular and practical plans.

After you have made your survey of the board's combined opinion (excellent congregation-participation), appoint some one person, or a committee of not *more than three* to be responsible for initiating action on the approved plans and projects. They are to *assign* and *sell* various church organizations on carrying out the ideas. And don't forget that the organizations should be *sold* on the ideas instead of just being told.

You have undoubtedly noticed the extra wide margins at the left and right sides of most pages. These are "working margins" designed for you to use as a place to make notes, regarding ways of carrying out the plans and projects on the page. So please use these wide margins to write in: notes for action . . . things to do . . . people to see . . . other things to read and notice.

As we said at the opening of the chapter, this is not just another book. It is a printed collection of proved plans to use. . . . So do use this like a textbook . . . a notebook . . . a plan book. Write on it or in it wherever the writing will be helpful and stimulate action.

In this book there are plenty of projects for individuals. That is where you and I come in. They concern you, as an individual, or some other member of the church. He may not even be a so-called "regular attender." Yet when you or the committee ask him to assume a special assignment you will be surprised how this can and will increase his interest in the church, and his appearance in the pews.

So let's all do two things after we've read the book. *First,* write out our opinion of the first five projects to start. *Second,* plan what *individual* projects we will take on, and then *start them at once.* Let's not talk about all the things that need doing and then bemoan the delays. You and I can and should start *now.*

"Remember it's better to light one candle (our own) than course the darkness."

MORE POWER FOR
YOUR CHURCH

Opening Prayer

OUR FATHER, we thank Thee for Thy Blessed Son, Jesus Christ Our Lord, and for the Church He established. Illumine our minds as we seek effective ways to declare the Christian message and to offer the fellowship of the Christian church to our neighbors. Grant that we may be receptive to every creative proposal that will enable us to bring Thy love to the people.

May we realize anew the opportunity and the obligation that lie in the command "Preach the Gospel to every creature." Thus the means that bring the masses to our services are sacred because they are also the means by which the unsearchable riches of Christ are brought to the individual. Let us share our experiences in the ministries of music, prayer, preachings and Holy Silence to the end that all may share the blessings of Thy Love. We pray that this volume may be of help to every reader.

Amen.

Bishop G. Bromley Oxnam

Chapter 1

GETTING MORE PEOPLE
INTO CHURCH

THIS IS A FAVORITE chapter of the author for two reasons. First, its caption was almost selected as the title for the first book, instead of *Building Up Your Congregation*. Second, this chapter was voted one of the seven most helpful, most needed chapters, in the advance survey made among 2600 clergymen and lay workers.

While no sincere church worker is interested in *just* getting people into church, this is usually one of the necessary *first steps* in exposing more people to religion. Most of us must get into church first *before* religion can become a bigger influence in our lives.

There are so many proven ways to get more people into church or into synagogue that we hardly know where to begin. This desirable and needed form of evangelism is being accomplished week after week by inspired individuals, organized groups, committees, councils of churches, and individual hard-working clergymen. The religious press carries a continuous flow of proven plans for building up a congregation. Any lay worker who is charged with the responsibility or accepts God's challenge to bring in more worshipers should subscribe to his own denominational publication, plus a general interdenominational magazine like *Christian Herald, Christian Century, National Council Outlook* or *Protestant World*. The religious publications offer a rich storehouse of ideas and plans which can be adapted to your church . . . your neighborhood . . . and your city.

In this chapter we will describe some of the plans which have brought more people into houses of worship. You'll find other proven ideas in other chapters of this book. The problem is not to find them, but to *start* using them in your house of worship.

1. George E. Sweazey, secretary of the *New Life Advance*, points out that "in Spain Protestant churches are not allowed to advertise—not even by a notice on the door saying, 'Preaching at 11 a.m.' No cross or symbol is allowed to mark their meeting place. They are utterly dependent upon person-to-person advertising. Because there is no other way, the church members are extraordinarily zealous in giving invitations to the church, and Spanish Protestant Church membership is said to have doubled or tripled in the past twelve years."

2. When Dr. Joseph Sizoo went to the famous New York Avenue Church in Washington the congregation had become very small. They stayed small until some of the men of the church had an informal meeting to discuss the problem. Each man promised to tell several others during the week about the splendid services at the church. By this method alone, within a year the congregation had more than doubled.

3. A prominent leader said: "The great discovery about evangelism in our generation is that it is best done by training and assigning lay church members to go out and make calls. This method, often called 'Visitation Evangelism,' is bringing more adults into Protestant Anglican and Orthodox churches today than are all other methods combined—bringing more than mass evangelism ever did in its heyday. Experience during two decades has worked out highly practical and spiritually sound methods for this. There are several excellent books on the subject. I would recommend 'How to Increase Church Membership and Attendance' by

Crossland, Abingdon-Cokesbury, $1.75, and 'A Handbook of Evangelism for Laymen' by Bryan, Abingdon-Cokesbury, 50¢."

Tidings of 1908 Grand Avenue, Nashville 4, Tennessee, offer four briefer leaflets on this same subject.

4. "The good people of Jacksonville, Florida, rode to church—*any* church—free of charge last summer, thanks to a generous good-will gesture by Wiley Moore, president of the Jacksonville Coach Company.

"On Sunday morning, all a churchgoer had to do was get on a bus and tell the driver, 'I'm going to church.' After services, 'I've been to church' won him a free ride home.

"The possibility of persons using that as an excuse for a free ride on Sunday didn't bother Mr. Moore much. 'I figured if anybody cheated, it would be on his conscience,' he explained, 'and that would drive him to church anyway.' "

"To fill our churches we must advertise more," the Reverend Guy Perdue, minister of the White Rock Methodist Church of Dallas, Texas, advised. "God was the original advertiser. He hung out the stars to let 'the Heavens declare the glory of God.' "

The bus company in Buffalo took people to church free on the Sundays in Lent. Perhaps there is an equally public-spirited transportation company in your city. It's worth finding out.

5. St. Matthew's Lutheran Church in White Plains, N. Y., secured a 25 percent increase in attendance by training the entire congregation for evangelism. Prior to the beginning of their official program, each member was sent a copy of a special booklet, entitled, "Let's Put First Things First." Prepared under the direction of John H. Wagner, this booklet gives the details of a complete program of evangelism. As this plan worked, it's worth sending for this material.

6. The Reverend E. Hoyt Kerr, Jr., pastor of the First Presbyterian Church in Clarksville, Arkansas, se-

cured a 20 percent increase in church attendance through the following program:

"Our plan involves the signing of an enrollment card or a registration of each person present each Sunday. The results of this signing are tabulated in a notebook each week. The notebook contains, in alphabetical order, the names of each member—or close friend—of the church. Then before the service the following Sunday each absentee—not each family that is absent but each person—is sent a postal card reminder which also contains the coming sermon topic and any important announcements."

This plan is used once a year for a two- or three-month period. It is used at different times each year . . . spring . . . fall . . . or summer.

7. Several synagogues in the East have a special service which helps one fulfill that religious axiom, "The family that prays together, stays together." It is known as *"Family Night Service"* and is held the first Friday in each month. All children with a birthday that month attend this service *with* their families. Here is an ideal way to add religious significance to a child's birthday and to make it an occasion for worshiping *together*.

8. The Reverend Gerald V. A. Barry of Christ Church, Riverdale, N. Y., sends each member a birthday card every year. But it is not the usual type of greeting. This card arrives the week of the birthday and announces that on the next Sunday "we will remember you in our prayers . . . we hope you will worship with us on that day." Few churchgoers can resist going to church on their "Birthday-Sunday."

9. During the past 10 years more than 5,000 attended Sunday church services in Philadelphia, yet an hour before services not one had planned to go.

They went because 75-year-old Fred Werner, layman at Holy Trinity Church, asked them to go.

Leaving home about an hour before church Mr. Werner patrols principal streets and parks of downtown Philadelphia on the lookout for servicemen.

With a friendly smile he says to them: "Come on boys and go to church with me. It won't hurt and it won't cost you a cent." Mr. Werner says of his direct technique: "I don't talk religion to the boys . . . I'm not a sheep-stealer. I just figure if a boy is lonely and in a strange town and hasn't anything else to do, he might as well be in church."

Usually, he says, from half a dozen to 40 servicemen respond and accompany him to church. A decrease in the number of servicemen after World War II didn't lessen his activities. He brought in foreign sailors.

This is a method which can be adopted in hundreds of cities. As the Information Service Bulletin of the National Council of Churches says,

"Though people come into the Church in groups, it is very frequently under the influence of one strong, deeply converted man or woman within the group. One such layman is worth his weight in gold."

10. The Reverend H. P. Alexander is a retired Presbyterian minister who has an enviable record of getting more people into the six small churches he has built up in Oklahoma and Kansas. The secret of his success was to call in the families . . . call on families . . . and keep calling on families. All families! He called on farmers who hadn't been visited by a clergyman in almost 20 years.

11. Getting more people into church on a mass scale was dramatically illustrated by the successful state-wide crusade of the Iowa Methodists. In a single week these inspired workers rang enough door bells to convert more than 11,000 to active membership. The drive was directed by Dr. Eugene Golay of Nashville, Tennessee, as an associate of the Methodist United Evangelistic Mission. Despite severe weather 32,518 people were interviewed.

More than 6,000 professed the Christian faith for the first time and 5,022 others transferred standing membership—mostly inactive—to local churches. This was all accomplished by two-member teams who visited non-churchgoers and persuaded them that "the Church is never more needed than now."

This state-wide crusade is additional proof that countless thousands are ready to go to church, if only someone will talk to them about it. God bless Bishop Charles W. Brashares of Des Moines and the Iowa Methodists for their leadership in setting an example which should be followed in other states by other denominations.

12. The Church of the Ascension, Fifth Avenue and 10th Street, New York, has kept its doors open around the clock since 1929. Is it worth it?

The church released figures for the last eight months in 1951. Total attendance during the night hours from 9 p.m. to 6:45 a.m. was 10,441, about equal numbers of men and women and preponderantly adults. About one-fourth were members or constituents of the church. There were only 23 requests for relief.

Is yours a church which can duplicate this "Around the Clock" service?

13. The DeWitt Memorial Church uses a "block captain" technique for stimulating church interest among tenants of the apartment buildings on New York's lower East Side. "Under the plan, a member of the congregation living in each of the 16 buildings of the new Lillian Wald Houses that cover a 16-square-block tract near the church is the church's representative for his building.

"His job is to call on each family, acquaint it with the church's work and services and extend an invitation to join the congregation.

"Each block captain also organizes children in his building for Sunday school attendance. He meets them in the lobby at a set time on Sunday morning and shepherds them to and from Sunday school."

The Rev. Donald J. Walton has found that this block captain plan has resulted in greatly increased church attendance and Sunday School enrollment.

Chapter 2

LET THE PEOPLE KNOW
EVANGELISM THROUGH
EDUCATION

*By Bishop Wilburn C. Campbell**

I<small>N THOSE DAYS</small> when it was fashionable to be a "parlor pink," a well-to-do lady was much moved by the earnestness of a follower of Karl Marx. What most touched her American sentimentalism was the condition of his clothes and shoes. She replied to his importunities with a generous bill and these words, "Young man, I am touched by your sincerity. Here is some money with which you can get some shoes." After accepting the money, the young man replied, "Thank you, madam, but I shall use this money for printing more leaflets for the Cause."

In these days when Communism has swept over a large area of our world and is a proven foe of Christianity, is it not obvious that much of the power of Communism comes from two inseparable sources: a devoted discipleship and education? Rightly or wrongly, a Communist has been trained by a carefully calculated system of indoctrination and education. He is articulate. He is convinced of the truths of Karl Marx as interpreted by Soviet Russia.

So, too, were the early Christians. Our Lord taught, indocrinated, and educated his apostles and disciples. Nor was it a simple matter to become a Christian in the early days. To be admitted into the divine fellowship meant that one had to know the Faith. The very word "propaganda" was originally a Christian word meaning

---

* Bishop Coadjutor of West Virginia and First Executive Director of Presiding Bishop's Committee on Laymen's Work.

to propagate the Faith. One had to be trained. One had to be taught. It was because the Christians knew in whom they believed that they were able to subvert the wisdom of the Greeks and the sophisticated worldliness of the Romans.

Yet, if there is one glaring weakness among Christians today, it is the degree of religious illiteracy. Christians simply do not know the Faith. When you do not *know the Faith*, you are not apt to be a disciplined follower of the Faith.

There are many and varied techniques for attracting more people to the Church. More power will be in the Church only when these people are convinced, converted and consecrated. This means education. Christian education among adults must be more vigorously pursued.

In addition to adult Bible classes on Sunday morning and the Wednesday evening prayer meeting, I would like to suggest adult Schools of Religion. Adult Schools of Religion are one answer to this problem of adult education. Schools of Religion do not take the place of the Bible class, the prayer meeting, or the educational program of the women's group or the men's club. Nevertheless, a School of Religion gets immediately to the heart of the matter and has a powerful part to play in any church program. It feeds people the strong meat of religion.

There is no hard or fast pattern for conducting a School of Religion. There are some general rules which experience has proved to be best.

First, definite registration should be demanded from those planning to attend. The school should be an invitational affair only in the sense that all interested persons may register. Those who come *must* register. Indifferent attendance inevitably breeds indifferent results. A crowded lecture room one week, because events in the community are propitious toward good church attendance, and then hardly anyone present the next week, because events in the community are unpropitious, will kill any School of Religion. If the Church believes that she has a message of life and death and that for a short period of time members of the congregation are privileged to hear and better understand the message, then those attending should be definitely committed in advance registration. Let us not overlook the psychology angle, either.

Second, a registration fee should be charged. The fee may be only twenty-five cents but it ought to cost something. Those who cannot afford anything should be given the privilege of earning, winning, or qualifying for a scholarship. The charge immediately creates a more respected atmosphere. In some places the registration fee has been as high as five dollars. In other places the fee has been more nominal. The amount is not important; the fee is. The fee also allows the School to do two important things: it makes it possible to bring in outside lecturers and it makes it possible to distribute good collateral reading material.

Third, a School of Religion should be placed on a high plane and approximate academic environment and standards. If possible, utilize a high-school classroom or arrange the parish house or Fellowship Hall to resemble a classroom. While good fellowship prevails always, the School should be called to order promptly and after an opening prayer the lecturer of the evening should launch into his subject. Avoid making the sessions worship services, hymn-sings, or missionary services. It is a serious school concerned about the high and holy call of Christian discipleship.

One of the pioneers in Schools of Religion was St. Luke's Church, Evanston, Illinois. The rector began by arranging a series of lectures, running one night a week for ten consecutive weeks. After a few weeks recess, the School held another series of ten lectures. Enrollment was open to men and women. Its continuation over a period of years with ever increasing enrollment indicates the need for Schools of Religion and the power which results from them.

In the city of Pittsburgh several churches combined to conduct a joint School of Religion for men only. The school held lectures one night a week for eight consecutive weeks. The registration fee was five dollars, and the school was limited to two hundred men. By placing a limitation on the number, a demand was created and a seriousness of purpose fixed. I was the rector of one participating church. These schools were the greatest single source of power during my ministry in that church. Incredible results came.

Indeed, just recently I was having dinner with one of the men and he looked over the assembled group of people having dinner with us and he asked me just how many *real Christians* I thought were gathered in that crowd. I estimated that probably thirty percent could be called good, intelligent church members. He emphatically shook his head and said, "No, there isn't more than ten percent here that could qualify. I know because I know these people. They are where I was three years ago. I thought the Church was a fine institution. I believed in the Church, I supported the Church, and with some degree of regularity I attended her services. Now I have been trained. I have been taught. I am on fire with the Church and the saving message of Christ. I am eager to teach Sunday School. I thrill every time I have the privilege of opening up young minds to the knowledge and love of Christ. When I think of how lukewarm my religion was three years ago and what it is now, I want to shout to the housetops to all people who think they are good Christians and tell them to learn more about the Church and her divine Head, Jesus the Christ. I want Christ to win."

Since the pattern for the School of Religion in Pittsburgh could be easily adapted by groups of churches or by a single church, let us see how such a school was launched.

First, two laymen and the minister from each church met informally one evening and explored the possibilities and the need for such a venture. It takes only a few men to begin—four in this case. The next step was to decide on attendance. The laymen decided against inviting women. They felt the men would be more relaxed and that the atmosphere would be more congenial for men who were shy about religion and who knew so much less about the Church than the average woman.

An evening was selected without too much regard for conflicting civic interests on the "best mousetrap" theory. The courses were in due time decided upon, lecturers secured, a folder printed, registration tickets sold, and the school held. After the school a steering committee of fourteen men was chosen to explore the desirability of having another school. This committee was enthusiastic about having an annual school, inviting only men, and extending an invitation to all churches of the area. The series was shortened to six weeks and the fee was reduced to three dollars. The income was ample to provide for the finest lecturer and for books and pamphlets which could be given away free.

An interesting corollary developed. The women of the churches demanded a School of Religion for women. A school for women was duly held. Then, the following year, the men and women conducted a joint school. It is interesting to note that the men's interest in the school waned a bit when it became a mixed school. Maybe the men of Pittsburgh were shy—and then maybe all men are embarrassed in the presence of women who know more than they do and are more articulate.

What subjects proved most interesting? If doctrine is given modern relevancy, it ranks the highest of any subject. People want and need to know the doctrine of God, particularly in days when the doctrine of God is being denied by humanists, secularists, materialists, and Communists. People want to know the doctrine of Christ and of man. What does the Church teach about immortality? How can prayer be more effective? What is the true relationship of the Church in history? Church customs and the whys and wherefores of Church services are likewise most popular and help make real churchmen out of lukewarm members.

A School of Religion does not depend on importing lecturers and attracting crowds of men. It can be held wherever or whenever two or three are gathered together and the spirit of learning hovers near. In one small church the minister has a twenty-hour series of instructions which he endeavors to have every member take. He asks a couple to invite to their home two or three other couples, regardless of church affiliation. This group meets once a week during the course. This is the familiar "cottage club" type of school. It is not an aimless, wandering evening of fellowship in someone's home.

A School of Religion is not a general "bull session." Such sessions inevitably follow each lecture. It is well to have light refreshments served each evening. But education is the essential purpose and merit of a School of Religion.

Another variation of a School of Religion is the "Parish Seminary" for laymen. In many churches there are laymen who, as they reach the retirement age, are anxiously seeking an avenue of future work and activity. There are also men who, if they were to live their lives over again, would have entered the ministry. Now it seems the door is closed to them. After a careful screening of the manpower of this church, the minister invites one or more of his men to enroll in his "Seminary" for laymen. This seminary can be conducted along the lines of a correspondence school. The minister assigns readings with papers to write. A periodic meeting of the seminary should be held. Men who successfully pass the seminary course are then given certificates of achievement and should be commissioned at a church service.

These men will continue to seek their livelihood

through secular employment but on Sundays or on any given occasion are trained and prepared to be assistant ministers to the congregations. Indeed, in some cases, men have resigned from their secular vocations and gone into the full-time ministry from just such a seminary for laymen.

In my own Diocese of West Virginia I have created a West Virginia Seminary for laymen on a diocesan basis. Two of the clergy and myself comprise the faculty. The laymen study all during the year, writing papers, reading books and covering assigned material for study. Then in the summer at our summer conference ground we have an eight-day "in residence" session. Men literally work and study and pray the clock around. When they have successfully completed the course, I commission them Bishop's Men and license them to function as lay preachers throughout the diocese. The seminary is a three-year program. The details are not important. What is important is that these men willingly, freely and gladly give their time to study and work for the Church. These are hand-picked men. They are men in whom I have confidence; they are men who are leaders in their churches. Nevertheless, practically every man, after the first year's course, comes to me and says, "Bishop, now I think I know a little something about what Christ taught and wanted us to do and be. 'Thy Kingdom come, Thy will be Done' are no longer just words of a prayer. They are my marching orders from Christ. I thank God that my eyes have been opened, my vision enlarged, and my mind trained. Now I think I can begin to profess the faith of Christ." Here is power for the Church.

Schools of Religion, knowledge itself, will not save the world, but we cannot follow the Truth until we know it. When we know and follow the truth, then shall we indeed be free.

Chapter 3

GREATER INSPIRATION THROUGH MORE CONGREGATION PARTICIPATION

Sports, music and religion have one basic factor in common. Those who personally participate get far more out of it than those who are merely spectators. People in the pews who are listening are more like spectators than when they actively put themselves into the service by praying, singing or reading responses. There's nothing like participation to build morale and give a sense of belonging.

Many of the churches which are showing the greatest growth are those in which more and more of the service is being given back to the people in the pews. Here are some of the many ways in which your church can increase its congregation participation. Yes, they will result in more inspiration.

1. During "Laymen's Sunday," held every third Sunday in October, laymen read the Bible lessons, among their several activities in this service. This does something to deepen the reader's religious life. From that Sunday on, his religion, his attendance at church services mean more to him. So why not let this experience of pulpit reading of the Bible be enjoyed and shared by more members of the congregation? Why not have the Bible read by laymen at least once a month? The congregation likes this change of pace and it permits the clergyman to save more of his energy and thoughts for the sermon.

The Reverend Robert Anthony of the North Presbyterian Church in Flushing, Long Island, carries out this congregation participation regularly. So does Dr. Samuel Harkness of the Winnetka, Illinois, Congregational Church. To vary the practice, have the good ladies read the Bible lesson every now and then. In addition to the good it does them and others, they deserve the recognition for the overwhelming amount of church work done by the distaff side.

2. In Grace Church, Utica, New York, a group of laymen read the litany each weekday noon. In addition they pray for peace and pray for parishioners having anniversaries.

3. Has your church ever used a prayer hymn? St. Joseph of Arimathea in Elmsford, New York, uses the first verse of the hymn, "Lead Us, O Father, in the Path of Peace," in the latter part of the Reverend Walter McNeely's closing prayer. The First Presbyterian Church in Sebring, Florida, has a Prayer Hymn right after the first lesson. Listening to "God Be in My Heart" is just the right sort of musical background for one's personal silent prayer. Why not try letting a prayer hymn lift the praying souls to greater heights? How about starting this next Sunday?

The First Presbyterian Church of Sebring, Florida, opens its 11 a.m. Sunday service in a most unusual and tuneful way. The organist plays the Westminster "grandfather's clock" chimes at 11 o'clock. If you have a chimes stop on your organ, try this opening on special Sundays. If your congregation likes this chiming introduction, use it once a month as a change of pace.

4. Better congregational singing is one of the surest and easiest ways to increase congregation participation. This can be done simply by singing favorite, well-known hymns. One key to which hymns are most popular and best-loved is a list of those which are sung on Sunday radio programs. For example, the Fred Waring program, sponsored by the General Electric Company,

closes with hymns that people love to sing. Another source is the hymns played on the bells at the famous Bok Singing Tower at Lake Wales, Florida. Mr. Anton Brees, the world's master carillonneur, tells us that the following hymns are favorites with the millions who come from all over the United States to listen at this mountain lake sanctuary:

> Hymn of Thanks
> Faith of Our Fathers
> The Old Rugged Cross
> In the Garden
> The Bells of St. Mary's

"The Word of Life" TV program asked listeners to send in their favorite hymns. Out of thousands of letters, these were the best-loved:

> The Old Rugged Cross
> What a Friend We Have in Jesus
> In the Garden
> It Is No Secret
> The Love of God

Of course you will always get better congregational singing when the service includes such standard favorites as:

> Dear Lord and Father of Mankind
> Onward Christian Soldiers
> America the Beautiful
> Lead Kindly Light
> Jesus Lover of My Soul
> Come Ye Thankful People Come

One of the best ways to find out the individual favorites of your own congregation is to make a "Favorite Hymn Survey." This is described in detail in the book, *Building Up Your Congregation*.

For the best congregation participation in your church singing, make sure that the opening and closing hymns are favorite hymns. Let the people in the pews sing what they know best, even if you schedule the same favorite every month or six weeks.

5. There are some churches which cannot afford the time or money to have an adult choir. Or they do not have enough musical talent among their members for an adult choir. This is not a serious problem. A junior choir of girls from 12 to 17 singing favorite hymns is an acceptable alternate to an adult choir.

St. Joseph's of Arimathea, at Elmsford, New York, does this, even without choir practice, for their junior choir. The Rector frequently uses hymns in place of such canticles as the "Te Deum," etc. to promote greater congregation participation. A decimeter (sound measuring device) would show that the singing at St. Joseph's is the height of congregation participation.

St. Mark's Methodist Church in Brooklyn, New York, goes so far toward youth singing that it has a choir of "cherubs." These tots (2-5 years old) look like cherubs in their white surplices, scrubbed faces, shining hair and little mouths open in song. They appear at the Christmas and Easter services and other special features. Think of little children singing and you hear silver bells on a soft summer's night; the twinkle of a brook running deep in green woods; the laughter of angels.

6. Some of the best-loved hymns are the glorious resurrection ones for Easter. Notice how much better the congregation sings such inspirational music as: "Jesus Christ Has Risen Today."

There is no reason why those lovely popular hymns should be sung only at Easter. The truth and inspiration of Christ's resurrection is with Christians all through the year. So why should we sing about this joy just during the all too brief Easter season. Why not plan to sing Easter hymns at a "Resurrection Sunday Service," the first Sunday after Labor Day? That's when the

fall season of church services starts. There's no better
way to begin another church year of worship than with
Easter hymns and a sermon on Christ's resurrection . . .
what it means to all of us.

R. W. Dale, the great English Congregationalist
preacher of over half a century ago, had his congregation sing an Easter hymn almost every Sunday morning. A visitor to his church commented, "When I first
attended the service there, I was surprised to hear on a
November morning the hymn, 'Christ Is Risen, Alle-
lujah!' I mentioned it to Dr. Dale afterwards and he
said: 'I want my people to get hold of the glorious fact
that Christ is alive, and to rejoice over it.' "

7. For many years leading clergymen and laymen
have longed for some way to add more congregation
participation to the wedding service. It is true that in
some wedding ceremonies the Lord's Prayer is repeated, or some responses given. But even the Lord's
Prayer doesn't answer the longing of those who would
like to see a wedding service participation which enables the married people of the congregation (usually
in the majority) to renew their own wedding vows.

At last this need has been filled by a special wedding
hymn with words by Catherine Haydon Jacobs and music by Lee Hastings Bristol, Jr. (Mr. Bristol, interestingly enough, is a descendant of another hymn-tune
writer, Thomas Hastings, who wrote—among 1,000
others—the tune TOPLADY to which "Rock of Ages"
is usually sung). This inspirational wedding hymn by
Mrs. Jacobs and Mr. Bristol is reproduced in this book
with their permission.

Copies can be secured from Lee Bristol, Jr., Room
1155, 630 Fifth Avenue, New York, New York. To
enable the congregation to join in the singing of this
wedding hymn, it is suggested that enough copies be
ordered for everyone. These attractive little leaflets
make an interesting personal memento to carry away
from the wedding. Some people order them far enough

WEDDING HYMN

1. Dear Lord, a man and woman bring
     Their consecrated love.
   Hear Thou our voices as we sing;
     Receive their vows above.
   Remember them as children who
     Are Thine through hope instilled.
   O, God, our Father, bless these two,
     Thy sacrament fulfilled.

2. Through paths untraveled and unknown
     Dear Lord, speed Thou their ways
   And bid the radiance of Thy throne
     Illuminate their days.
   Grant them a lasting faith renewed,
     Courageous hearts that dare
   To blend with selfless gratitude
     The holiness of prayer.

3. Before Thine altar, Lord, they kneel
     In humble reverence,
   Entrusting earthly woe or weal
     To Heavenly consequence.
   Receive their union through Thy rite
     Ordained within this hour,
   Fidelity in Thy clear sight,
     Thine everlasting Dower.

4. Before Thine altar, Lord, may all
     Who took the marriage vow
   Kneel once again! Let them recall
     Their spoken pledges now,
   Their love to each as theirs to Thee
     Beyond our silent claim.
   O, Father, bless this marriage, we
     Ask now in Jesus' name.   Amen.

Catherine Haydon Jacobs

WEDDING HYMN
(C. M. D.)

"JOEL"

LEE H. BRISTOL, Jr.

ahead of time so that a local printer can imprint them with a personalized identification at the top of the page. This might read as follows:

Wedding Hymn

sung at the wedding

of

_____   and   _____

on (date) at (name of church and town)

By now, my dear reader, you may think that the author has spent too much of your time and your book discussing hymn singing. For that normal reaction, I don't blame you. Yet, I was encouraged by many people to go all-out in discussing this important part of church services. One big encouragement was the following item in the *Episcopal Churchnews*.

BISHOP SAYS INSPIRING HYMN
WORTH A THOUSAND SERMONS

"In California a hymn is worth a thousand sermons. At least this was the opinion implied by the Right Reverend Karl M. Block, Bishop of California, when he addressed the first Diocesan Church Music Conference recently in San Francisco. Said the Bishop: 'The spiritual upthrust gained from the lilting songs of the church, the very antiquity of some of the chants, and the beauty of the familiar, will catch and change a person more often than a dozen sermons.' Calling for close association between rectors and organists, Bishop Block said, 'Get to know your rector and you'll know what's in his heart.' "

8. Speaking of the relationship between clergy and organist leads us logically to the relationship of clergy, congregation, and choir. To cover this vital subject the author was able to secure the help of an experienced specialist in that field . . . a Mr. Paul Swarm. He is Director of the Church Music Foundation (P. O. Box 7, Decatur, Illinois), a non-profit corporation dedicated to serving church musicians of all faiths and creeds and to improving church music in America. By conducting local "workshops" and other programs and by publishing helpful reference material, the Foundation has done much in its short existence to further its objectives. Here is his sound advice on contacts with the clergy.

CONTACTS WITH THE CLERGY

A successful church music department can be achieved only with the complete support and cooperation of the clergyman. For most church musicians, the pastor is definitely "the boss." A weekly conference for detailed planning of musical services and for frank discussions of personnel problems is a necessity.

When considering a position you should meet with the pastor to discuss the kind of program that will meet the needs of the congregation. What are the worship traditions of the church? What is the cultural background of the congregation? Ask the pastor to place these music department functions in order of importance: (a) worship aid, (b) evangelism, (c) community prestige, and (d) church school.

The clergyman will respect you for giving him a copy of your weekly schedule for interviews, choir rehearsals, and organ practice. It will be an advantage to live near the church so that you are within walking distance of work, meals, and recreation. You should have a telephone number where someone can record messages for you.

To earn the encouragement and admiration of the clergyman:

A. study constantly
B. keep your word
C. give honest appreciation
D. admit mistakes
E. do not criticize predecessors
F. never interrupt
G. do not argue

Progress is slow because people resent sudden change. Whenever you have a suggestion, be sure to mention it only three times. If you make a suggestion more than three times, you create a reverse reaction by arousing stubbornness. This rule will teach patience, because it may be clear that an annual request might be more effective than a weekly one.

Remember that there are no ideal jobs. When confronted by difficult situations, consult the pastor and music committee. Share your little problems and successes to gain the friendship of the church secretary, the organ maintenance man, and the custodian.

By showing your pastor the orders-of-service from other churches you will be able to secure his cooperation on three important points.

1. The words of anthems should be printed in the bulletin.

2. There should be a weekly music corner in the Sunday calendar. This can be used to announce choir auditions, special rehearsals, recognition of loyal choir members, and historical notes about the service music.

3. Your name should appear with that of the clergyman. Most progressive ministers list their names with other staff members and church officers on the last page of the Sunday order-of-service.

9. In an effort to promote greater congregational participation, the Reverend Anson Phelps Stokes, Jr., recently began a once-a-month morning congregation rehearsal in Manhattan's large St. Bartholomew's Church

after the 11 o'clock service. At that rehearsal the congregation practices responses and canticles to be used at services during the coming month.

10. Not long ago before a Christmas Midnight Service at the imposing Cathedral of St. John the Divine, New York City, a clergyman came out before the congregation and declared: "The complaint is sometimes made that we leave all the singing to our choirs and don't sing ourselves, and so, with the Bishop's permission, we are going to ask the congregation alone to sing several carols before the choir begins its procession. As some of these carols are a bit high, I would suggest to you that you take a big breath before you begin!" That cathedral can seem cold and austere, but it did not seem so that night. An enthusiastic singing congregation gave it real warmth.

Hymn singing, of course, is only a part of congregation participation, but it is an important part. Do your pastor and organist avail themselves of the *Hymn Society of America? Hymn festivals? The American Guild of Organists?* Here—capsule fashion—is a note about all three.

The Hymn Society of America

The Hymn Society of America is a national organization founded in 1922 to increase interest in hymns and hymnology in America, and to raise the standards of hymn texts and hymn tunes as well as the standards of their use by congregations. The Society's main activities are: public meetings, hymn festivals, anniversary celebrations, new hymn and tune projects, and publications—including papers of the Society.

The society regularly publishes its attractive, informative magazine, *The Hymn*, which is edited by the noted hymnologist, George Litch Knight. This magazine contains a wealth of useful material. In addition, the Society publishes a number of inexpensive hymn leaflets containing words and music suitable for congregational use at festivals. The Society publishes much on the great hymns and hymn tunes of the past, but also promotes the writing of new hymns and tunes to meet new needs today. (For further data, write: The Hymn Society of America, 297 Fourth Avenue, New York 10, N. Y.)

Hymn Festivals

Recently the Society published an unusually interesting paper entitled "The Hymn Festival Movement in America"* by the widely-recognized authority in this field, Dr. Reginald L. McAll. In this practical, idea-packed paper Dr. McAll not only traces the history of hymn festivals but ably discusses (1) the different types of festivals; (2) how best to plan for them; and (3) samples of outstanding recent festival programs. Dr. McAll gears his suggestions not only to the large-scale, community-wide type of festival but also to the modest small-scale village parish type as well.

In his paper Dr. McAll says, "The National Federation of Music Clubs has a strong department of church music, in which hymns are featured. Member clubs frequently plan hymnic programs, sometimes joining with other groups for community-wide hymn festivals. 'Hymns of the Month' are suggested and each month they are given vigorous promotion. In many communities carillons play each Sunday the current 'Hymn of the Month.' Local 'Hymn of the Month' chairmen notify the churches in their communities, many of which feature it. It is also included in the repertoire of seasonal community 'sings' and is usually given a place on local radio programs of religious music."

The American Guild of Organists

One of the most important forces in the church-music life of the nation is the American Guild of Organists,

*35¢ a copy. Hymn Society of America

a national organization founded in 1896 with chapters now located throughout the country, President S. Lewis Elmer declares, "The purposes of the A.G.O. are: to advance the cause of worthy church music; to elevate the status of church musicians; to increase their appreciation of their responsibilities, duties and opportunities as conductors of worship; to raise the standard of efficiency of organists and choir directors by examination in organ playing, in the theory of music and in general music knowledge and in choir training; and to grant certificates as Fellows, Associates, or Choir Masters to members of the Guild who pass such examinations; to provide members with opportunities for meeting, for the discussion of professional topics; and to do other such lawful things as are incidental to the purposes of the Guild." A lot to handle, that! But they do it!

The Guild is non-sectarian. No examination is required for membership as a Colleague. Examinations are held, however, annually in New York City and other centers for those wishing ot try for the degrees of Associate and Fellow (which the N. Y. Board of Regents has authorized them to confer).

Under the able leadership of James Bleecker, the Guild's Public Interests Committee has begun publication of a series of helpful "how-to-do-it" pamphlets for organists and choirmasters, containing pertinent hints for planning new programs, etc. (For additional data, write: The American Guild of Organists, 630 Fifth Avenue, New York 20, N. Y.)

11. There is an extra benefit of more congregation participation which has been proven for many years by the Reverend W. Hamilton Aulenbach. While the lay readers take over part of the regular Sunday service, he ducks out to the Sunday School where he gives a combined class meeting his story for the day. Simultaneous church and Sunday School services are one of the many reasons why this participating congregation has grown

from 400 to more than 1400 contributing members, and the Sunday School has expanded from 85 to 375 students.

Another reason is that the Reverend Mr. Aulenbach believes in scores of committees . . . in getting as many as possible of the members working on one committee or another. In this growing church everyone gets a job, instead of having most of the activities taken care of by the faithful few, or those fine old-time families. For example, they have a Ministry of Sound in charge of the church's amplification system . . . a Ministry of Light for color effects during services . . . a Ministry of Grounds in charge of landscaping and gardening. The more "Ministries" (or committees) the more participants and the fewer spectators in the glorious program of a growing church . . . growing in Christian services.

12. One of the most logical forms of congregation participation is to make every-member surveys on: sermons, services, church activities, etc. Examples and full details of making services more inspiring are found in Chapter 6, starting on page 64.

There is a clergyman in Ponca City, Oklahoma, who knows that more congregation participation is right for the congregation and right for the church. He has found that it is a sure way to increase interest and attendance. That clergyman is the Reverend Charles W. Shedd of the First Presbyterian Church. Here are three different and three successful ways he develops more congregation participation.

The first was a service of calling on Sunday morning. When the people came to church at both the 8:30 a.m. and 11:00 a.m. services, he gave them a five-minute sermon and said that this was one service which they would conduct. They were dismissed from the church and were given a card on which was a name of a member of the church who had not attended regularly for some time. In spite of the fact that they have two services to accomodate the congregation, they still have, in the church of 1500 members, a good number of people who do not attend at all.

The people were asked to go call at eleven o'clock that morning on those who were not in church. You can imagine the reaction. For instance, one man in shorts, watering his lawn said, "You can imagine my surprise —there I was watering the lawn when a couple came to see me and said, 'There was a service going on at our church and we left it to come and tell you we missed you.'— I'll be there next Sunday."

Another special service was held one Sunday when the theme of the sermon was "Is There An Everlasting Hell?" The sermon immediately followed the opening hymn, then the congregation was divided into six different seminar groups. These groups went to various places in the church for twenty minutes discussion session. Each group had an appointed leader and each group presented two questions for discussion. These questions were then returned to the Reverend Mr. Shedd and his assistant who answered them in the closing twenty minutes of the service.

Another rather unusual feature of the church is the Westminster Youth Church which is organized on the basis of Elders, Deacons, and Trustees—like the adult church. They have a five o'clock vesper service on Sunday afternoon at which they have been featuring a "God In The Funny Paper" program.

Chapter 4

TURNING MAN-POWER
INTO CHURCH-POWER

"NEVER UNDERESTIMATE the power of a woman" is the slogan of a well-known woman's publication. Few people do. Men aren't so highly regarded, it seems. Churches, clergymen, even laymen themselves, are underestimating the power of men.

We men, at least most of us, sit back and watch while the little ladies carry on the main part of church work. The women make and serve the chicken dinners; they sew, knit and mend for the needy. They take care of choir and altar. They are the missionary conscience of the church. They run the bazaars, the socials, and most money-making affairs. True, we men usually foot the bills, pay for the tickets, or allow ourselves to be dragged out for the occasions. Yes, we're nice when some hard-working gal talks up a wonderful value in a handmade apron.

But how many major or helpful activities are started, and carried out, completely by men? Outside of the every-member canvass, board meetings, the men's club dinners, or Boy Scout sponsorship, do we males make much of a contribution toward keeping our church going and growing?

When we remember that the original twelve who spread Christ's word were *men*, we realize how far we've slipped from our duty, opportunity and privilege. We once had the alibi of being busy, everlastingly working to make a living. No more. With the eight-hour working day and five-day week in so many communities, the old excuse doesn't hold water.

One specific situation which should be ours to solve is the problem of getting more men to attend the Sunday services. As it is now in most churches, women outnumber men in the pews by a most discouraging percentage. This can be corrected in two ways.

First, by our making it an established practice—a regular habit—to attend worship services ourselves, with our wives and families. Out of our 168 hours of time per week, let's give God's hour back to him by being in church on Sundays. It does something for us. It is amazing how much better the service makes us feel the rest of the week. It does something for others, too. Each one of us sets the example for at least twenty other people who follow what we do, who consciously or unconsciously imitate many of our actions and activities. Some of these think they can lead a "good life" without going to church, and they point to us as an example.

Second, we should all assume the duties of Sales Manager of Church Attendance. Or, we can call ourselves Vice-President in Charge of Building Congregations, if we like a more impressive title. In either case, our steady job is to invite men, with their families, to worship with us in our church. We should ask these nonchurchgoers on Thursday or Friday, so they will have plenty of time to arrange their Sunday schedule. When we are turned down, we'll keep on at regular (but not annoying) intervals asking them to come. As Sales Manager, we should set for ourselves a yearly quota of new men and families to get into the church. It may be two or six or ten. But set the quota and then work regularly at achieving or exceeding it. That is the greatest con-

tribution which most of us men can give our churches
—more valuable, ministers say, than money.

There are many activities which the men of the
church can take over, and put over. Why not a definite
Christian objective for your men's club each year? This
could be increased contribution to foreign missions,
local missionary work in your community, a clothing
campaign for Korean children, a teen-age club or other
recreation for the young people in the church. Why
shouldn't we men organize a stag Saturday painting
party and paint the church rooms that look unworthy
of God's house? Our church is a sanctuary which should
invite reverence.

An annual Father-and-Son Sunday helps to increase
male attendance. Wives, mothers, and daughters are
welcome, too. But for just this Sunday, fathers and sons
sit down in front.

Instead of having Laymen's Sunday only once a year
in October, why not another Men's Sunday in May? At
that service we men could read the Bible lessons, give
the prayers and perhaps even the sermon. That's a
tested way to step up male attendance. Some churches
have different men read the Scriptures every Sunday.
Why not start this practice in your church?

Have you ever asked your minister to pray for business men? Today business men need such prayers more
than ever. Business workers and executives can't help
gravitating to those churches where their pressing work-
day problems are recognized and an effort made to help
in their solution on a Christian basis.

Many men like a garden. A churchmen's garden club
will appeal to those who do. It's a privilege to create
and maintain a church garden that is a joy and inspiration for members, visitors and passersby. A good place
is the front yard of the church facing the street, the
garden shape a well-proportioned cross.

These are just a few of the obvious ways we men can
be real builders, not merely well-behaved pew-warmers.
You will think of other helpful, Christian things to do.

Mr., Mrs., Miss_____

Address_____

_____Phone_____

Business Address_____Phone_____

has indicated an interest in participating in the following areas:

☐ Attendance at Worship Services

☐ Affiliation with_____
                                        (Organizations)

☐ Daily Personal Devotions   ☐ Family Worship

	Has	Will		Has	Will
Teaching			**Youth Groups**		
Children	☐	☐	Counselor	☐	☐
Youth	☐	☐	Member	☐	☐
Adults	☐	☐	**Men's Work**	☐	☐
Music			**Women's Work**	☐	☐
Choir	☐	☐	**Visiting**		
Instrument:			Sick	☐	☐
			Visitors	☐	☐
_____	☐	☐	New Members	☐	☐
			Absentees	☐	☐
Ushering			**Church Dinners**		
Morning	☐	☐	Assist in Kitchen	☐	☐
Evening	☐	☐	Serve Tables	☐	☐
Office Work			**Church Maintenance**		
Typing	☐	☐	Carpentering	☐	☐
Bookkeeping	☐	☐	Painting	☐	☐
Mimeographing	☐	☐	_____	☐	☐
Floral Arrangements	☐	☐			

Name.

Other:

_____ ☐ ☐

_____ ☐ ☐

_____ ☐ ☐

_____ ☐ ☐

Interviewed by_____

Date_____

The Judson Press   Form W. No. 3—Price, $1.25 a hundred

But don't stop with thinking about them. Write down your ideas, discuss them over the phone with a fellow member, talk about them with your preacher or a church official at next Sunday's service.

Dr. Charles O. Wright of the First Baptist Church in White Plains, New York, makes sure that their manpower is geared into church-power . . . in writing on cards. Reproduced on this page is the handy card on which each new man (and woman, too) puts down how he would like to personally participate in the various activities of the church. This gives the Reverend Mr. Wright and the church organizations a visible inventory of the available man-power.

You can get a supply of these cards from The Judson Press, 703 Chestnut Street, Philadelphia, Pennsylvania, for only $1.25 per hundred. Ask for form W No. 3. This card is one of a series of cards and folders developed by the Council of American Baptist Men. Headquarters at 152 Madison Avenue, New York City. The Director of this active laymen's group is Edward Parsons.

Very few churches have an up-to-date and adequate library of religious books. Although this needed project is listed under the chapter on women's organizations, it is a religious building plan that is worthy of the personal interest and support of any red-blooded male Christian.

Here's a congregation building plan which some man in your church can duplicate. Maybe *you* will volunteer to be its starter and sponsor.

A chain of ribbons promises to fill Emanuel Evangelical United Brethren Church, Cleveland, Ohio, to its very rafters.

In a unique "Church Loyalty Crusade" each man, woman and child attending the church this month is given a colored ribbon every Sunday to give to a friend with the friend's promise to be at church next Sunday.

The first Sunday of the campaign ribbons were distributed to 105 attending the service. The next Sunday, Mother's Day, a crowd of 197 nearly filled the auditorium, anteroom and balcony to capacity. All received ribbons to give to their friends for next Sunday.

As a feature of Mother's Day, Mrs. Emilie Hartwig, 85, was given a bouquet as the oldest mother present, and Mrs. Richard Spears, 21, received flowers as the youngest mother. Some 75 mothers were given potted plants, "To watch grow, signifying your growing with your children."

You business executives may have the opportunity of getting a religious basic theme or church-going slogan included in the advertising for your own company or for your trade association. Look how effectively the Washington Automobile Trade Association did this in the following well-read newspaper advertisement.

You will be interested to know more about the basic theme "Bring Your Problems to Church this Sunday . . . Millions Leave Them there." It was developed as one of the many sound and effective appeals by and for the "Religion In American Life Campaign." From reading about it on pages 278 to 289 you'll see they have many things your executives can use.

We like the little folder put out by Paul Swarm, President of the Church Music Foundation of Decatur, Illinois. It is entitled "How to Hold a Church Position Without Working." Inside you get the answer in these three short sentences:

> Don't fool yourself
> It can't be done
> Study your profession and go to work

That is sound advice for us business men. But Paul means it for choirmasters. He has developed a manual work book which some man in your church should get and give to the choirmaster or organist. It is entitled "Guideposts for the Church Musician." One section tells "Fourteen Ways of Maintaining Choir Interest." Are *you* the man who will be a hero and helper by giving this great guide to your choir? It is written for all three faiths!

By now you may be saying the author is certainly lining up a lot of jobs for *one* man to do. Of course, you cannot do them all, even if you want to disprove that dire Old Testament prediction, called to my attention by Charles Brower . . . a good friend of mine at B.B.D.&O. It is from Ecclesiastes, Chapter 26, Verse 29, and reads as follows:

A Merchant shall hardly keep himself from doing wrong:
and a huckster shall not be freed from sin"

We are sure you'll keep from doing wrong by doing right by those jobs in this list which you can do *best*. Jobs which are *not now* being done in or for your congregation and church.

At All Saints Church, Syracuse, New York, two laymen read morning prayer and two others read evening prayer, *every day of the week* except Sunday. At the beginning of their effort to have DAILY services at their church these men found they were all alone each day. But now after several years of this daily worship lead by 24 laymen, they find that other laymen and women stop by the church during weekends for prayer and meditation.

Most laymen serving are business men. The work started under the leadership of W. Dexter Wilson, an insurance executive, who for 20 years has been a leader in central New York's laymen's work.

Did you ever see your minister cutting a stencil or mimeographing a church bulletin? If you did you should have a guilty feeling about it. It is not his job. He has far more important things to do. A qualified layman should do this or be responsible for getting it done.

Yes, men, this *is* your business. It is the biggest and most important business in the world. The Church needs you and you need the Church. Away with petty dislikes, controversy, and personal criticism. Let's see the Church for what it is—the one means of saving the world. Let's concentrate on the one institution that reaches into the personal lives, the family lives, and the community lives of all of us.

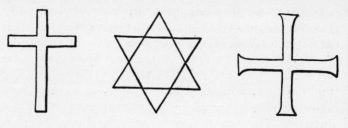

Chapter 5

WHAT ABOUT
LAYMEN'S MOVEMENTS?

By Lee Hastings Bristol, Jr.*

I<small>T IS ONLY RIGHT</small> that *More Power for Your Church* include some mention of laymen's movements. After all, wasn't the early Church, in a sense, a kind of laymen's movement? And hasn't much new power and vitality come to the American Church from the phenomenal growth of laymen's groups and their activities during the past ten years?

This is not said to suggest that laymen are taking over the Church. Far from it! This is said merely to point out that laymen all over the country are more and more extending the work of clergy at the laity level and are trying—in their own lives—to recognize the relevance of their faith to everyday living, at home, in the community, or at the office and shop.

And all this is as it should be, because the New Testament is packed with reminders that Jesus Christ intended the spreading of the Gospel to be done not merely by clergy but by laymen, too, "the royal priesthood of *all* believers."

In tackling this inestimably important work, laymen are helped by principally three factors:

* Assistant Advertising Manager of Bristol Myers Company.

1. *There are so many more laymen.* 1952 estimate: U. S. Protestant, Anglican, and Orthodox laymen (men only) : 22,000,000; clergy: 120,000.†

2. *Laymen are out where the people already are.*

3. *Laymen are non-professionals.* As such, they get a better hearing in the community or at work. They are amateurs. The fact that a layman's testimony carries added weight with the man in the street is no indictment of the clergyman. It is simply a fact of human nature which your own pastor or rector would be first to admit.

It should be said, however, that laymen's movements have a tremendous contribution to make to the spiritual life of our nation. If we shrug smug shoulders and say, "Count me out," we shall want to remind ourselves of what we are permitting to "go by the boards." Chances are that the loss is more our own than it is a loss to the laymen's movement of which we steer clear.

The main objective of a laymen's movement should, of course, be one of changing souls. As St. Paul puts it, "If any man is in Christ, he is a new creature." And isn't the acid test of a man's faith whether or not he meets life *differently* because of the spiritual resources his faith has given him?

There are, of course, many pitfalls to launching laymen's programs. Too detailed an organization will get the group bogged down with "tremendous trifles" and cause members to lose sight of their important objectives. Unless there is some study and knowledge, there can be no really intelligent action taken. That is why laymen's schools, as described by Bishop Campbell, help the laymen-amateurs to avoid the pitfall of merely *talking* about worship and prayer fruitlessly without understanding that there are techniques to worship and prayer which can give a spiritual program "wings."

Mere numbers are no mark of success and can cause

† According to Mr. E. Urner Goodman, General Director of United Church Men of the National Council of Churches.

harm. Although laymen's groups will sometimes assume large proportions, it is important that any movement be based on one individual going to another. As Bishop Campbell puts it, "The cell movement was the beginning of Christianity. It is part of the dynamic force of Communism and should be continued in our own Christian life in these days. It is when two or three are gathered together that the Spirit of our Lord begins to do things a most forceful way."

In this way, we laymen find ourselves swept into a real fellowship. It is not, of course, the familiar fellowship many associate with a parish supper of potato salad and poor tea! It is a fellowship with God and one's neighbors, a fellowship where we talk with ease about our faith and develop those rich friendships which fellowship of this kind has a unique way of offering.

During the past ten years the growth in national laymen's movements has been extraordinary. Both secular and church press have been full of accounts of more and more laymen's groups springing up. Magazines and newspapers increasingly often carry accounts of the growing influence of laymen's movements on the spiritual life of our country today—among churchgoers and non-churchgoers alike.

As a friend said to me a few days ago, "Lee, it's exciting! If laymen are this much concerned and really *care,* look out! Something's really going to happen!"

What that "something" will be depends on how wholeheartedly laymen of America open the door to the Author of their Faith!

ABOUT SPECIFIC GROUPS

The following brief descriptive "catalogue" of particular laymen's movements cannot include a presumptuous comparative appraisal of the various programs. Obviously, different people will have to be reached in different ways. That is true of sermons, and it is just as true of laymen's movements. The following list of thirty-four organizations is divided into two parts—fourteen *national* laymen's movements which are inter-denominational or non-sectarian, and twenty *national* laymen's movements which are denominational. The list is by no means complete. In some cases names of other laymen's movements were not known, and in some instances the data on other programs was not received in time for inclusion in this chapter.

NON-DENOMINATIONAL GROUPS

American Sunday-School Union:

1816 Chestnut Street, Philadelphia 3, Pennsylvania (John H. Talley, Recording Secretary and Treasurer)

The Society was first organized in 1817 as an outgrowth of a still earlier group. In 1845 the Commonwealth of Pennsylvania granted Articles of Incorporation as a non-profit, religious corporation. The program of the Union is under the supervision of a board of officers and thirty-six managers. Its express purpose: to establish and maintain Sunday Schools, and to publish and circulate moral and religious publications. While the Union is not officially connected with any particular church groups, it has its strongest acceptance among evangelical churches. Union Sunday Schools are set up in small, needy, rural areas, especially where religious sentiment is too divided denominationally and the community seems too small for churches of any particular communion to go to work effectively. Approximately one hundred sixty missionaries, working under nine district superintendents, are now working in some forty states.

Carolina Project:

30 Cathedral Avenue, Hempstead, New York (and) 603 North Blount Street, Raleigh, North Carolina (Robert B. Doing, Executive Director)

This movement was founded in January, 1952. The name of this project was suggested by the name "Manhattan Project" which was used to describe the U. S.

atomic research program. It is primarily directed at the deepening of each individual's spiritual life from the point where a man realizes his life is not what it ought to be and wants to do something about it. The program calls for regular worship, financial gifts to support Christian work in the world, evangelism, prayer, meditation, regular group meetings, and a full-hearted attempt on the part of members to come back at every situation consistently like Christians, no matter where they may be, no matter what that situation.

Christian Business Men's Association:
(The Gideons International), 212 East Superior Street, Chicago 11, Illinois (D. J. DePree, President, 43 Pine Street, Zeeland, Michigan)
The well-known Gideon association, which dates from 1898, today boasts about 16,000 members in the United States and Canada. They have placed over 21,000,000 copies of Bibles and Testaments in hotels, hospitals, motels, schools and penal institutions. Over 11,000,000 New Testaments have been given to service men and women since before the outbreak of World War II. The Gideons describe themselves "as an extension of the arm of the church." More and more their program of Bible distribution is being extended abroad, and so the organization is fast becoming truly international. American tourists in France currently report large Gideon-sponsored signs saying, "Lisez la Bible!"

International Christian Leadership:
2324 Massachusetts Avenue, N.W., Washington 8, D. C. (Abraham Vereide, Secretary General)
Founded in 1935, International Christian Leadership is best known by its breakfast groups which have sprung up all over the nation. The I. C. L. purpose is (1) to produce and develop men and women committed to Christ in key positions of leadership throughout the world; (2) to make them conscious of their responsibilities and possibilities; and (3) to equip them with techniques for exercising constructive influence and helping

people with personal problems. The essence of the I.C.L. is a system of small group meetings—breakfast or luncheon get-togethers, campus or legislative groups, etc., etc. There is one such breakfast group in Washington made up of Senators, for example, and another composed of members of the House of Representatives. Both meet (separately) each week while the Senate and House are in session and are looked upon, says Senator Ralph E. Flanders, as "a necessary part of the work of Christian members of the House and of the Senate." By writing to headquarters, you can learn of one of the small groups in or near your community.

Laymen's Missionary Movement of North America:
  19 South LaSalle Street, Chicago 3, Illinois (Harry B. Ansted, Executive Secretary)
  The Movement was founded in 1906 by seventy-five laymen of several communions to promote interest in national and international missions and to further their support by laymen of all churches through (1) Men and Missions Sundays (observed nationally each October since 1931), (2) Mass Meetings, (3) Conventions, (4) Fellowship Dinners, and (5) Radio and Television Programs. A "Speaker's Manual," containing articles by prominent missionaries, clergy and laity, is available each year to those participating in the Men and Missions program. Men and Missions Sunday falls on the second Sunday in October. The Movement is a service organization. "It has no missionaries of its own. It handles no mission funds. It controls no mission boards or stations. It seeks to enlist men . . . for the cause of national and international missions."

Laymen's Movement for a Christian World, Inc.:
  347 Madison Avenue, New York 17, New York (Weyman C. Huckabee, Executive Secretary)
  Founded in 1941 by Wallace C. Speers and others, this movement is a national, non-sectarian association of business men who are trying to build Christian principles into the everyday life of the world. Its member-

ship consists of laymen of many faiths in the United States, Canada, and abroad. As an organization it has sponsored Laymen's Sunday nationally; it has worked to get the United Nations to open its General Assembly sessions with Prayer and set aside a permanent room for meditation; it has led representatives of Labor and Management to meet and consider the application of Christian principles as a "norm" in settling their differences; and has successfully called 50,000 men and women in some 50 nations to pray regularly for world leaders and the United Nations. Laymen will find here an informal, not overly-organized group of concerned business men who welcome new recruits and new ideas on how to get Christianity into even the "garden variety" of everyday experiences.

Laymen's National Committee, Inc.:
     Vanderbilt Hotel, New York 16, New York (Mrs. Sara B. DeForeest, Treasurer and Executive Director)
     The Layman's National Committee was founded in 1940 as a non-sectarian, non-profit organization "to encourage belief and faith in God, daily reading of the Bible, religious education, the attendance at houses of worship and Sunday Schools, and to strengthen religious life in America as a basis for national as well as individual living." Chief among the many activities of the Committee are National Bible Week, which was inaugurated in 1941 and is observed annually the third week in October, and National Sunday School Week, which was inaugurated in 1945 and is observed the second week in April. The Committee is not affiliated with any other organization, is made up of laymen of all faiths, and does not solicit or accept contributions from churches. Eighty-five percent of its revenue in contributions comes from corporations. In promoting observance of Bible Week and Sunday School Week, the Committee has had the support of the nation's leaders from the President on down. Governors have issued proclamations. Over a hundred mayors have given radio talks

in behalf of these projects each year. Ninety-three thousand items of publicity were distributed about Sunday School Week in 1952 alone! The Committee demonstrates great understanding of promotion techniques and rare thoroughness in the way it utilizes all major media to put over its program: television, radio, newspapers, menu stickers, posters, etc., etc. Until recently there was no such thing as "membership" in the Committee. In response to an expressed need for local chapters, however, local groups are more and more appearing on the scene. These are given great freedom by headquarters in developing their programs, so that they best fill local requirements.

Moral Re-Armament:

Caux, Switzerland (Field offices in many major cities; New York City office: 640 Fifth Avenue)

Founded by Frank Buchman, Moral Re-armament was well known until 1938 as the Oxford Group Movement. Today the movement has about a thousand full-time workers throughout the world. Working through teams and so-called "task forces," Moral Re-Armament endeavors to change people spiritually both as individuals and as members of a community. They direct much of their program emphasis toward what they call "civic achievement" and have done so with real success. They make abundant use of the theatre to convey ideas, but much of their idea-planting is done at the individual level through person-to-person evangelism.

Pocket Testament League:

156 Fifth Avenue, New York 10, New York (Alfred A. Kuntz, Executive Director)

As its name might suggest, the Pocket Testament League, founded in 1908, is a movement made up of people who agree to carry a Bible or at least a New Testament and read it every day. Hundreds of thousands of New Testaments have been given to American service men by the League. Many have been distributed also in prisons, schools, and missions. The League has also developed its own missionary movement with trained teams. More than 11,000,000 specially prepared copies of the New Testament have been distributed in Japan, China, Formosa, and Korea.

Religion in American Life:

(RIAL), 289 Fourth Avenue, New York 10, New York (Earle B. Pleasant, National Director)

For the first time in the history of organized religion, all the resources of national mass advertising have been placed at the service of religious institutions through this non-sectarian movement. American business, through The Advertising Council, underwrites and provides a national campaign of advertising in all media during each November in which everyone is urged to attend and support the church or synagogue of his choice. RIAL, which was founded in 1949, seeks to help local communities to organize church attendance campaigns during November and assists these communities in making full use of the national advertising for the benefit of local religious groups. In 1951 more than 3,000 communities used this advertising campaign for local RIAL programs. The Religion in American Life movement is sponsored by a National Laymen's Committee composed of representatives of the three major faiths and headed by Charles E. Wilson, former director of defense mobilization. It is supported by 22 national religious bodies.

Religious Education Association:

545 West 111 Street, New York 25, New York (the Rev. H. E. Wornom, General Secretary)

Founded in 1903, the Religious Education Association welcomes as members all those involved in or concerned about religious education, no matter what their faith. The purpose of the Association is "to inspire the religious forces of our country with the educational ideal, to inspire the educational forces with the religious ideal, and to keep before the public the ideal of religious education and the sense of its need and value."

Working through its own local regional and national groups and through helps provided by its bimonthly publication *Religious Education,* the Association is currently attempting to mobilize interested leaders of all faiths and professions in a widespread search for the best means of providing more adequate training for all American young people.

Sermon Project Committee:

Mayville, New York (Mr. Paul L. Norton, Chairman)

Mr. Paul L. Norton and an able corps of like-minded cohorts have prepared the Sermon on the Mount in the form of mats for reprinting in either standard-size or tabloid newspapers. The carefully executed layout is arresting and contains a number of illustrations. Under the banner headline "Can you spare 9 minutes to read a message 19 centuries old?" the Sermon (sometimes with offers of reprints) is reproduced *in toto* in the modern Goodspeed translation. A local newspaper, for example, may reprint the Sermon as a public service or under the sponsorship of some organization or individual. The Sermon Project is "sponsored by a group of people who believe Christ's Sermon on the Mount is a message for everyone."

United Church Men of America:

National Council of the Churches of Christ in the U.S.A., 120 East 23 Street, New York, New York (E. Urner Goodman, General Director)

The United Church Men program represents the union of the men's work efforts of the nineteen communions now members of the National Council. In practice it attempts to bring together in Christian fellowship and action the men of the twenty-nine great Protestant, Anglican and Orthodox communions in order to give practical expression to their allegiance to Christ in (1) helping laymen to render more effective Christian service in their everyday lives and occupations; (2) encouraging churchmen to strengthen the life and work of their local churches, their respective denominational agencies, and the local, state, and national councils of churches; (3) providing an effective means for sharing successful experiments by agencies for laymen's work within the different communions; and (4) encouraging interdenominational community cooperation between both clergy and laity throughout the nation. There are three primary areas of activity: (a) to bring new strength and vitality to men's work in the several denominations and in each local church; (b) to focus upon projects—local or national—which laymen should unitedly undertake; and (c) to launch a crusade, national in scope, which will dramatize the great relevance of Christianity to world problems and the determination of churchmen to bring their faith more and more into the everyday life of the world where it must be to count.

World Brotherhood:

(Formerly the National Conference of Christians and Jews), 381 Fourth Avenue, New York 16, New York* (the Rev. Everett R. Clinchy, D.D., President)

In 1928 the National Conference of Christians and Jews, or World Brotherhood as it is now to be called, was formed to promote intergroup understanding, cooperation, and to combat existing prejudices. Brotherhood is understood by members of this movement as "giving to individuals of every group the same respect and opportunities you want for your own group." Nationally, in other countries, and in local communities World Brotherhood works *through* (not in competition with) people and organizations in five trunkline institutions: (1) schools and colleges; (2) churches and synagogues; (3) civic and community organizations; (4) industrial groups; and (5) press, radio, television and movies. The purpose of this World Brotherhood movement is "education to develop attitudes, habits, and motivation for universal brotherhood." Laymen are

* After 1953, the location will be 46th Street and United Nations Plaza, New York.

needed to work in the five commissions. There are Brotherhood offices in sixty American cities.

DENOMINATIONAL GROUPS

American Baptist Convention:
National Council of American Baptist Men, 152 Madison Avenue, New York, New York (Edwin W. Parsons, Executive Secretary)
Founded in 1922, this laymen's program attempts to meet the problem that most churchmen will be claimed exclusively by secular activities and organizations outside if the Church does not make her claims "early in the game." This Council, made up of laymen from every state of the convention area, endeavors to stimulate loyal interest on the part of the average churchman in (1) his own spiritual development, (2) the work of the local church, and (3) the national program of the American Baptist Church. This is done by monthly men-of-the-parish get-togethers or by means of dividing the men of a local church into groups of five men, each with its leader and a specific program to follow.

Augustana Lutheran Church:
Augustana Brotherhood, 609 Safety Building, Rock Island, Illinois (Pastor C. Oscar Leonardson, Executive Secretary)
Founded in 1922, the Brotherhood's program is inter-synodical in nature, as it is used by all Lutheran groups (except for the Missouri Synod) at the present time. The Brotherhood follows a ten-point program of objectives. It is this group which promotes the Lutheran Scouting program, awards thirty-two scholarships to students at eight colleges, and undertakes other specific jobs "to evangelize, to educate, and to energize the manpower of the Church. Remarkably complete material is available which is attractively prepared, genuinely spiritual, and yet does not expect laymen to "bite off more than they can chew."

Church of the Brethren:

National Council of Men's Work, 1142 East Euclid Avenue, McPherson, Kansas (R. E. Mohler, Executive Secretary)

Originally set up in 1929, this program has undergone a number of subsequent changes. The purpose of Men's Work is to (1) help laymen more deeply appreciate the relevance of their faith to daily living and (2) help laymen to find the area in which they can serve the Church most effectively. Each year at annual council meetings about six projects are chosen which council members would like to see stressed throughout the Church. In addition, each region or church district may also suggest projects for the Church to undertake nationally or within a particular area. Local Men's Work groups are organized in individual churches, and their activities are largely congregational in scope. (It is suggested that inquiries be addressed to the General Brotherhood, 22 South State Street, Elgin, Illinois.)

Colored Methodist Episcopal Church:

Department of Lay Activities (Inquiries should be addressed to W. L. Graham, Executive Secretary, Paine College, Augusta, Georgia)

Working through local, district, and conference groups, the Department of Lay Activities of the Colored Methodist Episcopal Church has as its basic belief that the supreme mission of the Church is "to redeem human society from selfishness, greed, and hatred by the transformation of individual lives." Activity is encouraged among laymen. By pointing up the need for Christian stewardship, the Department hopes not merely to increase Church funds, but to develop a substantial Church-conscious nucleus of laymen leaders. If strong leadership can be built up, the spiritual life of the Church will be increased immeasurably and its influence appreciably extended in the community.

Congregational Christian Churches of America:
    Laymen's Fellowship, Pembroke 1, Kentucky (Walter
    A. Graham, National Director)
    The Laymen's Fellowship had its beginning in 1936.
It exists to strengthen the churches through a pledged,
active laity and to better the community by trying to get
those laymen to translate their Christianity more and
more into a 24-hour-a-day program in whatever areas
their careers take them. Every man belonging to a Congregational Christian Church is automatically a member
of the Laymen's Fellowship. There are no dues, no
membership cards. Out of the 5,651 churches, approximately 2,750 thus far have men's clubs. Generally, the
program consists of periodical meetings with a speaker,
panel, or forum discussion. State-wide organizations also
have monthly meetings of officers and usually schedule
two state-wide meetings a year: one, a weekend retreat;
the other, a state-wide Conference. A growing number
of states, associations and local churches promote
"Schools of Churchmanship" to instruct and train laymen on the job they have to do.

Disciples of Christ:
    Christian Men's Fellowship of Christian Church, De-
    partment of Men's Work, 222 South Downey Avenue,
    Indianapolis, Indiana (Rev. William H. McKinney,
    Executive Director)
    "Men's Work," as set up by the Disciples of Christ,
calls for each church to hit upon the men's program best
suited to its particular local requirements and in keeping with the overall objective of drawing laymen into
active participation in the total life of the church. The
Fellowship is a joining together of a number of laymen's
groups which existed within the Church. Each state follows its own prerogative of choosing a name, type of
setup, etc. These state leagues, which are known by various state names (Ninety and Nine, Christian Men's
Brotherhoods, etc.), are all part of the national Chris-

tian Men's Fellowship of Christian Church. The manual "Why and How of Men's Work" is one of the best available, because it not only touches on the many overlooked pitfalls of setting up laymen's groups, but also deals *thoroughly* with what just about any type of local group might want to adopt as its program in fulfilling the Fellowship's objectives. There are numerous practical suggestions in the manual to give the newest local group a headstart in launching a program.

Episcopal Church:

Brotherhood of St. Andrew, 701 West Market Street, York, Pennsylvania

Here is an organization, founded in 1883, made up of many local chapters all banded together nationally and chartered by Act of Congress for only one purpose—the spread of Christ's Kingdom among men and boys. Just as Christ chose His twelve, so also He called the "Seventy." The Brotherhood members feel their job is to help build up that larger group. Following a definite rule of prayer and service, members try to follow the example of the Apostle Andrew who brought his brother Peter to Christ. In addition to the regular Men's Department, the Brotherhood also has a Junior Department for boys. The Brotherhood operates in parishes and missions in small chapters or cell groups, banded together to follow a program of prayer and service. "The genius of the Brotherhood program," members maintain, "lies in personal service or the person-to-person contact in every category; hospital calls, Baptism and Confirmation calls, new member calls, shut-in calls and other types of Evangelism in personal work." Personal assignments are an important part of Brotherhood work, and personal assignment record pads are furnished. Through local chapters, diocesan assemblies and through national leadership, the work is promoted at home and abroad. Yes, abroad, for the Brotherhood exists in fourteen countries—with autonomous groups in Canada, China, England, Japan, the Philippines, etc.

(The Brotherhood's American Committee for Japan, called K.E.E.P.—the Kiyosato Educational Experiment Project—has as its threefold program: (1) setting up the first Christian student centers in Japanese urban areas; (2) developing Christian democratic centers in rural areas, e.g. the famous Kiyosato project; and (3) building up laymen leadership for the Episcopal Churches in Japan. Col. Paul Rusch, Director, 2720 North Greenview Street, Chicago 14, Illinois.)

Episcopal Church:

The Presiding Bishop's Committee on Laymen's Work, 281 Fourth Avenue, New York 10, New York (the Rev. Clarence R. Haden, Jr., Executive Director)

Formally organized in June, 1942, the Committee has representatives at the national level, representatives at the provincial level, and parish representatives at the diocesan level, forming a chain of leadership so that ideas may originate with the parish and work up to the national group, or originate with the national group and work down to the parish. The purpose of this chain of leadership is to put into practice the threefold program of (1) worship (2) education, and (3) evangelism. The founders believe that a program using these three points will be more effective than imitation Church Rotary Clubs, or organizations concerned only with money raising. The first executive secretary made an effective case that if money raising is not mixed up with laymen's work, in the long run more money will be raised.

The goal of the Committee is not so much a national program setup as it is parish setups at a grassroots level. Many dioceses have successfully completed their chain of organization and have their own committees with key men representing every parish. Some of these are known as Episcopal Churchman's Associations, and were organized by Bishop Wilburn C. Campbell after a year of study and research aimed at finding out what laymen's movements should be like. Through the Episcopal Churchman's Associations, ideas can be initiated on a parish level, or an area level, or on a diocesan level. It enables laymen to move freely up or down and makes it possible to carry out successfully any ideas that a parish or group of parishes may have.

Evangelical and Reformed Church:

National Churchmen's Brotherhood, 1720 Chouteau Avenue, St. Louis, Mo. (The Rev. J. Kenneth Kohler, Executive Secretary)

With approximately 23,000 members of its 621 Chapters, this Movement is the result of a merger of the Evangelical Brotherhood of the Evangelical Synod and the Churchmen's League of the Reformed Church in the U.S.A. The purpose of the Brotherhood is enlisting and coordinating the manpower of the churches through study, prayer, fellowship, and service for a deepened personal spiritual life and a stronger support from within of the program of the local church and the Church nationally and internationally. Local chapters are given flexibility, so that individual churches can tailor to measure a program which is best suited to their own local requirements and yet still in line with national Brotherhood objectives. An attractive, loose-leaf Revised Handbook has been prepared which covers "from soup to nuts" the whole program of the Brotherhood—from objectives to practical suggestions on how best to achieve those objectives. The nine-point program of "hints for successful chapters" is but one of the many remarkably well thought out guides available in this handbook.

Evangelical United Brethren Church:

The Brotherhood, 1900 United Brethren Building, Dayton, Ohio (the Rev. W. R. Montgomery, National Director)

This program is an outgrowth of the Otterbein Brotherhood (founded in 1908) and the Albright

Brotherhood (founded in 1903). All male persons over sixteen years of age are considered members by virtue of their church membership. The purpose of the Brotherhood is (1) to organize churchmen into fellowship and service; (2) to promote study of the Bible, Church History, and the Evangelical United Brethren Church; (3) to enlist men in winning others to Christ and the Church; and (4) to stimulate active interest in community betterment and in national and international welfare. Meetings must not be ends in themselves. Although the minister is the key man, the local brotherhood group "must not be built around him," warns a Brotherhood brochure. Efforts are made to keep local groups from becoming "just another community or service club." Twenty-seven definite projects are suggested as points of departure in Dr. Montgomery's brochure, "A Brief Statement on the Why and How of Brotherhood."

Methodist Church:
Methodist Men, General Board of Lay Activities, 740 Rush Street, Chicago 11, Illinois (Robert G. Mayfield, Executive Secretary)

This group, which has borne the name Methodist Men since 1942, is a combination of the laymen's movements of the three formerly autonomous churches which in 1939 were finally unified into the Methodist Church. To seek daily Christ's way of life and win others to it and the Church are basic aims of the Methodist Men program. With a present goal of 4,000 local clubs, this movement already boasts over 3,000 and continues to grow. Service and study are the keystones in this movement: service to the Church and community, study of the Church and its teachings. Writes the Executive Secretary, "We do not claim to have a program which is unique . . . we are simply trying to challenge the men of our Church into a more vital Christian experience."

Orthodox, Old Catholic, and Anglican Communions:
Catholic Evangelical League, 54 Weston Avenue, Wollaston 70, Massachusetts (Mr. H. J, Mainwaring, Secretary-Treasurer)

This program is directed toward providing a meeting-ground for individuals who are mutually interested in individual-to-individual evangelism among non-church-goers. Members are recruited from the Orthodox, Anglican, and Old Catholic Communions. The League publishes a quarterly *Catholic Evangelican*.

Presbyterian Church, U. S.:
The Men's Club, Division of Men's Work, 8 North Sixth Street, Richmond 9, Virginia (the Rev. S. J. Patterson, Secretary)

This program "endeavors to relate every man to the work of the church and the work of the church to every man. . . . It seeks to teach men the history, the aims, the beliefs, and the program of our Church, all built upon a solid foundation of Bible study." The program is aimed at accomplishing these ends by developing among its men "skills of prayer, evangelism, friendliness, stewardship, teaching and social service, against a background of personal spiritual development." Local clubs get to formulate their own statements of purpose in keeping with their own needs and in keeping with these over-all objectives. Local clubs may choose their own names for their groups. In "Presbyterian Men," a local church manual, there is a suggested constitution and many ideas for implementing these club programs. Fifteen leaflets are listed under available helps: twelve of these are contained in Men's Work Packet No. 1 for local leaders; three are contained in Men's Work Packet No. 2 for presbytery, synod, and assembly leaders. If the suggestions made in this material are followed, a well-balanced "diet" of activities and emphases should result.

Presbyterian Church in the U.S.A.:

National Council of Presbyterian Men, 156 Fifth Avenue, New York 10, New York (Dr. Paul Moser, Executive Secretary)

A distinctive feature of the technique for program and projects of the chapters developed by the National Council of Presbyterian Men is the EVERY MAN plan. The plan is not only now used by the Presbyterian Church but by churches of other communions as well. The plan calls for briefing a sufficient number of men in every parish on the program and strategy of the Church, indicating the program of the General Assembly's agencies, so that there will be one leader for every four men in a church. Each group is known as a Unit. The job of the Unit Leader is to pass on to every man in his Unit the training which he had. The national annual meeting of this National Council of Presbyterian Men is attended by over two thousand. The Council publishes suggested programs as needed which become part of a loose-leaf notebook. A monthly news-letter is published for officers and leaders of the Movement. A vital element in the program is the Presbytery Councils of Presbyterian Men which are set up geographically, corresponding to the presbyteries. These councils act as advisory groups to the local chapters of Presbyterian Men.

Religious Society of Friends:

Quaker Men, Five Year Meeting—Men's Extension Plan, 101 South Eighth Street, Richmond, Indiana (L. Glenn Switzer, President, Box 247, East Pasadena 8, California)

The Men's Extension Movement was started in California in 1923. The men there felt the need of a more active group within themselves to help challenge men to a more fully dedicated service to the Christian way of life. The program is an extension of the men's groups throughout the Friends organization through personal visitation. Christian Citizenship awards are made to young people. Father and son programs are conducted and personal visitations made throughout the Meeting and communities. Great stress is placed upon the work of the individual laymen in the Meeting. Men try (1) to seek daily Christ's way of life, bear witness to it in business and social life, and engage in definite Christian service; (2) to cooperate in the general program of the church; (3) to study the Society of Friends, its organization and its doctrines; (4) to promote personal evangelism, especially among men and boys; (5) to develop Christian fellowship in the Society of Friends by promoting Christian understanding; (6) to cooperate with other units of Friends' Men united in the promotion of local, Yearly Meeting and general projects of Christian service.

Reformed Church in America:

Reformed Church Brotherhood, Department of Adult Work, 156 Fifth Avenue, New York 10, New York (the Rev. Bert Brower, Director)

The General Synod in 1949 set up the Brotherhood in order to give laymen of the Reformed Church a greater voice in the Church. The Brotherhood puts out a "Know Your Church" chart, study materials, a periodical News Sheet, project suggestions. It conducts Leadership Training Courses and tries wherever possible to "start the ball rolling" on local programs to interest laymen in person-to-person evangelism.

Southern Baptist Convention:

Baptist Brotherhood Commission, Commerce Title Building, Memphis 3, Tennessee (Lawson H. Cooke, Executive Secretary)

Under this Commission comes a real program of man-to-man evangelism—at home, at work, "in fact everywhere and upon every occasion when one man might appropriately speak to another about his Lord." Men of the local brotherhoods are urged to meet regularly at church and go in pairs to homes to try to win other lay-

men to the cause of Jesus Christ. The Baptist Brotherhood promotes the Man and Boy Movement where men
are asked to look around in their own communities, find
some boy not now enrolled in Sunday School, and take
him four successive Sundays. Does it work? Numerous
local brotherhoods find that many boys are won to the
Church in this way every year. Also a part of the Commission's program is the Cooperative Program, which
aims at prompting intelligent, "scriptural giving" and
draws laymen into more active appreciation and support
of the financial needs of the Church, not merely at the
local level, but also at the national level and overseas.
Another program adopted by the Commission is support
of the Baptist Foundations which have as their purpose
the encouragement of "giving and administering funds
to build, undergird, and stabilize the boards and institutions owned and operated by the state conventions
and the Southern Baptist Convention."

United Lutheran Church in America:
    The Lutheran Laymen's Movement for Stewardship,
    231 Madison Avenue, New York 16, New York
    (Henry Endress, Executive Secretary)
    The general aims of the Movement are to promote
the objectives of The United Lutheran Church and,
specifically, to promote the cause of Christian stewardship in local congregations. This the Movement does in
following a simple seven-point program. The Movement is an association of men joined together to promote Christian stewardship and greater application of
the Christian faith in daily life. Organized in 1907, the
L. L. M. now numbers 1,154 men, who contribute from
$100 to $1,000 a year to underwrite the cost of the program. Members get no pins, badges or cards. The Movement is short on organization, long on purpose. "Their
philosophy is simple," says Carroll Thompson. "They
believe that when Christians understand that all worth-
while things come as gifts from God, they'll respond—
by giving back a portion of what they've gotten and by

living their Christian faith clear across the board." With "cells" of able laymen leaders shouldering more and more the job of raising funds, offerings in the last five years have jumped from 27 to 52 million dollars! Recently, a junior group was founded to give men 25 and under a chance to participate on the basis of $25 annually and men from 26 to 35 a chance to do so at $50 a year.

United Presbyterian Church of North America:
    Department of Men's Work, 209 Ninth Street, Pittsburgh 22, Pennsylvania (the Rev. Lee Edwin Walker, Executive Secretary)

This program is an attempt to answer the question of "how the active can activate the inactive" and had its beginning in the 1948 General Assembly in an effort to have all men meet regularly to become better acquainted with the program of the Church and to provide a nucleus of manpower "harnessed for Kingdom action." The program, governed principally at the local level, goes by such names as the Men's Brotherhood, The Men of the Church, etc., depending on the wishes of the local congregation. A program of six simple, major objectives has been outlined, and a number of unusually well-written pamphlets for a loose-leaf binder have been prepared. The pamphlets take men from the "how to begin" stage all the way through the setting up and completing of full programs of effective action. "We are not going to 'dazzle' men into . . . activity," declares the author in one leaflet, ". . . programs can possess the 'come again' quality without being cheap and sensational." To have good programs ten qualities are listed as important for leaders to bear in mind. Those ten "oughts" of programming could well be taken as a check-list guide for any program planners—be the planners Presbyterians or what-have-you.

OTHER DENOMINATIONAL GROUPS

A. M. E. Zion:
Department of Men's Work (Dr. Victor J. Tulane, President, Howard University, Washington, D. C.)

National Baptist Convention of America:
Laymen's League, 809 Virginia Blvd., San Antonio, Texas (I. H. Swaizey, Executive Secretary)

National Baptist Convention, U. S. A.:
National Laymen's Movement, 310 Loyola Avenue, New Orleans, Louisiana (James E. Gayle, Executive Secretary)

Chapter 6
IMPROVING
THE SERVICES
THROUGH
EVERY-MEMBER SURVEYS

IN AUTHOR Bruce Barton's office hangs one of the most helpful and significant of framed sayings, which reads as follows:

> "There is one person wiser than Anybody
> and that is Everybody"   (*Talleyrand*)

This wise observation was made by Talleyrand years before modern research and scientifically planned surveys were developed. Yet that axiom is a keystone of market research.

In a survey you don't reach "everybody," but you do contact enough of the everybodies to uncover facts, trends, statistics, reactions, and suggestions which are far wiser than "anybody." That is why more and more successful companies use research, use surveys, to reach the everybodies. They use this proven technique to find out what customers or potential customers think about their products . . . competitors' products . . . service . . . and the company as a whole.

For the same basic reason, more and more churches and clergymen are using every-member surveys to find out what their own congregations think about the following subjects: Sermons, methods of delivering the sermons, congregational and group activities, church services, and what the people *believe.* One of the first to use this technique was Dr. Albert G. Butzer, beloved minister of Westminster Presbyterian Church of Buffalo, New York. His questionnaire on what the congregation really believed provided the factual basis for a series of mid-week sermons which drew standing-room-only congregations. The story of this survey and its technique is fully described in *Building Up Your Congregation*. Since then a growing number of churches, all over the country, have used surveys and questionnaires to increase the usefulness and inspiration of their services. Space limitations permit us to comment on or reproduce only a few of them. If your problem is not included in these examples, call on a local advertising agency, or discuss it with a local sales or advertising manager. They will help you develop a questionnaire and a survey technique which will throw a lot of light on your problem.

The Rev. John McCombe, Pastor of the Asbury Methodist Church in Crestwood, New York, sent out the following questionnaire to 500 key churchmen.

1. What are some questions asked by people you know about religious beliefs and practices?
a. About God, *b.* About Jesus, *c.* About Eternal Life *d.* About Christian Brotherhood, *e.* About applying Christian practices to daily life and family living, *g.* About other related subjects.

2. What events making the headlines in the news are most interesting?
a. Which of these headlines should be discussed by church groups, and why?
b. What parts of the newspaper do your friends read first?
c. What are some of the reasons for the feeling of insecurity so prevalent among people today, especially in and around New York City.

3. What should people expect of the Asbury Church when they join the church?

4. What should the Asbury Church expect of people when they join?

5. What topics would you like to see included in the preaching program?

Here is an interesting and comprehensive "Check List on Beliefs" developed by the Rev. W. Leigh Ribble of The Grace and Holy Trinity Church of Richmond, Virginia.

(Mark the statements which come closest to what you believe)

1. I believe that by nature people are (check one)
___ Good
___ More apt to be bad than good
___ Neither bad nor good
___ Bad
___ More apt to be good than bad

2. (a) I believe (check one)
___ That God is personal. He rules the universe and controls our lives, subject to our free will. He is interested in us and can be reached through prayer and worship.
___ That God is not personal but is force and power. The Universe is directed by natural laws.
___ That because of ignorance I neither believe nor disbelieve in God.
___ That there is no God. Belief in God is a primitive superstition which we have outgrown. We are on our own and must make the best of it.

(b) Do you hold this belief (check one)
___ With deep conviction, regardless of cost?
___ With a feeling that it probably is the right one but you are not sure?
___ With the idea that it makes no real difference whether it is right or wrong?

3. (a) I believe that Jesus Christ (check one)
___ Was a noble man only. A great prophet or teacher to be respected but not worshiped.

___ Was a great leader but he did the world more harm than good.

___ Is divine. Is truly God and was truly human. Lives today and helps me through my faith in Him.

___ Never lived at all but is a symbol of good like Santa Claus or the goddess of Liberty.

(b) Do you think that your beliefs about Jesus Christ (check one)

___ Make no real difference in the long run?

___ Have a deep influence on your life for good or bad?

___ May have a good influence but you are not sure?

4. I believe that the Holy Spirit is (check one)

___ Natural force or power making the universe work. It is not personal.

___ God in action in human life and who gives us strength and help in all our needs.

___ Such a vague idea that this article of belief makes little difference to me personally whether it is true or false.

5. (a) I believe that the Bible (check one)

___ Is true, word for word, and must be believed in every detail.

___ Is a book of good literature and fine moral teachings but is no more true than the books of other religions.

___ Is an inspired book which, while its parts differ in quality and accuracy, yet presents the Word of God to the World (i.e. that God speaks to us through the Bible).

___ Is a book with no meaning or use for us today.

(b) During the past year I have read from the Bible (check one)

___ Daily.   ___ Once or twice.
___ About once a week.   ___ Several times.
___ Several times a week.   ___ Not at all.

(c) Do you think that (check one)

__ The Bible and science so contradict each other that you have to choose the one and reject the other?

__ That you can accept both the teachings of the Bible and the findings of science if you can interpret both correctly?

6. Concerning death, I believe that (check one)

__ A person truly dies but that God will raise from the dead those who have faith in Him.

__ There is no real death. The soul is immortal. At death it separates from the body and lives on forever in the spirit world.

__ Immortality consists in living on in the memories of loved ones or in the lives of children, or by being reabsorbed by nature and by our physical energies being taken up in some form by plant and animal life.

__ With death all is over. The candle is blown out. There is nothing more.

7. (a) I believe that the Church (check one)

__ Was organized by people to help them live good lives and to teach the world high ideals.

__ Is an organization of doubtful value. It may do as much harm as good.

__ Is an outworn institution. It does not make any difference whether I belong to it or not.

__ Is created by God and that His will is that all people should belong to it. It is the true home and refuge of all mankind.

(b) During the past year I attended Church services (check one)

__ Once a week.   __ Now and then.

__ Once a month.   __ Not at all.

__ Twice a month.

(c) How many times did you take Holy Communion during the past twelve months?

__

8. (a) Do you say your prayers privately
___ Every day?
___ Once or twice a week?
___ Now and then?
___ Only when you are worried
or in trouble?
___ Not at all?

(b) Is there regular Family Prayers in your home?
___ Yes.   ___ No.

(c) Is grace said regularly in your home at meal-
time?
___ Yes.   ___ No.

9. (Under each head check at least three reasons in
the order of their importance by numbering them 1, 2
and 3)

(a) I go to Church services because
___ It gives me a lift for the week.
___ It helps me to live close to God.
___ I like the service and church atmosphere.
___ I want to meet people.
___ It makes me feel better.
___ Everybody should go.
___ I learn how to live.
___ I am in the habit of going.
___ God will reward me.

(b) I say my personal prayers because
___ It is a habit learned in childhood.
___ I need help and God will give it.
___ It makes me feel good.
___ It helps me to know God and His will for me.
___ I get relief from anxiety.
___ They remind me of my duty to God and to
others.
___ All people ought to pray.
___ It is bad luck not to pray.

10. As a Christian do you agree or disagree with the
following propositions? (Write *true* or *false*)

— It makes no difference what you believe. It is what you are that counts.

— Christianity is the only true religion and Christians should work to convert the whole world.

— Other religions (Buddhism, Hinduism, Mohammedanism, etc.) are as good as ours. We should not disturb other people in their beliefs nor try to force our religion on them.

— The Church should not concern itself with politics.

— The Church should confine its interest to spiritual matters and let secular matters alone.

— The world is getting better all the time. By social planning, science and inventions, progress is always onward and upward.

— Whether I am a Christian or not is my own personal business. It is of no concern to anyone else.

— Religion is all right for those who want it. If you don't have it no harm is done.

— To be a Christian it is enough to live by the Golden Rule.

— To be a Christian it is not necessary to believe that Jesus Christ is God.

— The best rule of life is "me first" because no one else is going to look out for me.

— A living dog is better than a dead lion. The most miserable person living is luckier than the noblest person dead.

— Power corrupts. Absolute power corrupts absolutely.

— Either men will be ruled by God or they will be ruled by tyrants.

— We can be morally perfect if we try hard enough.

— If a man does me a good turn I'll do him a better one. If he does me an ill turn—God help him!

— Forgiveness (of sins) is a beggar's refuge: we must pay our debts.

__ I cannot help being what I am and how I am.

Are you interested in joining a group to learn more about Christian doctrines? Yes __ No __ If so, what time would you suggest? __

The Rev. Roger C. Schmuck of St. George's, St. Louis Park, Minn., worded his sermon subject survey: "If you could hear only five sermons the rest of your life, what five topics would you like to hear discussed?"

The topics which got the most votes will form the basis for the Rev. Mr. Schmuck's Sunday sermons during Lent. They are: Immortality. Is there a life after death? How can we find the key to the pearly gates? How can we keep faith in the face of adversity? Is greater faith developed by adversity? What can we do to secure and maintain world peace? How can adults keep children from losing faith? When all goes well with our lives, how can we keep from feeling self-sufficient and independent of God?

The Rev. Mr. Schmuck went to his flock for the topics after he decided he wanted his Lenten series to meet their needs and to answer their questions on the Christian religion or spiritual life.

Quick magazine reports, "Churchgoers soon may find a suggestion box beside the traditional poor box. The Rev. Charles Brackbill may have started a trend when he polled his Elizabeth, N. J., parish, found most felt his sermons 'clear, thought-provoking.'" This 30-year-old minister handed out questionnaires to his congregation and took them up the day before New Year's. The questionnaires (unsigned) asked the congregation how they liked the sermons . . . was the preacher getting his message across . . . should a sermon be about modern times and modern living . . . are there any disturbing mannerisms in the delivery of the sermon. (If yes, what are they?) For example, is the preacher's voice: grave, sing-song, monotone, belligerent, harsh.

The Rev. Mr. Brackbill urged his members to be

ruthlessly honest. He stated that one of the reasons for the survey was the competition for people's time offered by newspapers, radio and television. They all tend to predigest most everything for the public. As a result, says the Rev. Mr. Brackbill, "Today's sermon must talk cold turkey. You can no longer scare people into religion or out of false ideas."

This helpful study was reported in Elizabeth and New York newspapers as well as in *Newsweek* and *Quick* magazines. This shows the news value of church surveys. If you make one, be sure to send the findings to the newspapers.

A recent survey published in *This Week* magazine revealed that most people go to church to hear the sermon. That is one of the reasons more and more clergymen are asking members of their congregation: "What sermon subject interests you most?"

Through this survey technique, clergymen are able to prepare sermons which they know will be of real help to the parishioners. And the churchgoers know in advance that the sermon will give them more help for the coming week.

There are more than 5,000,000 sermons preached each year. Therefore, the matter of sermon subjects is one of the most vital importance to the entire religious field. That is why the July, 1952, issue of *Guideposts*— leading interfaith inspirational magazine—carried the following Sermon Questionnaire.

If your church would like to make a similar survey, just write Guideposts in Pawling, New York for reprints. You can put them in the pews before the service begins or pass them out during the service after the minister or head layman has explained their advantages . . . and asked cooperation in filling them out. Place pencils in the pews for checking and filling in the answers; this should take 3 to 4 minutes with the organ playing proper background music. Every-member surveys are the finest sort of congregation participation

Sermon Subject Survey
Guideposts
Pawling, N. Y.

Your name and address
(may be omitted if anonymity is preferred)

_____

Section 1

_____

Please mark with an "x" those *two* subjects among the following on which you believe a sermon (or sermons) would be most helpful to you:

Immortality ☐
How can I make prayer more effective? ☐
How can I take my religion into my business life? ☐
How religion can eliminate worrying ☐
The religious approach to economic problems ☐
The religious approach to international problems ☐
The religious approach to social problems ☐
Happier families through religion ☐
How can I make the greatest contribution to life? ☐
Ways to increase religious faith ☐

Section 2

I would like to hear a sermon given on the following subject or problem:

....

My religious persuasion is.......................................

I attend a house of worship (please check one)

Regularly ☐
Occasionally ☐
Seldom or never ☐

If you wish to make a survey in your own church, additional copies may be obtained from Guideposts, Pawling, N. Y. Prices: 50 copies for $1.00; 300 copies for $5.00; 1000 copies for $15.00.

Results of this survey will be published in a fall issue of Guideposts.
For further information about Guideposts, see pages 23, 24.

13

. . . a subject discussed in detail in the chapter starting on page 17.

The First Lutheran Church of Shelby, Ohio, held a workers meeting and discussion using the following questionnaire.

FIRST LUTHERAN CHURCH
QUESTIONNAIRE

1. Do you think our Church should inaugurate a program of some sort to call on or check with the new families moving into our community? Yes ___ No ___

2. Do you think a Song Service with a good Chorister conducted on Sunday evening would be a good thing for our Church and Community?   Yes ___ No ___
Would you attend such a Service?   Yes — No —

3. For Future Leaders in our Church would you recommend that a Future Leaders Class be conducted each Sunday during Sunday School Hour?
                                Yes ___ No ___

4. Would you recommend that the Church Council Officers appoint a Special Committee whose duty it would be to speak to members of our congregation who are capable of rendering service to the Church and see if such persons won't volunteer to use their talents in the work of the Church?   Yes ___ No ___

5. Which of the following methods do you favor in meeting the Financial Program of our Church in 1952?

    a. Conduct a regular "Every Member Canvass?" ___

    b. Conduct a "Loyalty Week" when the membership of the Church would call at the Church and register their Pledges?   ___

    c. Conduct a "Mailing Campaign" by sending letters, literature and Pledge Cards requesting that such Pledge Cards be filled out and returned to the Church Office?   ___

    d. Conduct a "Stewardship Campaign" among each of the major organizations of the Church and ask for no Pledges?   ___

6. Do you think meetings similar to this one tonight are of any value to our Church? Yes ___ No ___

7. This space is given to you for any remarks or suggestions you may wish to make to your Church Council.

These examples will show you how other churches improve their services with Every Member surveys. This is a proven plan worthy of being considered seriously by nearly every church. How about yours?

You may be one of the readers who wonder why we have not included in this chapter any results or findings from the use of these surveys. This is a very logical question to occur to any reader. The answer is, we hope, just as logical. If we reprinted the results of these surveys fewer churches would carry them out among their own congregations. Others might be guided by the findings of this research work done in other churches. This is not sound. There is no substitute for the use of these surveys among the members of your own church. Then *only* are you sure of what is in the hearts and minds of your own congregation.

Chapter 7

PROJECTS FOR
TEEN-AGE GROUPS

Baked bean suppers . . . hymn sings . . . and even religious movies are not enough to keep a young people's group growing in interest and in numbers. (However, all are real helps in the over-all plan.) Young people look for, and live on, action. They want to be doing things . . . different things . . . as much as possible.

Group leaders and adult advisers have the constant problem of directing youthful enthusiasm and energies into paths which develop character and religious principles. Their activities should also benefit the church . . . the congregation . . . and the community. To help in this planning we give you herewith a list of some projects which can help you in the fine work needed for these future leaders of the church.

1. The Bells. This is a great project for the God-fearing young people of our nation: To go to their places of worship and ring the bells or chimes or carillon from 7 p.m. to 7:15 p.m. every Saturday evening, to remind hearers to worship God, to tell the world that we are a God-fearing people, and to wordlessly ask people week after week to work for true brotherhood through all the world.

The inspiration for this project: Upon hearing of the century-old custom in Europe of ringing Roman Catholic, Anglican and Protestant church bells from 7 p.m. to 7:15 p.m. every Saturday evening, the 1950 Brotherhood Week committee for Washington, D. C., adopted as one of the Brotherhood Week features the ringing of the church bells of the nation's capitol every Saturday evening of 1950. The bells were first rung on February 18th, the eve of Brotherhood Week.

A project is born: A church youth group in northern Virginia, hearing of this feature of the Brotherhood Week plans in Washington, decided to ring the bells of their own church at the same time that the Washington church bells were being rung, and to ask young people of other churches near Washington to do the same thing.

Ringing the bells on Saturday night is not the only time your church should use this truly religious music. They should be rung daily at 12 noon. This reminds listeners of all that church and Christ offer them.

The Hitchcock Presbyterian Church uses its bells to play hymns when the men are coming home from the Scarsdale, New York, station at night. What a fine welcome back to one's neighborhood!

St. Bartholomew's in New York City uses its bells for a special purpose on Good Friday. At the close of the service the chimes toll thirty-three times to denote the years of our Lord's life on earth.

St. Paul's Cathedral in Buffalo, a typical downtown church, plays favorite hymns on its carillon every weekday noon. When repairs were needed for its bell tower, the neighboring business men were big contributors. This is the best testimonial that the bells are appreciated and loved by those who hear this traditional ministry of religious music.

2. Youth Counseling. Compton Hill (Congregational Christian) Church in St. Louis is in a blighted tenement area with a city mission job. The minister, Kenneth Murphy, writes in *Advance*: "We have instituted a youth counseling program that has become an integral

part of our program. We give basic vocational and personality analyses to as many of our young people as possible—750 tests thus far. With these as a basis, we do our counseling. Dr. Nathan Kohn, of Washington University and our associate minister for counseling, who is nationally known in the vocational field, is in charge of this program. Adult members are also interested in this program and come in for their own testing."

3. *Presbyterian Life* magazine carried this stimulating story of how Kentucky youth sponsored religion in high school:

"Teen-agers of a Kentucky town united recently to stage a week-long religious emphasis program in their high school.

"The young people were members of Protestant churches in Elizabethtown, Kentucky. Early last fall they went to the Ministerial Association and requested an extended program of religious talks and meetings for all the youth of the town. With the help of the churches and the school, they planned and carried out the *town's first Religious Emphasis Week.*

"In the high school each day a radio worship program was prepared by the young people. They wrote a devotional guide which was used for home-room devotionals. Out-of-town speakers addressed the school in daily convocation programs and individual conferences and consultations were held.

"A mass meeting led by the young people was held each evening in a central church. The boys and girls led prayers, sang in a forty-voice chorus, played the organ, and ushered. One of the high-school cheer leaders led singing.

"Evening meetings were overcrowded and every young person in the high school attended the meetings."

4. Historic Christ's Church in historic Tarrytown, N. Y., makes teen-age boys an integral part of its church

life by forming a Junior Vestry. This body of willing helpers meets once a month. If a member fails to attend three meetings in a row, he is notified by letter that if he has no excuse for the three absences he is no longer a Junior Vestryman.

This Vestry appoints a committee to help on these important activities: ushering, music, finance, and property. Naturally, the Junior Vestrymen are regular in their church attendance. Here is the service of Installation used by the Rev. C. Kenneth Ackerman of Christ's Church:

WARDEN "Reverend Sir, I present unto you these persons to be inducted as Junior Vestrymen and Associate Junior Vestrymen in the service of God and in this Parish of Christ Episcopal Church, Tarrytown, New York."

MINISTER "Shortly after the Day of Pentecost, when the Apostles received power from Almighty God to carry on the task of building His Church, the numbers of new converts increased so rapidly that assistance was needed to minister to them. And we read, 'Then the Twelve called the multitude of the disciples unto them and said, It is not reason that we should leave the Word of God and serve tables. Wherefore, Brethren, look ye out among you seven men of honest report, full of the Holy Ghost and wisdom whom we may appoint over this business.' You young men of the Junior Vestry have been selected to follow in that tradition. Therefore, that this present congregation of Christ may know your fitness and resolution for this task, you shall answer plainly to these things which we, in the name of God and His Church, demand of you concerning the same."

MINISTER "Are you ready and willing to accept the office to which you have been appointed?"

VESTRYMAN "I am."

MINISTER "Will you earnestly give yourself to this office by your faithful attendance at the services of the Church; by your ready and willing acceptance of the duties of your office; by your loyal support of and cooperation with the Rector of the Parish in the discharge of his canonical duties; by doing all in your power to promote the welfare of this Parish and of the whole Church of which this Parish is a part?"

VESTRYMAN "I will earnestly endeavor to do so, the Lord being my Helper."

MINISTER "By reason of the promise you have just made and by virtue of my office as Rector of this Parish, I heartily welcome you into this official relationship and hereby install you into the respective offices to which you have been appointed; and on behalf of this Parish, I declare that you are now charged with the responsibilities and privileges of said offices."

MINISTER "Let us pray. (All kneel and recite the Lord's Prayer)
"O Lord, we beseech Thee to pour Thy Heavenly Blessing upon all who are engaged in serving Thee through Thy Holy Church, especially these Thy servants called to be Junior Vestrymen in this Parish. Prosper Thou their understanding, grant them strength and wisdom for their task, and perseverance therein. Grant that by their efforts and example they may win others to zealous and faithful service in the work of Thy Church, through the same Jesus Christ our Lord. Amen.
"O God, the Creator and Preserver of all mankind, grant that these Thy servants to whom we have entrusted a portion of the affairs of this Parish may ever act with courage, prudence, justice and love. May they be of one mind and of one heart in the upbuilding of Thy Church and in the spread of Thy Kingdom. We ask it in the Name and for the Sake of Jesus Christ our Lord. Amen."

5. Many loyal churchgoers in their teens are disturbed at the way their older brothers, sisters, and friends let their church attendance slide when they go away to school. It is too easy for the student to get out of the habit of Sunday worship. Therefore, college days become dangerous days for the away-from-homers. Before they know it, they become away-from-churchers, too.

Thinking teen-agers do not want this to happen any more than their parents and clergymen. One way to help solve this problem is to have it discussed by teen-age groups *before* they go away to school. Have some popular college graduates in the church tell how they met and solved this problem in their own personal lives. The clergyman can explain how he will write a fellow-minister in the school town to ask him to look up the home town student . . . and gear him or her into the life of the school town church. In the Episcopal faith the Reverend Roger W. Blanchard has developed some helpful materials in this work. As Executive Secretary of the Division of the College Work he prepared a "Letter of Commendation" which the student presents to the rector of a school town church; a duplicate of this is sent by the Rector to the College chaplain or school town clergyman. This "Letter of Commendation" is such a constructive factor in maintaining the church-going habits of students that we reproduce it here in full.

On the back of the right half, used by the clergyman, is a space for "Comments on Student." This includes printed subject headings for: Parish acitvities, Interests, and Miscellaneous Comments.

This same Division of College Work at Church Missions House, 281 Fourth Avenue, New York 10, N. Y., also produced two other folders of great help to teen-agers going away to school. One is entitled "So You're Going Away to College." The other is "The Local Parish and the College Student." The ideas and suggestions in these folders are so general and so constructive that they can be used by any church of any denomination.

6. Teen-agers like a real reason to meet and talk to the older members of the church. Also they want to help on vital church projects. They can do both when they cooperate in making the congregational surveys described in Chapter 6, "Improving the Services Through Every-Member Surveys." The teen-agers can distribute questionnaires . . . interview members . . . collect the filled-out forms . . . and then help tabulate the results.

7. Here is a project which a teen-age group can ar-

range and finance all by themselves. It is to get the local radio stations to broadcast that wonderful song "Let's Go to Church on Sunday Morning" every Saturday, at least once during that day. First, calls should be made on the station manager and on the program director. Explain how the majority of listeners will like to hear this lovely and inspiring song on Saturdays. That's because the majority of listeners are churchgoers; are religious-minded. Then find out if the station has a recording of "Let's Go to Church on Sunday Morning." If not, the teen-age group has the opportunity of buying one for the station. This builds good will and encourages the station to use it frequently. This song was recorded on a Capitol record.

8. When young people go away to college, it is widely recognized that this is the time when many drop out of church forever. At Colby College, Waterville, Maine, a religious census showed that over 10 percent of the students were Anglicans. Yet only five attended the downtown church. Several college students decided that they knew the reason. The downtown church was poor and dirty. It couldn't keep a clergyman over a year. Its parishioners fought among themselves. So the students got permission to paint and clean up the church, they never fought among themselves and showed a united front before the townspeople. The result was that although the college still didn't have a chaplain for them, they became a working lay team.

After a year, a young Army Chaplain, John Knight, came to serve at both the church and the college. In two years he had built the small downtown mission, for 75 years dependent on outside funds, into a self-supporting church. With his student aides, he opened up a mission in a cellar at a nearby town, and after two years, they have built their own church. This and many other examples at St. Mark's, Waterville, show that when laymen assume responsibility they can help their church help them. Thus college students without a chaplain helped a downtown church and got a chaplain.

9. Several Boy Scouts in a Syracuse Sunday School opened the eyes of a public relations director when he found out how they had got out of the habit of going to church. These youngsters had been faithful in their attendance during the year, until they went to summer camp. When they came back in the fall, they didn't show up in church any more. The lay leader went out to Constantia, New York, the next summer, and talked with another group of boys. They told him, "We're doing all right here, we seem to get along without church services such as we attend at home. So why bother?" The public relations man tried to talk to his bishops to point out the importance of picking up the ministry at the camp, which was formerly under the jurisdiction of one of their clergymen. But they didn't show much interest.

So several laymen got together and with the help of the Christian Boy Scouts Board Members and other clergy who were interested, arranged to have a morning prayer service read at the camp, even though it was inconvenient for the lay readers—but not for the Boy Scouts. The record next year showed that not one Boy Scout dropped out of the church after his being able to share in the ministry of the young lay leader at Trinity Church, Constantia.

10. The youth at the First Presbyterian Church in Ponca City, Oklahoma, don't just sit around discussing things. They have raised $3,000 for Sunday School supplies. They sent $750 for youth work in other countries. Last year they paid the expenses of 40 boys and girls at summer camps. In addition they raised funds to bring a twenty-year-old Ukrainian D. P. to Ponca City to join her parents and small sister whom the First Presbyterian adults had already brought to town.

11. Teen-agers are given a practical and personal training in the parable of talents by the Reverend W. Hamilton Aulenbach of Christ Church and St. Michael's in Germantown, Pa. Each year certain older

Sunday School students are given ten talents, or one dollar, and told to multiply them. The report of their Christian stewardship is given on a rally day. There one boy tells how he multiplied his talents five-fold by selling dish cloths and brings back five extra dollars. Another explains how he doubled his talents through sales of dish cloths. What a sound way to show why and how teen-agers should develop their talents.

12. The Rev. James E. Ewalt, pastor of the First Presbyterian Church in Pittsburgh, Pennsylvania, writes us this good news about their "Boys and Girls Club":

"We have been running it for three years now and grow more enthusiastic for it all the time. The morale of the faculty and parents is equal to that of the boys and girls. Here is a description of it. Immediately after school on Wednesday afternoons a swarm of eighty-five boys and girls from grades three through eight come buzzing into our Church School building. On the first day of each semester you find them bringing two cans of fruit or vegetables as their registration fee for their club. Having registered, the boys go to the gymnasium for basketball, volley ball, or group games under the leadership of a certain gym teacher and her high school age son. This drains off all that energy which has been pent up from the day's confinement in school. The girls go to handcraft classes where they are taught ceramics, weaving, leather crafts, and embroidery.

"Next comes the Bible hour, a forty-minute period where the Club is divided into four classes for definite Bible study. Emphasis is laid on the application of Bible teachings to everyday life. In the spring semester the pastor conducts his Communicant's Class at this hour. Then comes the supper hour when the club members for forty cents are served a nutritious dinner. A permanent committee of four women staff the kitchen and a rotating committee of four women (parents) each week handles the dining room duties. After the dinner, the boys and girls go to the assembly room where they are led in devotions by the pastor. Twice during the semester he gives a consecration talk. At other times he gives a junior sermon or shows a missionary film.

"After that, the girls go to gym class and the boys to handcraft where they made model trains and airplanes, pocketbooks, belts, lanyards, book-ends, and hammered aluminum bracelets. Cost for the handcraft materials is defrayed by a banking system in which the club members make weekly deposits to their own accounts. A price is set for the raw material for each article they make and is charged to the member's account. Returning to the assembly room the boys and girls sing hymns for fifteen minutes which are projected on a screen and then they are dismissed with a benediction.

" 'I have never seen my boy so anxious to go to Church,' was the remark of one father about this Club.

" 'You don't know how much we parents appreciate your having this Club. My child would not think of missing it,' was the comment of a mother.

" 'The kids that don't come here, just don't know what they are missing,' one member announced."

PRAYER FOR THE YOUTH OF TODAY

"Hear the cry of our souls, O God, for the youth of today. Shower upon them Thy special providence, that they who will lead tomorrow may follow Thee now, and be girded against the issues of life or death. Take their courage and refine it until it becomes like that of Him who set His face toward Jerusalem and dared alone the cross for Thee. Take their enthusiasm and turn it to moral passion. Temper their zeal with patience, their fervor with discipline. Let their hearts' devotion be no longer misguided, or claimed by those who trifle with the lives of men and barter the righteous for silver.

"Allow no easy road or pleasant prospect to lure them into a betrayal of Thee. Meet them at every crossroads of decision, that they may discover Thy presence when tempted to forget it. In the hour when the youths shall faint and be weary and the young men shall utterly fall, bring them to wait on Thee and renew their strength. In the day when they rush to save the world and take the kingdom of heaven by force, give them pause by Thy question thrice repeated: 'Lovest thou Me?'

"We pray for the young people who are perplexed and bewildered today, for all who are separated from their loved ones and from the work of their choice. Above their hindered plans, their thwarted dreams, may they see Thee who will never fail them, nor swerve from that which is right. Keep them from bitterness, despair, and the sense of futility. Guard them against weak resignation to the low estate of the world and blind acceptance of its follies.

"Help them to choose those of strong character and lofty aims as their friends. Enable them to keep their minds and bodies clean, as befits Thy dwelling-place. Assist them in every new opportunity to witness to Thee by word and kindness to others. Preserve their bodies from danger and their souls from the sin of war. Keep alive their reverence for all human beings, their uneasy conscience, their good will for friend and enemy. So may they glorify each shameful cross they have been made to bear, and through each sacrifice bring us all to repentance and sanity. We ask it for Thy goodness' sake. Amen."

by Marion C. Allen

In conclusion, we would like to recommend to those who plan and direct teen-age projects, an excellent book for stimulating discussion. Entitled, "Whatever You Do," it contains 96 well-written pages on stewardship and Christian vocation. The author, Clarence C. Stoughton, worked out these talks and discussions with a summer school class of boys and girls. In fact, some of the prayers were written by his students. All this assures that "Whatever You Do" is geared to the thinking of teen-agers. The last three pages give an outstanding list of books for further reading. These are published by the following denominations: Lutheran, Presbyterian, Methodist. Other suggested books are by the National Council of Churches of Christ in America and general publishers like Harper & Brothers.

For a youth leader, "Whatever You Do" is excellent reading. To stimulate group discussion there is a list of points "For Discussion" at the end of each chapter. You can get a copy for a nominal fee by writing The Muhlenberg Press, Philadelphia, Pennsylvania.

Chapter 8

GOOD WORKS
FOR YOUNG MARRIEDS
OR YOUNG ADULTS

All the "project-chapters" in this book are grouped under the table . . . "Faith Without Works is Dead." Today the faith of our young adults is far from dead. It's filled with good works!

Religion should and does mean more to our young adults than to almost any other group in this country! Why? Simply because young marrieds want their children to be raised in the same kind of God-living land which our fathers founded. A land where we can have "In God We Trust" on our coins . . . and really mean "In God We Trust." They realize that only through religion can their children grow up with those individual opportunities for development found only in a religious country.

So today you see groups of young adults adding their drive, enthusiasm and hundreds of worth-while "good works" to the life of churches, synagogues, shrines, and cathedrals. Instead of having a "return to religion" of older people, our younger groups are carrying right on with those Godly principles they learned in Sunday School. Yes, they are carrying on with *action*, not just holy thoughts. They do not stop with prayers and hymns. Their religion goes on good works to further God's way in this world.

Here are some typical, inspiring examples, and some projects which are worth the God-living energies of our young adults:

1. Nineteen young adults from the local Protestant churches in New Brunswick, New Jersey, spent a weekend renovating the building of the Piscatawayton Baptist Chapel. They painted the Sunday School room, hung curtains, put hymn book racks on the pews. On Sunday the group helped the Reverend Lloyd A. Williams conduct the church service. This is a perfect example of how we can love our neighbors with good works. The Piscatawayton Chapel was a "pilot" weekend camp project of the United Christian Youth Movement which sponsors similar activities annually throughout the country during the fourth week in January.

2. The "Couples Club" of the Westminster Presbyterian Church in Buffalo, New York, raised funds to buy pictures for the Sunday School rooms, to send the Junior Choir on field trips and to provide "sitter service" for babies during the regular Sunday service. This same group took over the responsibility of calling on newcomers to Buffalo . . . inviting them to the meetings . . . and introducing them to young adults of their own age. This friendly religious welcome prevents new people from being "strangers within our gates."

3. In a large midwest synagogue the young adults organize the "Family Worship Service" for the first Friday night in each month. At this 8 p.m. service they honor all children who will have birthdays that month. (Note: Would that more religious groups organized special services in which families would worship together as families.)

4. The Emmanuel Baptist Church is probably one of the few churches in the country to sponsor an orchestra. Its Clinton Hill Symphony is composed of interfaith members who rehearse Tuesday nights. This new and unusual activity has enabled Clinton Hill to meet a

basic need in a neighborhood which has no other social center.

5. The young adults of the First United Presbyterian Church in Cincinnati, Ohio, add an extra convenience to their baby-sitting service. A file of available sitters is always available to parishioners in the church office.

6. The First Methodist Church in Bridgeport, Connecticut, has one of the most successful and progressive young couples' clubs in this country. It believes in sharing the responsibilities so completely that a man and his wife are elected to each of the clubs' offices. The evening meetings of the young adult club feature a wide range of speakers. A local rabbi talks and brings with him some of the young people from his synagogue. A librarian discusses "Interesting Discoveries of Early Connecticut." A Y.M.C.A. staff member analyzes "Experience and Trends in Race Relations." A popular radio commentator talks on "What America Is Reading." An outstanding psychologist leads a discussion on "Being An Adult." Each year one outstanding leader in the cooperative program of the church is brought from New York City.

7. The Interracial Fellowship of Greater New York has a most practical good works program. Their young adults spend weekends working to clean up run-down tenements in New York's East Harlem. They paint, plaster and clean up. This is a useful way for young people to express their religious and social concern for their less fortunate fellow-men.

8. The Youth Fellowship Council of Virginia sponsors the training and sending out of Youth Caravans. The purpose of these caravans is to deepen religious experience of the young people in the churches visited, to strengthen the existing youth program, and to show others how to organize and plan a vital program. Each caravan team serves for a three-weeks' period, spending a week at each church.

9. In the spring of 1951 young adults of Grace Episcopal Church in Jersey City, New Jersey, met at the Rectory to discuss what Christians might do about the dreadful housing conditions in the church neighborhood. They formed the "Grace Church Social Action Committee." Then they studied housing laws, tenement codes, and, most important of all, the seats of responsibility for enforcement at City Hall. This church group found that an active informed committee *can* get results!

Approving this project, members of other churches joined the Social Action Committee. Now there are over 100 members in the four groups with a Central Action Committee. Besides improving housing, the committee is providing playground equipment for placement in vacant lots and defending civil rights. Jersey City can well be proud of her young adults and young marrieds.

Here are some of the worth-while projects which are ideal activities for young adult groups:

EARN money to buy the minister a tape recorder machine. Then he can take church services right into the homes of the shut-ins, elderly people who cannot get to church. The tape recorder brings them hymns, prayers, and the sermon. This extra service is now being carried by many ministers like the Reverend Gibson T. Daniels of Saugatuck Congregational Church in Westport, Connecticut, and the Reverend G. Earle Daniels of St. James' Episcopal Church in Cambridge, Massachusetts.

VISIT hospitals and prisons on Sundays . . . taking the inmates magazines . . . reading the Bible to those who want that spiritual uplift . . . writing letters or postcards. Inmates of hospitals and prisons would deeply appreciate getting a birthday card from the church on their natal days. This would be tangible evidence that the church cares about its children no matter what their age is, no matter where they are . . . lending them radios owned by the young adults' group.

COLLECT inspirational quotations for the church bulletin, so that each issue contains thoughts which give the readers an extra spiritual lift. These quotations will be found in our leading magazines, in speeches by great leaders, in newspaper editorials, or in the ads prepared by the Religion in American Life Campaign.

Many promising young men are unable to study for the ministry because of the lack of financial backing. This should become the concern of the parish, and particularly the men of the parish. To assure such a young man of an education is one of the greatest services you can render. So why not—

GIVE "scholarship plate banquets" to help support students who are preparing for full-time Christian service? This is an annual event of the First Christian Church of Portland, Oregon. The scholarship charge can run from $10 to $25 per plate depending upon the average income of the parishioners.

RAISE funds to buy a church flag to fly over the doorway on Sunday. This flag gives the front of the church a "Lord's-Day-Look" on Sunday. It reminds all who pass the church of God's love for His children, of all that churches and synagogues offer to worshiping families. The flag also reminds us to worship more frequently.

PROVIDE the church or temple with a rack for the back of the church. This rack is to hold booklets, religious books, and church magazines. This is one of the surest ways to increase the religious readings of the congregation.

MAKE SURE that all your church's or synagogue's printed material includes a basic theme or slogan. This could be: "Worshiping Families Are Happier Families," or "Families Who Pray Together Stay Together," or some basic theme developed by your group and approved by the adult board. Make sure it's used on all bulletins . . . Letterheads . . . printed folders and appeals . . . and in your newspaper advertisements.

FORM a "Bell Ringing Committee" to use your church's bell more frequently and more effectively. This committee will arrange to have some members ring the bell every Saturday night from 7 to 7:15 p.m. This is a century-old custom in Europe among Roman Catholic, Anglican and Protestant churches. The pealing of the bells at the close of the Jewish Sabbath and on the eve of the Christian Sabbath proclaims from our Nation's Capitol—

That we are a God-fearing people,
That each week we re-affirm our trust and faith in God,
And that each week we are dedicating ourselves anew to work for true brotherhood under God through all the world.

PROJECTS FOR YOUNGER MARRIEDS

Some of the more advanced young adult programs in America's houses of worship are modeled on the pioneering efforts of the First Community Church in Columbus, Ohio. Tucked away in a middle-class suburb, this far-famed nondenominational church has a congregation of over 5,000 drawn from all levels of the city's social strata. Under the inspired leadership of a tireless fifty-year-old pastor named Roy Burkhart, it has imbued in its members a spirit of Christian fellowship which many visiting clergy say is unmatched anywhere in the U. S.

To an outsider the Young Couples' Circles are the clearest demonstration of the way the Church has wrought extraordinarily beneficial changes in the lives of these young folk. A Circle is an informal gathering of ten married couples who meet once a month at one another's homes, with Dr. Burkhart or one of his associate ministers present. What goes on? There is seldom any definite agenda, but conversation always gravitates unaffectedly toward issues of real Christian living. It may center around an exchange of ideas on the significance of some Bible passage—which in turn, may bring up a moral principle and its pertinence in twentieth-century life.

Having discovered that Christianity works in somebody else's parlor, they begin to test it out in their own. This starts them on the adventure of re-examining their prejudices and hostilities in the light of their changing natures. They become more tolerant, less prone to self-pity and over-dramatization of their personal troubles. Perhaps for the first time, they look for the good in their neighbors rather than for the bad. The inevitable result is happier, better-adjusted young people. And perhaps the proof lies in the fact that of the more than 1,100 marriages performed by Dr. Burkhart only nine have ended in divorce.

No wonder Dr. Karl Menninger, director of the Menninger Psychiatric Institute, says of the First Community Church program, "It is the finest example of organized mental hygiene I have ever encountered."

Like freshly converted young adults everywhere, those at the First Community Church are forever exploring the relationship between a person's faith and his job. With a missionary zeal they have in several instances changed the whole atmosphere in their places of work. For example, a group of bank workers report: "It has meant more smiles and less impatience, fewer clock-watchers, less time out for smokes, less swearing, less grousing about higher-ups and lower-downs, and even fewer suspicions about anyone's lifting stamps from the stamp drawer!"

When young people adopt a religious faith, it isn't long, as Dr. Burkhart puts it, before they are anxious to "make a contribution to the spiritual and economic welfare of all men." Thus a few years back young adults at the First Community Church responded to the challenge of a Columbus judge who pointed to a neighborhood that spawned ninety percent of the city's juvenile delinquents. First, the young men of the church accompanied marauding boy gangs on their escapades, seeking their confidence and discovering the influences that forced them away from wholesome living. Then they sponsored a settlement house, organized picnics in the country, staged indoor pageants at Easter and Christmas, and gradually introduced devotional prayers. The project's success is reflected in the latest statistics on juvenile crime in Columbus. Today only eighteen percent of the city's delinquents live in this neighborhood.

The same deep-felt will to help others was shown when a district of three hundred Negroes in Columbus bemoaned the lack of a place for worship. Some of them had been attending the First Community Church but complained that it was too far from their homes. So young peoples of both races joined to build a church in the Negro neighborhood. They dug the foundation, hauled the bricks and lumber, and gave up every leisure hour until the building was finished. Not even the subtlest racial bigot could unshackle the bonds of fellowship and cooperation that exist between the two churches today.

Evening programs in the First Methodist Church in Bridgeport, Connecticut, contain such variety as an address by the rabbi who attends with some of the young people from the nearby synagogue; a librarian's discussion on "Interesting Discoveries of Early Connecticut"; a Y.M.C.A. staff member's analysis of "Experience and Trends in Race Relations"; the pastor's presentation of "What Actually Happened on Easter"; a popular radio commentator on "What America Is Reading"; the council secretary's presentation of "Cooperative Work of the Community"; a trip to New Haven to hear Dr. Frank C. Laubach speak on "Literacy"; the pastor's presentation of the organizations of the Church; "Being an Adult," led by an outstanding psychologist; and two of the older members of the church presenting its history and episodes in the building of the present edifice. Each year one outstanding leader in the cooperative program of the Church is brought from New York. Home friends who have traveled abroad usually find this young adult group one of the most interested audiences upon their return. Some Sunday evenings are supper nights; others just "snack" nights.

Social meetings, such as a progressive dinner party, moonlight boat ride, picnic, Halloween party, New Year's Eve party, and Christmas party, have been part of the program.

In addition to the bi-monthly programs, the suppers and the social gatherings, the young adult group finds expression in four other areas. One, the Labor Day Week-End Camp has become a yearly event. Program planning, fun, inspiration, and fellowship make up the program.

First United Presbyterian Church in Cincinnati, Ohio, (the Reverend G. Barrett Rich III, pastor) offers a helpful service to its parishioners. There's a file of available baby-sitters in the church office.

The first Toledo (Ohio) marriage preparation course for young people from Protestant homes ended with a notable accomplishment.

It succeeded in holding the attention for ten weeks, of more than two hundred youths seventeen to twenty-three and broke even optimistic attendance estimates.

When 193 youths jammed the classrooms of the Whitney Vocational High School on opening night, the course's sponsors—Toledo's Family Life Education Program—moved to more spacious quarters in the parish house of Glenwood Lutheran Church. Course subjects ran the gamut from "Dating and Courtship" and "Love and Sex" to "Mixed Marriages" and "The Creation of New Life."

"Laymen and ministers alike have not been alert as they might have been to discern symptoms and learn how to deal with them effectively before they reach an advanced stage," says Reverend Herman L. Barbery, Associate Pastor of the Marble Collegiate Church, New York City. "Mr.-and-Mrs. clubs, which make some discussion of marital counseling part of their yearly program, are helpful in encouraging parishioners to seek help."

Plenty of expert counseling is available through ministers, but people must be encouraged to seek it. Churches had better be showing individuals, *before* their marriage gets to the breaking point, where and when to ask for help.

Here is where your group comes in. Whether you are the Young Folks, the Young Adults, the Couples Club, or the Women's Group, you can spark the organization of a program of education for family living, a marriage institute, or whatever you wish to call it. Tell your church, "We want to plan it and take the responsibility for getting people there."

In the First Community Church of Columbus, Ohio, when a young couple begins to look forward to a family event they will meet with one of the ministers of the church in the Family Workshop. Their interest in the Family Workshop will be in the pre-natal group which meets regularly the fifth Tuesday of the month (where there are five Tuesdays). This is a fellowship of young parents anticipating their first child. In the three or four evenings together the church will try to unravel with them the concept of the family, preparing them for the psychological, physiological, and spiritual aspects of the forthcoming event.

With the family now three, with a pre-school child, it will center its interest in the Family Workshop for pre-school children. This group meets on the first Tuesday of each month. So it goes. There is a Workshop to follow the parent through the various stages of his child's growth: elementary school, the second Tuesday; intermediate grades, the third Tuesday; parents of adolescents, the fourth Tuesday.

Young adults not yet married will find their fellowship in the Cambridge Club. This is a regular Sunday evening fellowship of young people beyond the college age, either as graduate students or employed. The Cambridge Club group, which meets on Tuesday evenings for a prayer cell experience, is primarily a fellowship group. The prayer cell experience is a deeper spiritual search. The whole group also finds fellowship on occasional weekends at the church's camp.

Married couples with or without children are also grouped in fellowship groups known as Couples Circles composed of ten couples to a Circle.

FELLOWSHIP AND SCHOLARSHIP

How is the attendance at young adult meetings in your church? This vital area of church activity is always worthy of careful thought and planning. The young people of today face a troubled future; besides fun and games they seek practical guidance in Christian living.

Varied programs that provide an opportunity for learning and intelligent discussion of life's daily problems can also stress religion in daily living. Lectures by doctors, psychologists, teachers, businessmen, and other clergy that are followed by a discussion period will stimulate both interest and attendance.

Proven many times, this thesis was proven again by the young adult group of the First Methodist Church in Bridgeport, Connecticut. After the general business meeting and worship service, and preceding the social hour and refreshments, a varied program was offered.

One Sunday they were addressed by the rabbi of a nearby synagogue, who brought some of his young people, and another time a Y.M.C.A. staff member spoke on "Experiences and Trends in Race Relations," a pressing problem today. A leading psychologist provided a thought-provoking group discussion on "Being an Adult." Sometimes members themselves accepted responsibility for programs on the history of their church, its edifice and denomination. The pastor frequently leads the group on subjects like church organization, how its money is spent, and its purpose.

This is in addition to a full and varied schedule of social events that include group junkets outside the church. The attendance has grown and interest runs high. A democratic system gives everyone a job to do in preparing for these meetings. They earn what they learn while meeting in fellowship through Christ.

The youth at Arch Street Methodist Church represent Philadelphia's most active young-adult program. Every Sunday afternoon they conduct a supper forum meeting. They provide a Sunday night choir of fifty voices. And after evening service they join in a church "Friendly Hour" that brings to lonely hearts a wholesome touch of Christian companionship.

AUDIO-VISUAL AIDS TO RELIGIOUS RELATIONS

There are now available many movies on religious themes that can be used to add spice to the meetings of the various groups and circles in your church. In addition there are film strips, records, and tape recorders. All can be used by you to advantage. The cost need not be prohibitive; some are available on a rental basis and those you buy could be lent out to other churches in return for what they may have in their film libraries.

Your young marrieds would be interested in films discussing the problems of raising children, the home, religion, and many other such topics. Films, sound or silent, black and white or color, will add variety to the programs of the Young People's Groups and in the Sunday schools. Adults like them, too, and some churches include them in the services to illustrate some point. If followed by well-led discussion periods it will add another dimension to group activities. For information on films and film strips write to the Religious Film Association, 35 West 45th Street, New York 19, New York, or your denominational board.

An enthusiastic young adult at Westminster Presbyterian Church in Buffalo, N. Y. writes as follows:

"As you probably know, the young married groups at Westminster are very active. They bring a great many new people to the church who eventually join. I can't tell you how many newcomers to Buffalo have told us that they wouldn't have known what to do with themselves if it had not been for Junior Parish or Couples Club or Children's Activities. All the friends Ted and I have made together as a couple we have met through some activity at church. One of the pleasures of going to church for me is the exchange of greetings with the many people we know while waiting for our children. And you don't meet those people and get to know them on Sunday mornings. One of my pet subjects is the purpose of a church group. Beyond the purpose of making money for a favorite charity I feel that a church organization serves the individual member by helping him or her to make new friends, to gain new outlooks and activities, and to make a place for himself in the church. Then he can say 'This is my church.'

"The Couples Club at Westminster was formed about seven years ago. Four couples who had discussed the need for such a group asked eight other couples (ourselves included) to meet with the ministers to make plans. We decided then that the most important thing was to meet together as couples and to become better acquainted. Everyone still feels the same way. They have no money-making project, but of their small dues they have managed to give the church a few gifts— *pictures for the Sunday school and a trip to Rochester for the Junior Choir. They also run a 'sitter service' for babies during church on Sundays.* Their membership numbers about 250 with an average attendance of from 90 to 120 for their monthly dinners held at the Church. This year they have tried to vary the usual after-dinner speakers by showing a movie once and by going to a pop concert at Klinehaus Music Hall after dinner another time. For the last meeting in May they have usually had a dinner dance, but this year they plan to make it a smörgasbord dance. When the program as planned is finished, they always bring out cakes for everyone which helps people to sit around and talk a little longer.

The bowling alleys are opened and I think there are ping-pong tables, too. We usually play a short game of bridge in the library.

"I am going to tell you about Junior Parish and Children's Activities groups because they really feed the Couples Club. And I feel they are quite separate from the Women's groups.

"Junior Parish you know about, but I'll bring you up to date. The girls are all 'young marrieds' and can't be over thirty-five years old. Their only charity is Westminster Camp, which they support in full, as far as I know. And you know what a beautiful spot that is. Last year they made over $3,000. They now have an annual fashion show at the Statler on which they make around $2,000. (Most of that on their programs.) Then at the linen sale in November they sponsor the luncheon, the baked goods booth, flower booth, and doll and toy booth. Their membership numbers about seventy, with an average attendance of fifty at weekly luncheons. They now have two sitters in the children's building during the meetings—one for babies and one for toddlers. At their meetings they have the usual unpaid speakers. Their only strictly religious activity—and this applies to the other groups, too—is a series of Lenten talks usually by Dr. Butzer. During the summer they still follow my suggestion of seven years ago. They meet once a month at the home of one of the members. It is purely social and keeps the group together over the summer months. And it is fun to go to the various homes.

"The Children's Activities Group was formed about seven years ago when a few of the Junior Parish girls became thirty-five and hated to go into the Women's Parish and sew all day. It grew very fast because there were so many girls with children who couldn't keep up the fast pace of J.P. but wanted something different from Women's Parish. The average age is between thirty-two and forty-five. There are one hundred mem-

bers with an average attendance of fifty to sixty at
monthly luncheons. Because they had to be part of
Women's Parish, 60 percent of the money they make
goes there. The other 40 percent they keep for their
own projects, all concerned with the Church School.
They try to do whatever is needed for the school. We
have an altar guild which has flowers for the school
altars every Sunday. *We supply the uniforms for the
thirty children* in the junior choir and decorated their
dressing room. We have bought tables and special
chairs and books and toys every year. Last year we built
a partition in the upstairs parish hall to make two
separate Sunday school rooms and avoid some confusion. Our projects to raise money are a spring bridge
luncheon and a white elephant and clothing sale in the
spring. Then, of course, our linen sale activities, which
include the knitting booth, sewing booth, favors booth
(those felt angels I sent you last year) and the tea. The
luncheon meetings are similar to those of the Junior
Parish.

"Perhaps the greatest service of the Children's Activities Group is furnishing 'Parent Assistants,' as well as
some teachers, in the Church School. Almost each grade
has a Parent Assistant for the teacher. You can understand the need for this when you realize we have almost
1,500 enrolled in our Sunday school. Dr. Butzer feels
these social church organizations to be very important.
For example, at Easter we took in eighty new members,
a good many of those being people introduced to the
church through attending these outside clubs or organizations.

"This year there was formed an executive P.T.A.
group which draws its membership proportionately
from the J.P., Children's Activities Group, deacons, etc.
It sponsors and plans P.T.A. programs which have been
unusually well attended this year. After lecture programs in the Chapel, the parents meet at tables by
grades with the teachers and over coffee and petit-fours

get acquainted with their children's Sunday school teachers and his or her problem with little Iodine. The executive committee more or less acts as host and the members prepare and serve the food."

Chapter 9

PLANS FOR MEN'S CLUBS

Here is an outline of "good works" which are worthy of the "church-power in your man-power." Most of them can be adapted to any size church in any size town or neighborhood. Plan to discuss them with the other officers of your men's club.

1. Why not have a committee go to the local newspaper editor or editors to ask that once a week, the paper publish a religious statement or editorial by a local churchgoer. This can be rotated among the various denominations and faiths. This weekly "witness" is done well in the Miami *Herald* newspaper. The column is entitled "What My Religion Means to Me." The Nashville *Tennessean* also features a similar testimony written by local business men.

2. At the Grace Church in Detroit they have vocational groups who get together and discuss how they apply their Christian standards in their work. For example, a group of industrial managers met and talked on how they can use their religion in their weekday work. Then the union members talk with themselves as to how they can run their unions and their factory lives on Christian principles. The groups meet monthly. There is no permanent leader. There is a different chairman each season. The notes are mailed to each member after each meeting. Here is a practical and challenging project for your church. For more complete

details, write Ralph Hiteman of the Detroit, Michigan, Y.M.C.A., at 2020 Witherell St., Detroit, Michigan.

3. From upstate New York comes this example of what a Men's Club can do when an industry moves into or out of a town:

Often when industry moves a new plant into a town, there is a golden opportunity for your church to win some new members. A recent good example of this was when Pneumatic Tube moved from Detroit to Utica, New York. The minister and vestry of Grace Church in Utica did the following:

a. Wrote to clergymen of their faith in Detroit asking for the names of their members who would soon be leaving Detroit to come to Utica. These would be naturals to join up at Grace.

b. Wrote to the company and obtained their help to get the names and addresses of the men being moved into Utica.

c. Having obtained the names, they wrote a letter to those families saying that they were most welcome in Utica. Could the church and its members do anything to help the move? Only at the end, did it say that if they were members of another faith, it was hoped that they would join the local church in Utica, but if they had no church, they would be welcomeed at Grace Church. This Christian act of fellowship and welcome not only resulted in good new families, but it prevented many from dropping out of church altogether during the move, and won national recognition.

4. Men's Clubs can perform a real religious function by getting more firms to subscribe to *Guideposts* . . . the inspirational magazine . . . for all their employees. This monthly magazine builds the morale and spirit of of all who read it. Interesting articles tell how individuals have overcome trouble . . . achieved success . . . or started life anew, through their faith. Approved by all three faiths, *Guideposts* has one of the few calendars in the world which gives the holidays and Holy

Days for Protestant, Anglican, Roman Catholic and Jew. Leading firms like R. J. Reynolds and Hotpoint Electric send *Guideposts* to all their thousands of employees. A year's subscription costs only $1.33 so any firm can afford this proven morale builder. The address is *Guideposts*, Pawling, New York.

Here is how James J. Nance, now President of Packard Motors, announced *Guideposts* subscription to his top executives:

TO THE KEY MEN:

For some time past, I have been reading a small magazine called *Guideposts* which was originated in 1945 by a small group of practical thinkers, including Lowell Thomas, Eddie Rickenbacker, Branch Rickey and Dr. Norman Vincent Peale. This little magazine endeavors to translate religion into the practical terms of everyday living and business relationships.

I have long felt that the Key Men might benefit from reading the down-to-earth writings that it carries, but I have been hesitant about taking any action because I have always believed that a man's religion is an intensely personal and private thing, which he must work out for himself. I am, however, convinced that the magazine is nonsectarian, completely unbiased, and not at all preachy, and further, that it has only one purpose: to be helpful to those who care to read its messages.

With this in mind, I have entered a subscription in the name of each Key Man for *Guideposts* to be mailed to your homes. I hope that you and your family will receive it in the spirit with which it is sent, and that you will find it thought-provoking and beneficial in your daily lives, both in and out of business. I would be glad to receive your reactions to the magazine after you have received a few copies. With all good wishes.

James J. Nance

5. The church men of White Plains, New York, have developed an activity which bears duplication in other

cities. In 1945 they established the Laymen's Inter-church Council. Its objective is:

"To unite the Christian Churches of the City of White Plains in common programs for their mutual welfare and the benefit of the City, with special emphasis on increasing the influence of the individual churches and of the churches as a unit in the lives and work of the residents of this City."

Some of the Council activities include:

a. Observance of Laymen's Sunday (third Sunday in October).

b. Getting outstanding preachers for city-wide Lenten services.

c. Religious census of White Plains.

d. Cooperation in Christian Education for weekday public schools.

e. Youth program for high schools.

f. Reformation Day Service, on the anniversary of Martin Luther's historical event on October 31, 1517, in Wittenburg, Germany.

g. City-wide Visitation Evangelism, which brought many new people into the churches.

h. Cooperation with the American Bible Society in getting daily Bible readings broadcast over station WFAS.

Three to six men represent each of the churches in this Council. This group action accomplishes projects which would otherwise be impossible or impractical for individual churches. The Council puts extra steam behind a drive which goes beyond the power of one church.

6. Portland, Oregon and Cleveland are among an increasing number of cities which open city council meetings with prayer. Representatives of various faiths are usually invited to invoke seriously the Lord's guidance. Suggestions from councils of churches to city officials are sometimes instrumental in introducing this practice.

A resolution by your Men's Clubs and the Men's Clubs of nearby churches can be the means of getting your city to open its council meetings with prayer.

7. Many of the men in your club work for firms which publish company magazines. Here is an opportunity for them to spread God's word among fellow workers. These members should contact the editor of their house magazine and get him to include some religious editorial material in *each* issue. This can be an editorial . . . a prayer . . . or a sermonette.

The writing and selection of this material should be rotated among the three faiths.

Charles R. Riegler, Editor of "Johnson and Johnson's Bulletin," is one of many who have found and proved the value of using religious editorial material. He has used the back cover for inspirational ads and, in a recent issue, carried a short but inspiring sermonette by a local clergyman entitled: "Thought for the Month." Think what an inspired group of laymen could do to spread this religious editorial policy. In their talks with house magazine editors your fellow club members should point out today, more and more *general* publications are running more and more religious editorials. That's because their readers want this material and respond to it. Readership studies show that religious articles, stories and news get above the average reading. When you read a good religious piece in a general magazine, don't sit on your hands. Send a post card or letter to the publisher or editor. Tell him how much you liked it . . . urge him to run more religious material. When all we church-goers keep sending in our notes of appreciation to publication people, the quantity of religious material will be at least double what it is today. So don't sit on your hands!

8. Your Men's Club can be a powerful factor in getting your city to celebrate Christmas in a religious way. They can greatly increase the religious observance of this festival. For example, your Men's Club can organ-

ize a plan to follow Little Rock, Arkansas, in giving witness to the religious meaning of the Christmas season. On December 15, local churches of eight denominations, plus the Y.M.C.A., stage their annual Christmas parade. This portrays the Life of Christ. The procession of more than 40 floats go down the main streets to the steps of the State Capitol. Here a Christmas lighting ceremony takes place. The parade is so newsworthy it is televised by a Memphis station.

9. Here is an answer to a popular alibi for not attending church, which should be read at the next meeting of your Men's Club.

"If I were a layman, I'd go after my non-churchgoing male friends, who say, 'My parents made me go to church so often when I was a kid that I swore when I was grown and had my independence I would never go again.'

"The woods are full of that brand of opposition. The field is white unto the harvest. Such a man needs to be made to think. He needs to have his conscience aroused. Generally, he is a likeable sort, but the average parson hasn't a chance with him. He is allergic to parsons.

"But a smart layman he often respects. A business associate has a good chance of winning him, particularly if as much time is put on the 'Christian sales talk' as the average business salesman devotes to the task of learning how to sell his particular product. Generally he can be reminded that he has a good reputation in town. He is a success. He has the respect and confidence of his fellow men. Ask him why.

"The basic reason is that his father and mother saw to it that he was brought up in the Christian faith, that he went regularly to church, that he learned to believe in and respect Christian principles of human conduct. The truth is, he is blaming his parents for the very things that put him where he is today. Besides hurting the cause of Christ at a time when the world desperately needs his abilities and witness, he is ungrateful for the heritage his parents gave him."

This is quoted from that helpful and inspiring folder "If I Were a Layman" by James W. F. Carman. These folders are available at 3¢ each or $2.25 per hundred, from the Presiding Bishop's Committee on Laymen's Work, at 281 Fourth Avenue, New York 10, N. Y. If all the men in your club had a copy of this folder they could do a better sales job on and for the church.

10. Speaking of educating laymen, the Lutheran Laymen's Movement for Stewardship has taken a forward step by establishing a lay school of theology at Wittenberg College. It is designed to prepare laymen for increased responsibility in congregational administration, stewardship and evangelism. Classes include Bible studies, basic Christian beliefs, psychological problems, for laymen, practical church work, church history and sociology. Conducted by Hamma Divinity School, Wittenberg's theological department, the classes will be held on eight consecutive Saturdays. They will be repeated twice each semester in the future if demand warrants.

11. Students at Wittenberg College made front page news when they organized their own Chapel Council. The newly formed Chapel Council at this Springfield, Ohio, college is a full-fledged, self-governing church. Your Men's Club can help the students at your local college to organize their church and chapel services. In too many schools chapel services are being curtailed or dropped.

Our Men's Clubs can strengthen the determination of the college president to continue these religious services and help him make them more inspiring.

12. How long since your Men's Club offered to help the Sunday School? Providing some badly needed new equipment . . . visiting and providing speakers for opening services . . . getting religious pictures for the walls? By doing this and other helpful things one of your members may become so interested that he helps give new life and growth to the Sunday School. For example, Luis Weil, a top executive at Young and Rubicam ad-

vertising agency became so interested in the Sunday
School at Noroton, Conn., that he plunged into its work.
As a result of Mr. Weil's activities, the size of the Sunday School quadrupled in four years. This contribution
was made despite the fact that Mr. Weil is one of the
busiest advertising men in New York City. He proved
we men all have time to help our Sunday Schools if we
are inspired to find it.

The Hotel Biltmore in New York City has a prayer
room. Conrad Hilton is establishing a prayer room in
the famous Waldorf-Astoria Hotel in New York. Your
Men's Club can help spread this religious development
in hotel and community life. Suggest to your local hotel
manager that he follow the example of these two hotels
who serve their guests and fellow townsmen by providing the facilities for prayer and meditation. Then
help the hotel publicize the room and encourage its use.
It would be most constructive if your club could get
groups of people to use such local prayer room in
group praying for specific causes like world peace, industrial peace, religion in government.

13. At the risk of being accused of having a one-track
mind, we are going to close with the same idea which
ends the chapter on "Activities for Active Old Timers."
This idea or activity is just as right and logical for
Men's Clubs as it is for Active Old Timers. It is the
project of getting local plants to hold religious services
regularly. The men in your club *can* persuade local industries to follow the example of the Gerber Plumbing
Fixture Co., of Plymouth, Indiana.

Here is how their program led to greater church
membership according to the special news story in the
Protestant World.

An increase in church membership and a lessening
in industrial tensions among the workers of the crate
factory of the Gerber Plumbing Fixtures Company here
can both be traced to the ten-month old program of religious services in the factory on company time. The

interdenominational services started early this year at a request from a number of workers in the plant, are held every Wednesday morning as the working day starts, at 7 a.m., and last for 30 minutes.

Seven Plymouth clergymen take turns in leading the services. They are: the Reverend Ernest R. Armstrong of the Presbyterian Church, the Reverend William Van Winkle of the Assembly of God, the Reverend Ivan R. Woods of the Church of the Nazarene, the Reverend Milton Petsold of the Evangelical Reformed Church, the Reverend Merlin Cassell of the Church of the Brethren, and the Reverend R. Richmond Blake of the Methodist Church.

Max Gerber, president of the company, is convinced that the investment of half an hour of company time once a week has paid big dividends in improved management-employee relations, better interfaith understanding and increased church membership.

The common bond established by prayer and song has served to reduce the number of grievances that normally arise among people working together.

On the basis of their experience, those who have shared in this successful experiment in factory religious services believe that their success can be readily duplicated elsewhere as long as a few simple rules are followed. The services must not be imposed upon the factory workers, but must come in response to their demand; services must be interdenominational; attendance must be voluntary; ministers in the area must support the plan; and the whole plan must be under the eye of a committee representative of all company departments.

One of the clearest indications that such a plan can work elsewhere is the fact that the employees of three smaller plants near the Gerber crate plant have recently been permitted to punch the time clock on Wednesday mornings and then take time off to attend the Gerber services.

From the testimony of Gerber employees, the in-plant services have reached and won back to regular church attendance many who had long stayed away from the church of their youth.

We know of no better way to close this important chapter than by giving you A. Douglas Steffenson's companion poem to the hymn "Rise up, O men. . . ."

Kneel down, O men of God!
If thou wouldst greater things,
Gain heart and mind and soul and strength
Of Him, the King of Kings!

Kneel down, O men of God!
His kingdom tarries long;
But God's great day of brotherhood
Is born in hearts made strong.

Kneel down, O men of God!
The Church for you doth wait.
God's strength is far beyond the means
We yield to make her great.

Kneel at the cross of Christ!
And rediscover there,
As brothers of the Son of man
What strength there is in prayer!

Chapter 10

PROJECTS FOR
WOMEN'S CLUBS

GOD MUST LOVE WOMEN dearly. He made them so attractive in so many different ways. He gave them patience
and understanding to get along with their husbands and
children. He keeps them from being bored with house-
work. On top of all this, God blessed women with a
sixth sense—the sense of intuition.

Ever since the Church was founded, women have
been showing their appreciation for God's many blessings by being God's greatest helpers. No church could
get along without the *daily* support of the women.
Women do so much more church work than men, that
the men in many families should be ashamed for letting
the "little lady" do so much more than they do. For too
long church men have depended upon the clergy and
the women to do most of the church work. Too many
men have been visible examples of a description given
by someone who reworded a familiar hymn to read:

> "Take my wife and let her be
> Consecrated, Lord, to Thee;
> Help her now Thy will to see
> But please, dear Lord, don't count on me."

The authors and sponsors of this book do not agree
with the above last line. That's why there are two chapters on how men can do their share of God's work. Yet

there are three words in that last line which are true of women . . . "count on me."

Ever since the time of Mary and Martha, God has always been able to count on women. Women's organizations are always looking for new ways to serve God . . . to spread his religion . . . and to help others. Here are some projects which are worthy of being extended to and adopted by other women's church groups.

1. Wouldn't your group like to provide your church and clergyman with a valuable device that extends the ministry of service and of music? Of course it would! Especially as the cost is within the means of most women's organizations.

The device is a tape recording machine. With it your minister can bring your own church services to shut-ins, to the hospitalized and parishioners. They can actually participate in services which they are unable to attend. A tape recording machine brings your choir these unusual advantages. It can rehearse entire numbers without interruption. Then the choir leader can play back the rehearsal with individual group choir members to suggest improvement. Also the recording permits rehearsals when an accompanist cannot be present.

Many ministers use the tape recording machine for practicing sermons and developing a still better delivery. The Minnesota Mining and Manufacturing Company of St. Paul, Minnesota, can tell you all about the useful machines because they make the recording tape for them.

2. Here is a worth-while project which costs only the time and postage of individual letters. It is to encourage motion picture companies to produce more religious films to combat our godless common enemy . . . Communism. The production and showing of more religious films will also remind more movie-goers to attend their houses of worship more frequently. They show the unchurched some of the values of life which come only through a religious life.

How do you organize this project? Simply by forming a "Motion Picture Committee." The members report regularly on religious films that deserve the support and commendation of churchgoers. The committee urges the members to take four steps concerning religious films.

First: Have the family see it.

Second: Recommend the film to friends, neighbors, and relatives.

Third: Write the motion picture company, thanking them for getting out the picture and urging them to produce more religious films of similar high calibre.

Fourth: Write or phone the manager of the local movie theater where you saw the film. Tell him how much you liked the picture and encourage him to show more religious films.

The Johnston Office of the Motion Picture Producers recently began to consider having films reviewed by critics from the religious press. This project is worthy of support, and adoption by your religious journal.

Here is what Spyros P. Skouras, president of Twentieth Century Fox Film Company, says on religion and the movies:

"The screen will never cease to be conscious of its tremendous responsibilities to the cause of religion. Church and screen are joined together in the defense of the spiritual heritage of Western civilization against the threats of a pagan philosophy. Among civilized people no medium of communication is more sensitive to the spiritual aspirations of humanity than the screen.

"Combining all the classical arts, the screen has long been able to present religion as a living experience, identifying the individual in the audience with the characters he sees on the screen. The screen's unlimited scope, in terms of time and geography, can make people relive again the story of Calvary, or report events of the present moment showing the influence of Christ upon the minds and hearts of men. The camera can penetrate into the greatest cathedral or the smallest country chapel."

By organizing a Motion Picture Committee, your group can help increase the number and quality of religious films shown to the 70,000,000 movie-goers in this country.

3. Instead of giving just a certain percentage of money from your group's treasury for foreign missions, plan to earn or give money for a definite project. Here are some examples. Provide a horse and saddle for a missionary in the Philippines. Send automobile snow tires for a traveling missionary in South Dakota. Get a printing press or a cow for the Kiyosato Educational Experiment in Kiyosato, Japan. Dr. Paul Rusch can let you know more of the needs of this pioneering rural project to bring Christianity to Japan if you write him at 2720 North Greenview Street, Chicago 14, Illinois.

The Foreign Mission Board of your denomination can give you specific needs which can fit the earning or giving capacity of any size women's group. You'll get more support from more members and more nonmembers through this method of filling definite needs.

4. Does your church have a lending library of religious books? If not, here is a real opportunity for your organization. Nearly all of us churchgoers do not read enough religious books. We would read more of them if the books were made more available . . . easier to get . . . could be picked up in connection with services of worship. Yes, a church library will stimulate the religious reading of the congregation.

Most churches have plenty of space for a church library. Some handy man or home workshop hobbyist in the church can build the bookcases. A book collecting committee plus pulpit appeals will bring in the volumes. Families with means can be urged to buy one new religious book per month, read it, and then turn it over to the church's library.

Each month the church bulletin can list the new

books and two or three favorites, like *In His Steps, The Big Fisherman, A Certain Woman, The Robe, A Man Called Peter,* The Religious Book Publishers Association of 2 West 46th Street, New York City, can supply your local book stores, or you, with a list of 350 religious books which can make a church library complete. Get this list and then use it as a guide for your new additions.

5. Have your group put on a skit before the congregation, visualizing your activities. It's a lot of fun. And oh, so worth while! The Women's Auxiliary of the Diocese of Chicago produced such a skit, entitled "Visions of a Parish President." The skit *sold* the value of women's work so thoroughly that new support, new members, new cooperation came from many sources.

The skit is well-written. It combines serious thought and lighthearted humor. You can easily adapt it to the work of your organization. So why not write for a copy of this script? The source is Women's Auxiliary, Diocese of Chicago, 65 East Huron Street, Chicago 11, Illinois.

6. All of us like to receive greeting cards on our birthdays. We would enjoy having our church remember us on that day. Why not form a "Greeting Card Committee" among your organizations? It's the responsibility of the group to send out birthday cards to each member . . . get-well cards to the sick and temporarily hospitalized . . . congratulation cards to the parents of newborn babies. The good will and friendship generated by this activity is far more than the low cost.

Mary and H. C. Mattern are the world's greatest example of the good will and friendship developed by birthday cards. This remarkable couple have developed a birthday card list of names which exceeds 12,000 lucky recipients. And the Matterns keep this flow of friendship going out every day, despite the fact that they have no permanent home and are "on the road" constantly. Their motto, "God Bless You," "Keep Smiling Always," is known throughout the U.S.A. and the world.

7. In an inspiring article in *The City Church*, Mabel G. Wagner tells how Methodist women teach neighborliness in community centers. Under the title, "Chaotic Cities or Christian Communities?" she writes as follows:

"Home missions have a significant responsibility for creating a Christian America by reaching the neglected areas of cities and developing in them a sense of neighborhood or community. Feeling this challenge, the Woman's Division of Christian Service of the Methodist Board of Missions and Church Extension has neighborhood houses and community centers in cities all over the United States.

"How are we carrying the Christian gospel through these centers? By seeking those whom society has spurned and sometimes our established churches have neglected. Our workers take people where they are, trying first to meet their most pressing needs, be they spiritual, health, social, or whatever else.?

"Respect for every personality, regardless of race, nationality, or religion, is basic, stemming from Christ's teaching of the worth and dignity of each individual. Sometimes this means we are serving people of other faiths in our program. The missionary spirit—'Go ye into all the world'—impels us to serve all, even those of another faith if there is human need. We are not carrying the Gospel only to our own little group.

"Always there is hope that our workers and programs will be able to give inspiration and guidance in the religious fundamentals of life. Such a response may not come in a week or a month or even longer. Years later we may discover that an individual was lifted up."

St. Mark's Community Center in New Orleans is an example of this home mission work so badly needed in so many cities. It is located in the famous French Quarter. Here young and old are welcomed. Under Christian leadership a program of wholesome recreation is provided to help young people to develop a sense of neighborliness and responsibility for helping themselves and the community. This includes clubs, Boy Scouts, Girl Scouts, Explorers, crafts, game room activities, family night programs, truck rides for teen-agers, parties and outings. Home calls and personal conferences minister to special individual needs.

Wesley House in Atlanta, Georgia, and George and Marcy Center in Chicago, are similar projects where church women sponsor a Christian social center to meet the community needs.

8. Re-establish the fine old religious habit of saying grace at your meals. We in America have so much for which to thank God, that we should take these family gathering opportunities to count our blessings *out loud*. And also start the practice of ending your grace with . . . "And keep us ever mindful of the needs of others." That's one of the surest ways to keep your children conscious of Christian charity and Christian stewardship.

9. How about having a bush-planting party in the spring or fall on the church grounds? In this way your church property can have the background of one of the most beautiful and inspiring grounds in the city. Flowering shrubs are especially effective. A chairman of the Garden or Grounds Committee can tell the congregation a week ahead of time what plants and bushes are wanted. For a complete plan of a church garden project, read Chapter 18, starting on page 255.

10. Women are the ideal ones to increase religious reading in the home. They are the ones to subscribe to the magazine published by your denomination, and to an inter-denominational publication like *Christian Herald, Christian Century, National Council Outlook,* or *Protestant World.* Yes, the fair sex are the best ones to start carrying out the suggestions in Chapter 26 on religious reading, starting on page 334.

Your women's clubs can start by organizing a rebirth of Bible reading in the home. The need for this is found in the Bible survey made for Thomas Nelson & Sons by

Batten, Barton, Durstine and Osborn. One question in this survey was: "How often do you read your Bible?" (Survey included all faiths and the majority of denominations.) The answers were as follows:

When I feel the need of it	33%
Once a week or so	24%
Every day	22%
Once a month	3%
Less frequently	9%
Never	3%

No religious group can feel very proud of this record. Let's hope that your church members read the Bible far more often. An inspired questionnaire, asking the same question, would be an interesting piece of research for your club members. Simply distribute slips of paper asking the same question, then ask the members to answer it, not signing their names. After the answers are tabulated, see how their Bible-reading habits compare with the above percentages.

Then start an all-out campaign to increase Bible reading in your members' homes. Point out that every family *has time* to read the Good Book. For example, no one is busier than the star, Red Skelton, with his TV and radio shows, personal appearances, etc. Yet Red Skelton finds time to read his Bible every day. Urge your members to put a Bible on the night table next to the bed. Then it is more convenient for husband and wife to pick it up and read it just before they go to sleep at night. If you wonder where to begin, start with the "Sermon on the Mount," Matthew, chapters 5 through 7. That is the talk which 8 out of 10 college students wished they had heard given at first hand. It contained more familiar quotations than almost any other part of the Bible. Some people read the "Sermon on the Mount" once a month. Yet regardless of what you read in the Bible, you will feel better for the reading. Some families stimulate the Bible reading of their children by giving them a brand new Bible in a different translation, for example, the "New Revised Standard Version."

Other ways of increasing Bible reading in the home are as follows:

a. Let each member of the family have his own copy and share in the reading, using the version best suited and liked.

b. Sometimes read the life of Jesus right straight through.

c. The Sunday School lessons may be followed.

d. Also readily accessible are booklets of daily devotional readings, selections from religious magazines, or leaflets which the American Bible Society makes available such as "Stories of the Bible," "Men and Women of the Bible," "Poetry of the Bible," "Wisdom from the Bible," "Forty Favorite Chapters," "A Month of Devotional Readings," "Bible Alphabet," or "Daily Bible Readings for the Year," which takes note of special days and religious events. The address of the American Bible Society is 450 Park Avenue, New York 22, N. Y.

If your church is getting a new minister *and wife,* we sincerely recommend your sending for a reprint of an article which appeared in the July 19, 1952, issue of Presbyterian Life Magazine. It was entitled "Directions for the Care and Use of Your Pastor's Wife." The author, Margaret Johnson Hess, points out the unsoundness and unfairness of taking it for granted that the new minister's wife can, and will, take over *all* the activities of the previous parson's bride. She will be better at some things and may not be as good at others. That's natural! She may even do things which were impossible for her predecessor.

As is pointed out by the *Presbyterian Life* article, published at 321 So. Fourth Street, Philadelphia 7, Pennsylvania, the talents of wives differ just as do those of their husbands. So *don't rush* the new wife into a lot of activities. Let her look around . . . and then decide what she can do best with her talents. In the situation of a new minister and wife, the women in a church should remember those wise words St. Paul wrote to the new church in Corinth:

"Now about spiritual gifts, brethren, I would not have you ignorant.

"Now there are various kinds of gifts, but there is the same Spirit; various kinds of official service, and yet the same Lord; various kinds of effects, and yet the same God who produces all the effects in each person. But to each a manifestation of the Spirit has been granted for the common good. To one the word of wisdom has been granted through the Spirit; to another—" And Paul goes on to enumerate the different gifts.

Chapter 11

ACTIVITIES FOR
ACTIVE OLD-TIMERS

Let us thank God for the development of "geriatrics"—for all medicine and health habits created for
older people. It has given our churches a larger number
of longer-lived members and communicants than ever
recorded in the religious history of the world. These
fine men and women are a priceless asset to any congregation. Properly directed, the energies, talents and experiences of these "active old-timers" can give your parish extra ways to serve your community, your congregation and Our Lord.

The size of this group is described in an article written by Jean Begeman. Entitled "Work Longer, Live
Longer," it states:

"Primarily because of modern medicine's emphasis
on longevity, there are now three million more old
folks in the United States than there were 10 years ago.
There are today in the United States 13 million persons
65 years of age or over. Those retiring at 65 now have
an average of 13 years of life remaining and half of
them will live longer."

These fine people are growing more important in the
religious life of this country. Here are just some of the
ways their abilities and experiences can build your
church.

1. The Reverend P. T. Graetz of the United Congregational Church in Avon Park tells us about the un-

usual activities of a woman who àt seventy-two suddenly found herself confined to a wheel chair. Some people could have become either bitter or *resigned* to this confinement. But not this grand soul. She started a new Christian life for herself by devoting her wheel-chair time to writing comforting letters to people in trouble. Even though she doesn't know the recipients personally, her notes of cheer and encouragement are an inspiration which often comes at the most opportune time. If a person cannot compose individual letters, he or she can now find attractive and inexpensive greeting cards which express many of the desired sentiments.

2. Speaking of writing to troubled people, there is another badly needed project which can be done best by our "active old-timers." That is to write to newspaper editors, magazine editors, mayors, councilmen, and congressmen whenever there is a matter which involves the Christian living . . . clean government . . . and public welfare. In the rush of these days, the older people have the most time to write. They also have the more experience through which to give advice to public servants and the public press. Therefore, their letters will have more influence on our leaders and our publications.

In the case of publications, our older people especially should write to editors and publishers when they run good religious articles or stories. For example, when the *Saturday Evening Post* published its interesting article on "Unknown Facts About the Bible," all our "over-6oers" should have written the editor or publisher thanking him for running this article of such great interest to the millions of religious people who read the *Post*.

3. One of the best ways for active old-timers to invest their time is to attend public hearings on problems and projects which concern public welfare, the church, young people, morality, etc. For example, they can and should sit in on local meetings on narcotics, juvenile

delinquency, etc. There they can make their influence felt. And the officials conducting the meetings will be encouraged by the presence of responsible citizens. Being better informed through their attendance, our older people will become valuable sources of first-hand information. By passing this on to their friends, neighbors, and relatives, they can be a direct force influencing public information and stimulating public action.

4. Many churches have found that they can get more young marrieds to attend churches by having "baby-sitters" take care of children while their parents attend the services. No group is better equipped to "baby-sit" in homes or in the church house than our retired men and women.

One of the best ways to organize the valuable services of the active old-timers is to make a survey of their talents. First make a list of the names and addresses of all members who are sixty or over. Then send them a letter, or call on them with a simple form to fill out. On this 3x5 card list the activities which each is willing to do. Wording for the card can be something like this:

ACTIVE OLD-TIMERS
IN (*Name of Church*)

Name ....

Address .... Phone..........

Will be willing to do the following:
    write newspaper editors ( )
    write magazine editors ( )
    attend public hearings ( )
    watch babies during service ( )
    baby-sit in homes ( )

5. The Lutheran Church of the Reformation in Rochester, New York, has a project which is ideal for active old-timers. The Rev. Alfred L. Beck tells us that they have a working Home Department in their Sunday School through which calls are made on over fifty sick and shut-ins, *several times a year*. The lay visitor brings a copy of the Sunday School quarterly and news about the church. Often they pray together. In between the regular calls these shut-ins are sent cards on their birthdays, Christmas and Easter. This is an ideal way to show your shut-ins that they belong to a church which really cares about them.

6. The older members of your church are just the ones to remind public office holders of the trust which the public has placed in them. This can be done by mailing the following prayer twice a year to all office holders.

A PRAYER FOR GUIDANCE IN OFFICE

Dear Lord, the people have elected me
To speak for them in things
Of state; to Thee
I come for help . . .
I shall be tempted by
Those men whose god
Is gain; may I
Be true to country, self and Thee!

Stand with me, Lord, each time
I speak, when godless
Men would make a mockery
Of righteousness.
At voting time touch Thou my lips,
For I would not bring shame
Or fear to fellow men—
Nor cast dishonor on Thy name.

And give me courage to defend
The weak; to work to ban
All things that would destroy
The dignity of man.
Knowing, Lord, that
Thou answerest prayer when
Humble knee is bent, I ask these things
      —but
Only by Thy will. Amen.

Herman S. Garst

It would be a good idea to mail this prayer (printed on a government post card, or typed on an 8½x11 sheet of paper) to *all candidates* in your fall election.

7. Dr. Frank Fremont-Smith, of New York City, suggests an excellent activity for active old-timers: *be a Foster Grandparent*. In that special magazine for older people, *Lifetime Living*, he spells out his idea in the following way:

"Many older people love to be with children, and 'have a way' with them which is particularly successful. Too often, however, older people can't have this kind of association, either because they live too far from their grandchildren or because they have none.

"A foster-grandparent movement might do much for both age groups. The proposal is very simple: Older persons can 'adopt' a foster grandchild or two, and a child can 'adopt' one or two foster grandparents.

"I know that this idea has been tried unofficially many times. What is needed is some promotion for the idea, perhaps a central clearing house or newsletter for the exchange of ideas and experiences.

"In some communities a church can start the project, give the plan publicity, and arrange contracts between prospective foster grandparents and foster grandchildren. The mutual adoption would be informal and voluntary, of course.

"Foster grandparents can take their youngsters on

expeditions, play games with them, teach them hobbies or skills. Foster grandparents can become godsends to parents by taking over a child for an afternoon—either at the grandparent's home or the child's—might baby-sit, or entertain the foster grandchild who is ill or convalescent.

"Groups of foster grandparents might meet occasionally to exchange ideas and might even form clubs. Once a year a grand picnic might provide some publicity and a lot of fun."

8. *Christian Herald* published a challenging article entitled "Smut on Our Newsstands." It told how filthy sensual paper-covered books are degrading the minds of our young people. These detective stories or whodunnit murder mysteries lure purchasers and readers through their front covers with partially nude drawings of over-sexed girls. The stories mix sex, sin and murder in such a way that, according to Norman L. Hall of Houston, Texas, "this trash is contributing very heavily to the moral breakdown in our schools."

Legitimate book stores would not handle these degrading books, and many of the news dealers and other stores selling this paper-covered filth do not realize the harm they are doing.

Active old-timers are well suited to be a Committee, vigilantly calling the attention of the stores to the bad books on their sales racks. They should ask the store owners if they would like to have the minds and actions of their children or grandchildren influenced by this "Smut on Our Newsstands." Let's meet the challenge of this situation by calling on stands and stores, *continually,* until this filth is removed. You'll be surprised how few calls will be necessary because retail outlets value their good standing in the community. They don't want the ill will and bad regulation which can be given them by a Church Committee.

9. Our older fellow church members can lead a campaign to get Bibles placed in the reception rooms of

local offices. Bringing the Word of God near to visitors is already being done by leading companies like J. Walter Thompson Advertising Agency and Bridgeport Brass. The New Revised Standard Version of the Bible gives your active old-timers an extra reason to ask for this company cooperation. That's because most office visitors have heard about this new translation and will want to see how it compares with the Bibles in their homes. Reading the Holy Book while waiting for a business interview is one of the best ways to bring your religion into your daily business life, Lee H. Bristol, Jr., takes "Business-Bible-ism" one step nearer by keeping a Bible on his desk at the Bristol-Myers Company.

10. Local radio stations offer another opportunity for active old-timers. They can call on the station managers and program directors, asking their cooperation in broadcasting churchgoing reminders on Saturday afternoons and evenings. These include the playing of that inspiring and beloved song, "Let's Go to Church on Sunday Morning." If your station does not have the record, offer to buy it for them. It was recorded by the Capitol Record Co. and costs only 89 cents.

Other churchgoing reminders are station-break announcements (8 seconds between two recorded programs). These are worded as follows:

"Take someone to church with you tomorrow. You'll both be happier for it."

"Tomorrow be sure to worship in the church of your choice. You'll feel better for it *all week long.*"

"Churchgoing families are happier families. Make yours happier tomorrow by going to church."

"Families that pray together stay together. Defeat divorce by praying together on Sunday."

"This week look through the windows of your church or synagogue from the *inside.*"

11. The Nehi Corporation of Columbus, Georgia, and other leading companies open their sales meetings

with prayer. They know that taking God into their business sessions is one way to get the right guidance for their deliberations.

Your active old-timers can call on local companies that hold sales meetings and conventions, pointing out the good of opening the sessions with prayer.

12. The Holy Communion United Lutheran Church of Detroit, Michigan, has another activity which is suited for active old-timers. The Rev. Alfred G. Belles tells us that they hand-pick couples who are pledged to make at least three calls per month, on prospective or delinquent members. These callers have a meeting once every four months to compare notes, share experiences, and lend encouragement to each other. Why don't you try this proven plan in your church?

13. God bless the National Council of Jewish Women for their "New York Council Club for Older People." They organized meetings where men and women come together for fun and inspiration. This is a project for large congregations, downtown churches, or your local council of churches. After this older group is organized and functioning in your city, it can take on the projects in this chapter and many others which will occur to the active members.

14. *Protestant World* featured this story of how a New Orleans pastor gives a Special Service for shut-ins:

"The Rev. G. A. Schmidt, pastor of the First English Lutheran Church here, has taken a little leeway with one of the mandates of Jesus Christ and has come up with a new kind of church service which has proved very popular. The Rev. Mr. Schmidt, burdened with an exceptionally large number of sick calls one month some years ago, decided that Jesus's charge to his ministers to visit the sick need not be taken literally—if the 'sick' were actually infirm oldsters who could get out once in a while with a little help from their families.

"In short, the Rev. Mr. Schmidt thought that it would be a good idea—a real time-saver—if the 'sick'

could come to visit him—in a group. He also figured—
and has since been proven right—that these oldsters
would be cheered more by the gathering than by a visit
from one solitary minister.

"The Rev. Mr. Schmidt's idea resulted in a special
monthly meeting and communion services for people
who ordinarily are 'shut-ins.'

"The first Sunday of every month an unusual procession forms in front of the first English Lutheran Church,
just before noon.

"Groups of elderly members, some of them in wheel
chairs, many using crutches and canes, begin arriving
for the special service. The youngest of the group is
sixty-five years old. The eldest member is in his eighties.

"Relatives help most of them get to the church. The
others, who are without families, get assistance from a
group of volunteers who call for them and take them
home.

"The service is held in the basement of the church,
which is only a few steps below ground level, rather
than in the chapel on the structure's second floor.

"For most of them, the trip to the church is their
only journey outside of their homes each month. So, it's
quite an event.

" 'They enjoy worshipping together and visiting together afterwards,' the pastor says."

15. The Welfare and Health Council of New York
City has sponsored an older-person project which can
be and should be duplicated by downtown churches, by
larger older neighborhood churches, and by the local
council of churches. This is an *Annual Hobby Show
for 60-Plussers*. For six years this exhibit has been
awakening the public's interest in the creative poten-
tialities of people over sixty years old. Among the 2,500
exhibits last year was a model of a Normandy Synagogue carved by Herman Kasindorf, a bookkeeper and
office manager.

You'll find the exhibits are so interesting that you

can charge admission to raise funds for some worthy local cause. Only be sure to announce your Hobby Show one year in advance so that the 60-plussers have plenty of time to work on their exhibits.

16. St. Matthew's Cathedral of Dallas, Texas, brings new life and new achievements to old-timers through its "Golden Age Club." This is a 60-plus, non-denominational organization which meets in St. Matthew's Church. There are no dues. At the Golden Age parties the old-timers have fun, meet new friends, and start on projects such as making small gifts for shut-ins. More than one oldster has begged to learn a new handicraft, "so I'll be accomplishing something again."

Incidentally, the "children" of Golden Age Club members are much happier, too. For in their homes, instead of having beginning-to-be-querulous old women whose discontent made them feel vaguely guilty, they now have lively little white-haired ladies who enjoy every minute.

Episcopal Churchnews credits Christ Church with organizing the first Golden Age Club in Dallas. Now there are four. So you can see you can have more than one of these helpful clubs in a city. They draw members like a circus draws kids.

Headquarters of this movement are on the grounds of St. Matthew's Cathedral in Dallas, Texas. Write Canon Edward B. Ferguson for complete details on how to organize and operate a Golden Age Club. And also say a prayer for E. D. Farmer, who financed the start of this project through his E. D. Farmer Foundation for the Aged.

17. Your active old-timers can also do a job in getting local newspapers to run more religious material. They can call on the editor and publisher and urge him to take the following steps:

a. Run a religious prayer on the Saturday church page, like the *Schenectady Gazette*.

b. Put a daily prayer above each day's editorial, like the *White Plains Reporter Dispatch*.

c. Use that basic religious theme or slogan "Church-going Families Are Happier Families" at the top of the church page, like the *Scarsdale Inquirer*.

18. In Larchmont, N. Y., Mrs. Roy E. Booth, organized the Genarians Club to rout loneliness.

"Early in January 1947, she went with her idea to the Reverend Dr. Floyd E. McGuire, pastor of the Larchmont Avenue Presbyterian Church. Dr. McGuire was enthusiastic about the plan. He helped organize the group—a club open to all persons, regardless of creed or church membership, who insisted upon remaining socially active and useful.

"The name of the club was suggested by the group's first chairman, Mrs. Katherine Lafitte. 'Since most of us are septuagenarians or octogenarians,' she said, 'let's call ourselves simply—*The Genarians.*'

"And then another member dubbed them with an appropriate nickname, *The Geraniums*. The geranium flower is now the club's official badge.

"The club was successful from the very start, for it fulfilled a universal human desire—*the longing to belong*. As one of the members observed, 'I had come to town a perfect stranger. The neighbors were very friendly, but I was anxious to associate with people of my own age. Now that I've found them, I feel as if I had received a new lease on life.' "

Journal of Living

19. Our last project is one that is near and dear to the author's heart. You dear 60-plussers will want to do something about it, too! It's the proved plan of organizing a religious service for plants and factories. It's being done successfully all over the country. One of the pioneers and leaders of this great movement is Rollin M. Severance, owner of the Severance Tool Company in Saginaw, Michigan. His story is so interesting we want you to hear it in his own words.

So take over, Mr. Severance. Tell the reader all about the services in your plant.

"Some may consider our devotional period as a church project, and I might say that we do not think of it as a church project in the usual sense of the word as promoting membership, etc., in a recognized church. It is strictly a spontaneous practice first instituted at a time when I only employed four or five persons. During the years since that time there have been various pressures exerted from one angle or another to change or otherwise modify this program. We have seen many things which are related to this little time together each day about the word of God which we feel are not to be valued in terms of the amount represented by that portion of payrolls in the time involved. All that we have is given to us of God and it is only appropriate that we unitedly take the few moments involved in devotion and recognition of Him at the beginning of our work periods."

The devotional services include: the singing of well-known hymns, reading from the Bible and prayers for the men, their families and their work. These morning devotionals ease tensions and bring feeling of kinship and good will. The men are paid for their time attending the services. The prospering Severance Tool Industries is today one of the best examples of what happens when faith hits the factory . . . when companies mix worship with work.

As the *Christian Herald* says:
"The National Safety Council recently reported that relief of strain and tension, especially in dangerous work, is an imperative statistical factor in keeping fatalities and accidents at a minimum. The Metropolitan Life Insurance Company has found that a worker doing perilous work is in much greater danger when troubled

by domestic discord, ill health in his family, or any recent emotional disturbance.

"Prayer, Eastman found, is the best antidote to the tensions that beset modern man. In actual practice, prayer soothes and invigorates the spirit and strengthens the tremulous and fearful.

"Daily worship is being practiced both at great plants throughout the country and at smaller, more humble places of endeavor. There is a citrus grower on the outskirts of Phoenix, Arizona, who conducts daily services for his workers amid the orange groves. At several factories of the gigantic Goodyear Tire and Rubber Company devotions are held daily for all who wish to attend. The company not only pays for the workers' time but supplies a suitable room properly equipped.

"At the famed R. G. LeTourneau Technical Institute at Longview, Texas, and at all the LeTourneau plants, the meeting in daily prayer of students and employees has been a long-established practice. Is it mere coincidence that here, as at other plants which bring religion into the daily lives of the factory workers, statistics both for strikes and accidents show a remarkably low incidence? At the LeTourneau school, where qualified young men are trained in industrial operations, part of the curriculum lays emphasis on the need for prayer in the interests of harmony, higher production standards, and higher morale among employees.

The J. C. Penny Company, which operates several hundred retail establishments across the country, has promoted worship services in all its offices and stores. The same holds true of the Kraft Cheese Company, a mining company in Arizona, a dairy in Wisconsin, and a pop-bottling works in Arkansas.

"In these organizations there prevails a spirit of contribution and good will that baffles their competitors. Employers and employees alike realize that they are working for more than just the profit and wages they receive. They find in their work a sense of dignity and a sense of belonging. They are in partnership with each other and with God. They lift their heads high as they go about their task."

Active old-timers are God's chosen people to sell this plant-service project to local companies. They have more time and often have more influence with owners and management. So, "Rise up, O Men of God" and organize these services which bring man's religion into his daily business life.

Bernard Baruch, now in his eighties, recently said: "The constantly increasing life expectancy of Americans gives this country its big opportunity of the next half-century. No previous civilization has ever enjoyed such a maturing, healthy population. How wonderful an asset if properly used! How tragic a liability if abused!"

Chapter 12

USING YOUR RELIGION IN ECONOMIC, SOCIAL AND POLITICAL SITUATIONS

THE CHIEF AIM of Christian social work is to help people in need of such service develop strength from within that will enable them to live life in the full exercise of their capacities and powers. A unique quality of such service is that it is motivated by Christian love—Christian love with all the qualities found in that term and dedicated to the principal that all human beings have certain basic human rights regardless of the accident of birth in a particular area, or of a particular racial heritage. It behooves Christians to examine the nature and the sources of that strength which alone can give direction, endurance, and satisfaction to human beings as they journey from the dawn to the setting of mortal life.

The nature of that strength which denotes the fullness of life can neither be given away nor hoarded, it can only be shared. Thus, in order to help others to be strong, Christians themselves need to know about, and to draw upon, sources of strength for their own lives.

In our church heritage are to be found instruction and guidance in dealing with modern social problems as well as with the conduct of the individual; in attacking causes of human ills as well as relieving and treating the sufferer and the disabled. The principles are there; they have only needed to be interpreted anew as times changed and needs became more complex. Both Old and New Testament are replete with human emphasis.

The institution of marriage came in the second chapter of Genesis, the question of "my brother's keeper" arose in the third chapter, and the first condemnation of murder a few chapters later. Of course, in the Ten Commandments the charge is still more specific: "Thou shall not kill." And they go on: "Neither shalt thou steal." "Honor thy father and thy mother." "Thou shalt not bear false witness against thy neighbor." "Thou shalt not covet thy neighbor's house," etc.

A few books later on (Deuteronomy 15:8) : "If there be among you a poor man of one of thy brethren within any of thy gates in thy land which the Lord Thy God giveth thee, thou shalt not harden thine heart, nor shut thine hand from thy poor brother; but thou shalt open thine hand wide unto him."

Then, in Proverbs, almost at random, there are to be found such admonitions as:

"He that despiseth his neighbor sinneth; but he that hath mercy on the poor, happy is he."

"The righteous considereth the cause of the poor; but the wicked regardeth not to know it."

"Let not mercy and truth forsake thee."

"When the righteous are in authority, the people rejoice; but when the wicked beareth rule, the people mourn." Also see Isaiah 1:16-17; 5:8—Amos 2:6-7a; 5:11 and 12—Micah 4:3; 6:8.

And so on through the Old Testament. The references to personal behavior, the relations of man to man, and other matters of welfare in the community could be quoted at great length.

The New Testament's pages also seem clearly to sanction and enjoin all people to minister to human needs as an inseparable part of the ministry of religion. When asked what was the first and great Commandment, Jesus replied, "Thou shalt love the Lord thy God with all thy heart, and with all thy soul, and with all thy mind.

And the second is like unto it. *Thou shalt love thy neighbor as thyself.*"

At another time, to the young man with great possessiones who asked what good thing he should do that he might have eternal life, having already kept all the Commandments, Jesus replied, "If thou wilt be perfect, go and sell all that thou hast and give to the poor."

In the scene of the last judgement where Jesus pictured the Son of man risen to His Kingly glory, separating from the others those who were to inherit "the Kingdom prepared from the foundation of the world," the choice seems to have been made solely because "I was hungered, and ye gave me meat; I was thirsty and ye gave me drink; I was a stranger and ye took me in; naked and ye clothed me; I was sick and ye visited me; I was in prison, and ye came unto me." When the righteous, bewildered, asked when they had done all these things, the King and great Judge answered and said: "Verily I say unto you, inasmuch as you have done it unto one of the least of these my brethren, ye have done it unto me." That award was without geographical, racial, language, or any other limitations.

Other equally pointed injunctions on the ministry to living men came from Him:

"And who so shall receive one such little child in my name receiveth me."

"Wherefore by their fruits ye shall know them."

"Give to him that asketh the, and from him that would borrow of thee turn not thou away."

"When thou doest alms, let not thy left hand know what thy right hand doeth."

"Render unto Caesar the things which are Caesar's and unto God the things that are God's."

He blessed the merciful, the meek, and the peacemakers, and is recorded as performing such human services as curing the sick and palsied; cleansing the leper; healing the centurion's servant; curing the man with the withered hand, the maimed, the lame and the dumb; making the blind to see; and feeding the five thousand.

In the Gospels, the emphasis is on elementary service, on maintaining life, relieving pain, feeding, clothing, healing, giving a cup of cold water. These elementary forms of service to a neighbor's bodily life have obviously played a tremendous part in Christianity. This is not because the Christian ethic rates bodily need as the most important, but because this type of service is the most universally understood language of brotherly love; and love is often quite as much concerned to show something by what it does, as to do something. It is part of the Incarnational character of Christianity that the plainest forms of service are seen as the most adequate expression of the highest love.

Once this is recognized, it must also be recognized that there are many other levels of service, as many as there are levels of need. To live the fullest life, one's neighbors need much besides basic economic necessities. They need truth, education, companionship, play, joy, beauty, order, protection from the aggressive egotism of fellow men, just laws, hospitals, good government, and so forth. It is here where the church social services can and do play such an important part by providing in their own organizational and community relationships a demonstration of the meaning and significance of their essential message for life situations.

The measure of the vitality of any church is its integration in its own community. Just as a plant must have its roots in the soil if it is to flourish and not wither, so a church must have its roots in the community, if it is to remain vital and grow. It must adapt itself to the people about it, drawing from them fresh energy and inspiration, and giving to them the eternal values of life, intelligently and with careful consideration for their own particular needs. Each community has a personality of its own: cultural heritages which must be known, social and economic patterns which must be studied, and needs which must be met. Only as the parish knows these things can it serve its community effectively .

In general, churches enter the social welfare field from three approaches:

1. Development of operational programs.
2. Community social action and social education.
3. Participation in nonsectarian community services.

These three approaches are rarely separated one from the other. Denominations which may emphasize one or another of these procedures may also enter upon programs in the other two areas mentioned. Denominations which have operational programs on behalf of children, families or the aged see the necessity of preventive social action and constructive social education. They also cooperate fully with community agencies publicly and privately operated.

Similarly we see that church groups which are interested in social education and community action are stimulated to enter the social-welfare field in direct service to people in need.

Government under the Judeo-Christian ethic has largely taken over the provision of financial assistance and is in many areas providing various types of care for children, hospital care for those who cannot afford it, and even community centers in depressed areas. Many non-governmental community-supported agencies have more adequate resources than some church agencies, and so can do a better job with wider coverage. A lack of church support has lead many church agencies to hand over their assets to non-sectarian community groups.

There are many reasons why churches should maintain social-welfare services or contemplate the expansion of already existing agencies.

First, if a democracy is to be strong and healthy, there must be opportunities for citizens to join together in groups to assume real responsibility for solving community problems. Once citizens look to government alone to meet every community need, democracy ceases to exist in its present sense. The work of the church social agency gives to church men an opportunity to work at a special problem within the larger fellowship of the church.

Secondly, the church has an historic tradition as a social pioneer. In days gone by it developed new services to meet human needs. Despite the many governmental and non-governmental services now available, there is still a need for the development of new ways of helping people in trouble. For example, creative experiments are desperately needed to discover new and better ways of treating children who are delinquent, overly sensitive and withdrawn, or otherwise upset. Then, too, more effective means of meeting the problems peculiar to old age should be a special concern of the church.

Only after experiments such as these have demonstrated their value, will the community and the government be willing to provide them. If and when this happens, churches should not regret the loss of an agency, but rejoice in being free to go on to some other unmet need. This willingness to pioneer and then relinquish is of supreme importance. The resources of churches are limited. If they attempt to continue every project they start, a time comes when they no longer have the resources with which to pioneer. The task is something like that of shock troops which are sent in to establish a stronghold. After it is established, they remain only until reinforcements arrive, when they move on to other tasks. In the same way churches go on to new tasks in the war against social ills.

Thirdly, and most important, churches should continue to maintain and develop social-welfare agencies because they are the most tangible way in which the churches can express the social concern which inevitably accompanies the love and worship of God. When clergy and laity in large numbers become genuinely interested in social-welfare services the religious life of the entire church is enriched.

Church social work has two characteristics that distinguish it from other forms of social work:

1. A recognized theistic (God-centered) philosophy as its basic foundation.

2. Existing national, or sometimes international, auspices for its promotion and integration.

There are national boards for the coordination of social work in many churches, notably among the Methodists, Baptists, Episcopalians, Hebrews, Presbyterians, Lutherans, Roman Catholics, Disciples of Christ, and the Evangelical and Reformed. In these denominations one finds a variety of operating agencies and institutions in the health and welfare field, homes for children and for aged, hospitals under church auspices, city mission work, settlement and community centers, homes for convalescents and chronic invalids, and hostels for youth. There are agencies for child placement in foster and adoptive homes . . . congregate and non-institutional services for the aged . . . and work among seamen, immigrants, and services to the deaf and blind.

These denominations have definite policies with regard to their denominational social welfare. They have some institutions that are more or less loosely connected with the church and others which are church-owned and church-operated.

Other denominations have boards or commissions on social action and social education to stimulate their respective members on social issues, and to help solve or try to prevent social evils and problems. Notable among this group are the Congregational-Christian Churches, the Baptist Convention, the Disciples of Christ, and the Evangelical and Reformed.

The churches are keeping abreast of the social trends and developing standards of professional social work especially in those denominations which have their own social ministries in health and welfare organizations. Some churches have taken responsibility for leadership in social work and have represented their welfare interests before federal and state government agencies and in national and state voluntary agencies. Newer methods of social-welfare work are being tested, and the churches have pioneered in the fields of foster homes for children and for the aged. An interesting illustration is the non-institutional service provided by the recently established Service to the Aged of the Diocese of New York.

Certain churches are developing services of chaplains who are trained professionally to cooperate within an institution with surgeons, physicians, psychiatrists, and social workers. The value of pastoral services, in cooperation with other therapies which help to restore sick people to health, is demonstrated. Team work between chaplains and physicians and social workers in meeting the total need of patients is beginning to be a well-enunciated pattern in many of our institutions.

The range of possible activities of a social welfare agency within a church is wide. A review of types includes the following—found, in the main, in some of our larger cities :

1. Operation of child-care institutions and agencies. Both foster homes and institutions are necessary since many children thrive in foster homes, while certain others with special problems require an institutional setting.

2. Operation of homes for the aged. These homes are run on two different plans: (a) the life-contract plan, where the resident assigns his assets to the home and pays an admission fee, thereby guaranteeing him care for the rest of his life, or (b) the boarding plan, where the resident pays a monthly sum for board and room.

3. Hospitals.

4. Settlement and neighborhood houses, also some group work centers in rural areas.

5. City missions which in some instances include the operation of camps, temporary shelters, nursing serv-

ices, convalescent homes, and group-work activities among the foreign born.

6. Chaplaincy service to hospitals and correctional institutions, especially to federal and state prisons, state hospitals, and veterans' hospitals.

7. Service to seamen, migrants, and other transients, including hostels and recreation facilities. Help in locating missing persons, and counseling.

8. Work with the handicapped, including the crippled, deaf, dumb, and blind.

9. Case work and counseling service, making special use of the resources of religion, psychiatry, and vocational guidance. Such services may be directed to general family and personal problems, or to the special problems of particular groups, such as adolescents, or the aged.

10. Service to displaced persons; assisting them with their financial needs, rehabilitation, and resettlement.

11. Social education and action on problems relating to family relations, race relations, housing, civil rights, correctional institutions and services, public health, mental health, education and world order.

12. Conduct of, or cooperation in, surveys of community problems.

13. Group work in clubs, recreation centers, and young people's organizations.

14. Assistance to ministers and others needing information and counsel in referring individuals and families to agencies equipped to deal with their problems.

15. Cooperation in studying community needs and planning and organizing work to improve standards of health and welfare services of the community.

16. Cooperation with other agencies, religious and secular, governmental and non-governmental, professional and lay, local and national standard-setting agen-

cies, in united efforts aimed at more soundly conceived, more efficient, and more economical welfare service.

17. Relief and rehabilitation in Europe and Asia.

18. Educational efforts aimed to secure better understanding through the churches of important welfare causes.

19. Educational activities aimed to promote better understanding among ministers and social workers.

20. Information on, and, at times, support of, legislation on social-welfare problems.

21. Cooperation with court agencies on correctional problems, and the prevention of delinquency.

22. Cooperation in efforts to promote the welfare of children generally.

23. Assistance in securing capable church leadership on community boards, committees, and service groups.

24. Aid to new ministers in becoming acquainted with community problems and resources.

25. Assistance to social workers in finding resources in the churches to aid in appropriate cases.

26. Giving of relief to needy persons in the community.

27. Supplying information on the standing of agencies to responsible inquirers who have received appeals for contributions.

28. Practice and promotion of interracial and intercultural associations.

29. Initiation of new and experimental projects, testing their usefulness, and motions to deactivate some.*

Great and rapid changes in community life often create new community situations which are but little understood and which call for social action. Extensive

---

* Most of these points were listed by Sheley W. Harrison, in his address entitled "A Strategy for Christians in Social Welfare."

modifications in programs and methods of work have been made by religious bodies—modifications which have come about in many cases through studies of the new problems, and initiation of experiments to meet the new needs.

Two examples of new community situations which have called for social action on the part of church agencies have been in respect to (1) the control of alcoholism, and (2) the problem of narcotic addiction. Many hospitals now have special wards for the treatment of alcoholics, often in cooperation with Alcoholics Anonymous. More recently, church societies have become aware that narcotic addiction is a contagious social and psychological disease whose presence in any part of a community threatens the whole. The churches are playing their part in cooperation with other community agencies in removing the facilities for drug addiction.

It cannot be urged too strongly that members of church social agencies join and work with the organizations of other church agencies, as well as both public and private health and welfare agencies. All communities offer the services of such societies. The churches were the original founders of health and welfare organizations. Many of these gradually moved out into the community. However, they still look at the churches for partial support, either civic or financial; leadership; public educational programs; and volunteer service. The churchman as a Christian has a responsibility for using his influence actively in support of an adequate, efficient, humane and non-political administration of public social welfare agencies.

To help agencies give adequate service:

A. Know the agencies, their programs and personnel.
B. Know the standards for adequate service in the fields covered.
C. Give financial support to the private agencies and assist in their fund-raising campaigns, directly or through community chests.

D. Support public agencies' efforts to interpret their work and raise standards of personnel and services.

E. Serve on boards of directors and committees of agencies.

F. Act as volunteers in the service programs of agencies and institutions.

G. Serve, as in the case of the clergy, as chaplains or spiritual advisers to agencies and institutions; when people under your pastoral care are involved. Plan jointly with the social worker.

H. Take special responsibility for the church's health and welfare services.

Churches recognize the responsibility of sharing the great tradition of service with those of other religious beliefs. This recognition must be implemented both by the interchange of ideas and action. Persons of different racial, cultural, and religious backgrounds can only attain a true understanding of each other by working together for common goals.

The church agencies can undertake:

A. Joint membership with other churches in community enterprises.

B. Participation in councils of churches on a regional and state level.

C. Planning for unchurched areas to avoid duplication of effort, staff, and buildings.

D. Joint approach to such enterprises as weekday religious education.

E. Interfaith forums on civic and social problems.

F. Joint support to bring about social or legislative reforms.

G. Community-wide observations of special occasions.

The future of church social work and its successful prosecution will depend upon the way in which basic Christian principles are transfused into social work. There is a distinct contribution to make to the whole field, which can be made only by standing foursquare upon the Christian principle of the worth and dignity of the individual. The total personality of men and women must be treated, instead of thinking of their material needs and their spirits as separate categories. It will be necessary also continually to emphasize the spiritual content, as well as the religious motivation of social service in all community programs. This way lies the redemption of social work from a hundred percent secularism. A challenging future awaits if churches and agencies meet the total needs of men, women, and children.

One of the leading commissions on Christian social relations engages in a five-point program for its lay members throughout the Church. They are (1) the community, (2) industrial relations, (3) race relations, (4) social action, (5) world responsibility. By encouraging local study and action groups, and by making available facts and research material from the state and national headquarters, a real effort is being made to encourage church members to participate in problems which they formerly ignored as church members.

Every major segment of our present society is part and parcel of daily Christian responsibility. The farmer for years has been part of the Church and its annual program. Harvest festivals, timed to the changing of the crops, have been a historic part of Christian rural life. More recently, labor has been recognized by churches and has joined management as an equal partner in developing Christian community programs. Some Christian leaders took a very active part during the years when labor was making major advances.

In the political life of the nation, the various political, economic, and social groups that are *not* exclusively Christian are effectively represented. Any observer at a state capital or in Washington, in addition to watching local developments, knows that management and labor, the farmer and various officials are represented by effective spokesmen for their interest. Seldom is there present a man or woman who speaks for "those that have come together in My name."

One of the leading bishops of a church regularly gets together all the legislators of his faith at a Communion service and breakfast. After having worshiped together, he tells them, "I am *not* here to get the church into politics, I *am* here to get the Church and religion into politicians." Then they proceed to discuss legislation and other questions of great public interest *not* as Democrats or Republicans, and so as opposing parties, but instead as Christian laymen trying to see what is right. These meetings, informal and off the record, help develop better Christian citizenship, as the men attending more and more act in the public interest, instead of on behalf of a particular group.

As one reviews many of the advances made in human living, creating better housing, schools, medical care for those that need it, often one finds church leaders in front. Clergy and laymen have taken the lead in making their religion a seven-day-a-week affair, and in every part of their personal and business life, rather than just confining worship to an hour on Sunday.

Many American organizations have placed leading Christian laymen in positions of high responsibility. The Advertising Council has recently conducted lengthy panels on the influence of religion in American life, the various factors making up our economic system, and what the future holds for the development of this country. A look at the attendance list shows that professors, editors, businessmen, and scholars have shared in studying these problems.

How far these study groups go in reaching the men who guide American economic thinking is well illustrated in recent Advertising Council panels. The editor and publisher of *Business Week* magazine, Elliott V. Bell, a churchman of Pawling, New York, took a leading part with other outstanding citizens in analyzing what was right and best instead of just the easiest to achieve. Interestingly enough, this same *Business Week*, aimed principally at business leaders, printed several Christmas editorials including one urging a return to a Christian Christmas. After showing how commercialized Christmas had become, the editorial written by Dr. Gabriel S. Hauge, a Lutheran layman and son of a clergyman, who each week has the responsibility for preparing the editorials for this leading business weekly, pointed out how some businessmen have stopped giving Christmas presents to each other and instead are spending the money to send to camp children who have never been out of the slums. That type of a Christmas present was an idea born of a Christian heart and mind. The more the nation's companies remember their Christian responsibilities as they are seen through the eyes of devoted laymen, the more the Church will become a constructive force in the life of people today.

When a man is in jail, he cannot go to church unless civic-minded church men make available a chaplain to serve at such an institution. When a man is fighting a war, or is training at a camp, he is dependent on chaplains sent from home to minister unto his spiritual needs. *"Wherever thou art, there I will be with you always."* If this is to be so in fact, laymen must always be alert to the needs of those that aren't so lucky as to be able to walk or ride down the street to the nearest church.

Often when a political question comes up there are many conflicting points of view. Experience has shown that in many cases there are certain basic Christian truths which help point out a solution if they are followed and studied by church people. Many a political crisis has been solved through the good offices of devoted church people. Many a good law has been born as a result of a sermon or a talk of a church leader with a legislator. Many abuses in the political world have been checked by men and women whose basic background of the Church made them stop something bad, before it was too late.

On the economic front, often boss and worker worship at the same altar on Sunday and their children say the same prayers out of the same prayerbooks. Yet during the week and during basic economic discussions, the two parties sometimes act as if they had nothing in common. Much effective work has been done on the economic front by men of good will whose basic allegiance was to God before it was with any particular economic group.

In explaining to a gathering of leading church lay people how the Church for many years had played an outstanding and building part in creating a better tomorrow "in Christ's image," the following was said: "The Church has always weighed the State for justice. Amos and Isaiah show this without a doubt. The Church always should pass judgment on the moral righteousness of anything affecting life, be it spiritual, economic, or social." Of the one hundred leaders present, some white and some black, some rich and some poor, some old and some young, not one voted to disagree with this. That is why in your community, in building up your manpower, you may well wish to study and act in certain fields of economic, political, and social questions where you have a responsibility as a lay leader."

NOTE: *In the questionnaire sent to 2600 clergymen and layworkers, the subject of this chapter was voted fifth most important in the entire book. It was marked essential by 81 percent of the respondents. That evidence urges us all to do something about this challenging subject.*

Chapter 13

ARE WE STARVING OUR CLERGY?

By William B. Hartley[1]

DISGRACEFULLY LOW SALARIES for ministers are weakening our church system. If help comes, it must be from young people." The following article is filled with fighting words and ideas. It opens to realistic scrutiny an area of human affairs not usually available to even the most sincere church member. If some of its contentions arouse shame or resentment, it will have served well as a direct challenge to the churchgoer, and particularly to the new generations of young people now participating for the first time in church administration.

The Editors of Redbook

The Rev. Nathaniel Jackson sat at the desk in his study and looked, with a familiar sense of discomfort, at his monthly domestic budget. Sometimes he prayed after working out the family's budget. Although prayer made him feel better, it never changed the cold reality of a column of figures.

Where could he cut? Food for three persons would

[1] Reprinted with permission from the November 1951 issue of *Redbook* magazine.

come to $50—and that meant lots of frankfurters and no roast beef. Car expenses, including the monthly payment to the finance company, would be $57.70. *High*, the Reverend Jackson thought, *but how could it be otherwise? I made fifty calls last month.*

Gas, heat, telephone, electricity would total $36.25 on the basis of last month's expenses. Insurance and pension dues, $28. Church and Sunday School contributions, $12. These expenses, totaling $183.95, would have to be met out of a monthly salary of $200. Only $16.05 would be left for such needs as clothing, toiletries, books, religious periodicals, newspapers, medical care, household supplies, repairs, and young Jimmy Jackson's school requirements.

No new suit for Jim, he thought. *And we can't afford any sickness until I've paid for the car.*

The Rev. Mr. Jackson, brooding over his bills on the first of every month, would be startled to learn how fortunate he is financially. For his yearly salary of $2,400 is considerably *higher* than the average for American clergymen!

Everyone knows, of course, that clergymen are poorly paid. But few laymen realize how poorly our churches are paying their ministers. And even fewer among the laymen understand the shocking implications of the situation.

The recent phenomenal increase in church membership makes the problem of low ministerial salaries more important than ever before. As reported in the June 1950 issue of *Redbook*, thousands of young men and women are entering the nation's churches, participating in church activities, and gradually taking over church administration. These young families expect competence in their ministers. They expect intelligent sermons, guidance in personal problems, leadership of a high order. It's unreasonable to believe that they'll find efficient leadership in men hampered by financial insecurity. A minister, unless he's a saint or a genius, can't be expected to deal intelligently with the problems of

his parishioners when his own financial problem is up-
permost in his thoughts.

Ten years ago a minister could live on an annual
salary of $2,000. But rising costs have changed the en-
tire picture.

The current miserable situation is one which must
be corrected by the young, new church members. For
they are responsible for the future of America's
churches. Anything endangering that future is properly
their concern.

In attacking the problem, church youth should first
ask: *Just what is the job of our pastor, our minister,
our rabbi?*

The answer is surprising. No professional man has a
wider variety of duties. The minister must be student,
scholar, orator, businessman, spiritual guide, family-
relations expert, psychologist, welfare worker, and community leader.

He performs marriages, baptizes or christens babies,
conducts funerals, constantly exposes himself to illness
by visiting the sick, comforts those whose relatives or
friends have died. He makes professional calls on poor
and rich, young and old. A myriad of ecclesiastical
duties include interesting young people in church membership and teaching the responsibilities of religious
fellowship. With the assistance of elected or appointed
laymen, he also runs the business of his church or synagogue, worries about the investment of funds, and supervises such activities as church repairs and upkeep.

The personal problems of his members keep him
busy. He deals constantly with the problems of unem-
ployment, debt, divorce, alcoholism and delinquency.

At the same time he must address his congregation—
often twice on Sunday—with scholarship and percep-
tion. This takes an enormous amount of reading and
preparation. A man who delivers two sermons a week
prepares, in the course of a year's time, about 350,000
words of material—the equivalent of several books.

Yet this is only the beginning of his duties. He must

organize youth clubs, Boy Scouts and Girl Scouts, young-adult societies and various other social groups. He is obliged to contribute to every fund drive of his community. He is frequently expected to spend time on civic committees. A clergyman must be everything to everyone at all times—a living symbol of all the virtues and, at the same time, a man of social talent.

Yet even if he attains this pinnacle, his church members may not be altogether satisfied. They want his job to be the job of his wife and, in part, the job of his children. A lawyer's wife isn't expected to know the law and a doctor's son doesn't attend medical conventions, but the entire family of a clergyman is supposed to participate in his work. As one minister's daughter put it, "You live your life in a goldfish bowl."

The clergyman's job is a big one. For performing it to the best of his abilities, he is rewarded by a lifetime of severe economic strain. No other professional man is paid as badly. No family of a professional man is subjected to greater money worries.

The most recent national figures showed 112,509 clergymen of full active status, with total income derived from salary. Of every 100 of these men, less than two received incomes from salaries of $5,000 or more. About 16 in 100 were getting incomes between $2,000 and $4,999. *Around 82 in every 100 were being paid less than $1,999 per year!*

The highly conservative "Twentieth Century Fund Report on America's Needs and Resources," published in 1947, with estimates for 1950 and 1960, places the "average" minister's salary at $1800 per year or about $34.61 per week.

The "Fund Report" goes on to say: "He [the minister] is generally paid less than $2,000 a year, but may receive an additional $200 a year for special services at baptisms, marriages, and funerals. His cash earnings are usually supplemented by the free use of a modest village home, known as the parsonage or manse. But he must furnish his own car, and he has no expense account for necessary travel."

There are, of course, some exceptionally talented, fortunate, or politically adept ministers who earn good salaries. These are the big-city men who operate large plants with large staffs. But for every one of these unusually well-cushioned gentlemen there are hundreds of devoted, hard-working city and country ministers who barely manage to scrape along.

The "Twentieth Century Fund Report" says: "To make salaries 'adequate' would require an increase of about 50 percent in prevailing rates of compensation without allowing for needed adjustments to the higher postwar level of living costs."

The Baptists recently surveyed 243 ministers in 34 states—almost all northern and prosperous areas—and found that only 25 men were receiving average annual salaries of over $3,000. Of the 243 ministers, 237 were married, with 1.6 dependent children per family. Fifty-five did not have parsonages. Yet the Baptist situation is by no means the worst.

Not long ago, one of the large Protestant denominations examined the condition of 17 pastors in a New England test area. Of the 17, 11 were receiving less than $2,500 in cash salary per year. Four were receiving less than $3,000. Only two received more than $3,000. Nine had debts averaging $525.

Let's look at these men in another way. Fifteen will average only $377 more than the average office boy in a near-by large city—if they pay their debts this year. The six lowest-salary men will average only $36.66 cash salary more than the office boy's yearly wage. One would actually receive less!

Yet these men have responsibilities far beyond those of an office boy. They have wives and children. They must make financial contributions to their own churches, as an example to their parishioners.

What's the matter with our churches? Why do congregations that demand scholarship and extraordinary service from their clergy frequently pay them salaries below the levels of local day laborers?

There are many reasons. *Perhaps you are one of them.*

In 1950, the per capita gift for more than 87,000,000 church members was $30.58. In other words, the average church member gave $30.58 to support the entire works—his church budget, including salaries, *plus* home missions, foreign missions, special projects, and the like. The contribution hammers down to 58¢ a week.

This figure came to the attention of a Hudson River Valley clergyman whose parish is composed largely of New York commuters. He laughed wryly and observed, "That's less than one of my men pays for his daily martini in the Commodore Hotel—before rushing home to attend a trustee's meeting."

It is, indeed. It's also less than a tip in a good restaurant.

The person of wealth is not the big contributor to his church in relation to his own income level. The last valid report in this field shows that persons with incomes in excess of $10,000 per year kick in a mere 0.6 percent of income to church support. But those in the $3,000 to $4,000 group give 1.3 percent! And the people who are really strapped themselves—those of an under $500 per year income—also contribute 1.3 percent of income to church support. The clergyman can indeed bless the poor, for without them he would surely starve.

Dr. Benson Y. Landis, analyst for the National Council of Churches of Christ in the United States, has this to say: "The proportion of the peoples' money going to organized religion has been decreasing these latter years. In the 1920's the American people gave slightly more than 1 percent of their total income to organized religion. In 1946, the percentage was nearer to ½ of 1 percent."

There's a simple rule in modern economy, to the effect that income has to come from somewhere. Salaries don't just happen. America's young adult church members can begin the job of improving their clergymen's financial condition by looking first at their own pocketbooks. Can they give a few more dollars to the church?

They Can participate actively in church-fund drives —a function traditionally handled in most churches by older members. They can initiate the pledge system, or every-member canvass, in their churches; if a system already exists, perhaps it can be improved. For example, in most pledge requests a person usually is asked what his annual contribution to the church will be. A reply of $30 sounds pretty good. But supposing you were to ask a person what his *weekly* contribution will be. At present income levels, few church members can feel heroic about a weekly contribution of 58¢.

At a recent budget-raising meeting one shrewd church-fund solicitor told his fellow members, "I'll start this thing off by contributing $150. Who will contribute $149?"

Two hands went up in the back of the church.

"Who wants to give $148?"

So it went. Human nature being what it is, the fund was quickly oversubscribed.

The young men and women who have recently become active in church administration can properly view their church budgets with critical eyes. Is it possible to raise the minister's salary by replacing a paid choir with volunteers? Are the services of a janitor necessary, or can this task be taken over by young church members on a roster basis? And how about that new paint job for the Sunday School—can this work be done by the men of the church?

The financial burden of your clergyman will be lightened by provisions for a gasoline and travel allowance. Few laymen realize how much of a minister's income is spent on auto maintenance and travel. The Methodists, for example, estimate that the average cost of operating a car on a rural circuit is $500 a year.

Above the door of every church community hall or

recreation room there might well be a sign: "Are you a free-loader?" Many people are quite willing to benefit from church organizations without paying any fare whatsoever. One New Jersey church provides its community with an excellent recreation house and a multitude of activities. But many prosperous residents of the area make full use of the facilities without ever contributing a cent to the church. The minister sometimes wonders what these people enter on their tax blanks under the heading "Contributions."

Clergymen of all faiths often are at fault themselves for their own low salaries. Young ministers particularly are apt to sell their abilities short. Driven by the powerful urge to minister, they are inclined to settle for substandard salaries.

Minimum-salary plans can help to prevent this "underselling," and many are now in effect. As young men and women become more deeply involved in church and denominational affairs, they can do much to raise minimums. In the hierarchical denominations, where power is concentrated at the top, the problem is much simpler; it is a matter of finding the funds to jack up substandard minimums. Among the congregational or autonomous groups, the individual church must establish a living wage for the clergyman *before engaging him*. The priests of the Roman Catholic church as a rule do not have economic problems because their church assumes an obligation for the necessities of life for its clergy.

Many people shudder at the thought of closing a church because the members can't raise enough money to provide the clergyman with an adequate salary. Support from denominational funds, they say, should be sufficient to keep all churches open. Unfortunately, it isn't.

Churches which can't pay living wages usually are located in areas where population shifts have resulted in too many churches or too few church members. Union of churches of kindred denominations is the only answer in these overchurched sections. Union is definitely a challenge to youth, for traditionalists resent the idea. Older church members usually resist change with a stoniness no softer than the foundations of the building in which they worship.

The commendable desire to cling to tradition should be viewed with sympathy. But tradition won't pay the minister's bills or create a strong church.

Canadian Protestants greatly strengthened their church position when a number of denominations joined forces in a United Church. In 1939, the American Methodists welded their three splinters into a solid block, and Methodism has advanced vigorously since that union. Membership has increased by 1,575,460, and in 1949 alone there was an investment of more than $67,000,00 in new buildings and improvements. That good record speaks highly for the advantages of merger on a denominational scale.

Union is nearly always effective at a community level, as local churches frequently are demonstrating throughout the country. In one small Connecticut town of 3,000 population, for example, the uniting of a weak Methodist church and a weak Congregational church produced a strong Town church.

The vast group of young adults who are entering the churches in our time are learning that a strong minister makes a strong church. They must see how weakening are the effects of scandalously low salaries, with resulting indebtedness, on the men who are their pastors. Consider, then, the gloom that darkens every clergyman's day when he thinks of his old age and retirement. In an age of increasing protection for an increasing number of citizens, remember this:

Clergymen receive no federal old-age benefits.

Yes, almost every denomination has a pension plan of some sort. So many exist that a detailed study of them would fill six issues of *Redbook*. They are good ones, too—sound plans administered by competent men. But here is a sampling of what they pay:

In 1950, the American Baptists (formerly the Northern Baptist denomination) paid an over-all average pension of $539. In the same year the Congregational Board of Ministerial Relief made an average grant, including a Christmas gift, of $417 to retired ministers. (These were outright grants for ministers who had not joined the Annuity Fund Plan of the Congregational Christian Churches.) The average pension of those who retired during 1949 under the Service Pension Plan of the Presbyterian Church (U. S. A.) was $665.21. The Episcopalians have raised their minimum pensions to $1,500 in recognition of higher living costs. It must be remembered, however, that there are only about 6,500 Episcopal clerics, and thus the high Episcopal pension does not greatly alter a generally unfortunate picture.

There was a time when a retired clergyman might have eked out subsistence on these pensions. But today, with living costs soaring daily, they are totally inadequate. The problem was summarized thus by Dr. Frank J. Scribner, General Secretary of the Ministerial Relief Division of the Board of Home Missions of the Congregational Christian Churches, in his 1950 report:

"The figures released by the Bureau of Labor Statistics have shown a progressive increase in the cost of living since the early part of 1950. This index changes so rapidly that it is not worth while to quote figures which are sure to be obsolete before they can be printed, but at the beginning of the year it was recognized that the retail cost of all items stood at 180 percent of the 1935-1939 level. More than that, food costs (the major item in the budgets of our pensioners) stood well over the 200 percent mark. . . . The denomination cannot ignore this situation and the effect that it has upon the lives of its retired ministers."

The pension boards are not to blame for low pensions. In fact, they deserve the greatest praise for their work. Unfortunately, they are trapped by various inescapable circumstances.

One limiting factor is the recent installation of many

of the plans. The excellent Baptist plan, for example, was founded in 1921. It just hadn't been in existence long enough for its participants to enjoy retirement at half-salary after thirty-five years of service. Further, men were slow to join. Not until the late 1950's will benefit payments be fully satisfactory to plan participants.

Widows and dependent children are covered by most of the plans, for clergymen have an unfortunate habit of dying earlier than their wives. Ministers' widows can be expected to live alone for seven or eight years.

What can young church members do?

They can insist that their ministers be given pension protection, no matter how small. Most plans call for joint contributions by clergyman and church. A typical one for a minister receiving a $3,000 salary calls for the church to contribute $210 and the minister $90.

But it's difficult for a minister to declaim, "I think it would be dandy if you paid $210 a year to the pension fund so I won't starve to death thirty years from now. And by the way, I'll put in $90."

The young adult church man had every right to ask his pastor whether he belongs to a pension program, and to insist that church and pastor share the cost of this protection. He has this right because he expects an efficient ministry from his clergyman and he knows that worry about the future doesn't create efficiency.

Any lasting solution to the problem of low pensions must, of course, rest with the professional—the actuaries and the highly trained administrators of pension plans. But the stimulation of young interest in a problem of the aged minister would help to bring about a speedier solution.

This entire task of easing the clergyman's financial burden, in all its phases, is a big job. But it's a job that has to be done, if churches are to be well served. And it's a job that must be done by young church members, for it demands energy, initiative, and a fresh interest in church affairs.

SOME POSSIBLE SOLUTIONS

It was most cooperative of Wade Nichols, publisher of *Redbook* magazine, to grant us permission to reprint this challenging article. It challenges us all to re-examine the amount our churches are paying our clergymen for their twenty-four-hour, seven-days-a-week calling. Are we expecting them to get most of their reward in Heaven? Or are we raising enough money . . . increasing attendance enough . . . getting enough people to tithe, so that our minister receives a *decent living* from the congregation?

The problem of adequate compensation for the clergy is one which has worried congregations, church boards, bishops, and denomination headquarters for years, in some cases for decades. For the men of the cloth, who help us get closer to the greatest blessings in life, usually work for far less than those in a less strenuous profession, business, or occupation. No, this problem cannot be solved overnight. But there are several solutions which a church with a badly underpaid pastor might well investigate and act upon. These include the following.

1. Are there building maintenance items (like painting and carpentry work) on the yearly budget whose cost could be saved by getting members of the church to do the work? Then this saving in building maintenance could be added to the clergyman's salary. The laymen on the maintenance committee can secure many money-saving suggestions from a book entitled *Church Maintenance Manual* by Roger C. Whitman.

2. Perhaps the church can save extra money for the minister's salary by substituting a free junior choir for an adult choir where the soloists are paid. A fast-growing Eastern church, located in a suburban area, solved its music problem with a junior choir which sings six well-known hymns each Sunday. This eliminates the need for paid soloists (and even the need for rehears-

als). The congregation likes this ministry of music better because they are part of that ministry—they themselves join in the singing of the six hymns. So if your church can save money on music to augment the clergyman's salary, do consider the advantage of a junior choir.

3. In business we say: "There are few problems which a company has that cannot be solved by increased sales to more customers . . . to new customers." Likewise there are few church-budget problems or clergy-salary problems which cannot be solved by having more people worship in a church more frequently. Instead of asking more and more of the same old faithfuls several pewfuls of new faces in the church can add new life to the budget, as well as to the singing and responses.

So if your church needs to pay its clergyman more, you have another reason for using the proven plans in this book, for getting more people into church. But don't just read about these projects, get them started in your church. If you run out of things to do, get a copy of *Building Up Your Congregation*. This book is also filled with tested methods which increase attendance and increase giving.

Enthusiastic letters we have received from all over the country claim that the use of the ideas in *Building Up Your Congregation* (especially the chapter on Special Sunday Services and the one on Direct Mail) have increased church attendance from 25 to 50 percent. Some churches which used the financial-solicitation ideas had their mortgages paid off in full. But don't get this book till you have used up all the ideas in *More Power for Your Church* which you can carry out. Remember the more visitors . . . the more new worshipers . . . the more new pledges, the less your clergyman has to wait to get so much of his reward in Heaven.

4. A growing list of churches are able to pay their clergyman adequately because they are getting more of their faithful families to tithe. Yes, it takes times to get

this proportional giving started. But it is the surest way in the long run. And it brings so many blessings to the tithers.

For example, N. O. Bardal, treasurer of the Icelandic Evangelical Lutheran Synod of North America, writes us from Winnipeg, Manitoba: "By pointing out the value of giving a percentage of one's income, rather than talking in terms of dollars, our church tripled its income."

5. The fifth possible solution may come as a shock to both clergy and lay workers. That's because it's so new. So few people have thought of it. Yet it is proving so practical and helpful to everyone concerned that it should be duplicated all over this country. This is a new idea as well as a solution. We'll give you the new idea first. It is putting a parson on the payroll, and is being pioneered by the R. J. Reynolds Tobacco Company of Winston-Salem, North Carolina. This company is typical of American business, large and small, which is discovering that everyday religion can work miracles in both office and factory. John C. Whitaker, President, and James A. Gray, Chairman of the Company, are giving full support to the full-time minister they retained to be the "preacher-counselor" to their 12,000 regular employees. The Reverend Clifford H. Pearce of St. Paul's Methodist Church, Ashville, North Carolina, was the one called to lead in the new trend—the new experiment which is proving that "Christianity with its sleeves rolled up" is paying off at the assembly line. Before you get disturbed at that business appraisal of a spiritual service, read how the Reverend Mr. Pearce is bringing the benefits of religion to the R. J. Reynolds people during the "other six days of the week." His new office is always open for a private and confidential consultation on all sorts of problems. At his request an attractive prayer room or chapel has been built next door to his office. This enables visiting *fellow employees* to re-enforce their consultations with prayer

for divine aid and guidance. When not in his office, the Reverend Mr. Pearce is roaming through plants or offices getting to know people and have them know him as the company's preacher-counselor. He also holds prayer meetings, which in only two years have increased from two to fifteen per week.

His Christian advice—prayers and guidance—have helped scores of employees solve tough problems which otherwise would have ruined their jobs, lives, and homes. Yes, the R. J. Reynolds people are a lot happier and more contented with their work since Messrs. Whitaker and Gray put a parson on the payroll. Often groups come to work early, a half-hour before the time clock has to be punched, just to sing and pray in the cafeteria.

Doesn't this sound like the vital religion which God likes? Didn't Christ often take the message to where the people were: along the shore, at the well, mending nets, instead of waiting until they came to see Him? If you would like to read the full stimulating story which Clarence Woodbury wrote for *American Magazine,* write to the magazine at 640 Fifth Avenue, New York City, for a reprint from their January, 1952, issue.

Long before this you may have been wondering: "What on earth has all this to do with helping more churches pay their parsons a living wage (commensurate with 1952 living costs)?" The answer is simple. Why not consider allowing, or getting some local company to call your minister to the part-time post of preacher-counselor? Now don't say right away, "He hasn't enough time to take on any more assignments." Most ministers could *make time* for such a worth-while piece of part-time employment. How? Simply by not attending some of the hundreds of committee meetings which really do not require their presence. With this saved time the minister could be available at a company consulting room or chapel for two hours on Mondays, Wednesdays, and Fridays. In most communities there are several local firms which can afford, and

should avail themselves of, this new religious service for
their employees. It will solve problems which otherwise
cause industrial inefficiency and heartaches. It will solve
church budget problems which also cause hardships
and heartaches.

Chapter 14

NEW AND DIFFERENT WAYS OF RAISING MONEY FOR CHURCHES

J ESUS WAS INTERESTED in money. He referred to money and its uses more times than to any other subject —the Kingdom of God, heaven, hell, or salvation. The use of money serves as a thermometer to indicate a person's interests. "Where a man's treasure is, there will his heart be also."

The securing of funds is not an end in itself. Money is but a tool whereby we may accomplish our real purpose.

One of the best places to begin increasing the effectiveness of your church is in your church finance. Money is not only necessary, but absolutely essential to the success of your church program.

Of all the organizations and institutions, the church's business should be conducted on the highest plane possible, because of the purpose for which it exists. Good business is good religion, and good religion is good business.

Nearly two billion dollars were placed on the altars of churches and synagogues by living donors in 1951. This is approximately half the total amount given for all tax-exempt religious, educational, and welfare causes.

While the amount thus contributed was approximately $100,000,000, more than that contributed in 1950, this increase of 5 percent was not enough to offset the increased cost of services dependent upon these contributions.

The income of the people in the United States, as measured by their expenditures for food, shelter, clothing, etc., doubled between the years of 1850 and 1920. Between 1920 and 1945 it doubled again. But much (?) small change is still found in the offering plates! Is the proportion of our income that we return to the Giver of all a worthy acknowledgement of our stewardship?

You readers who have the high responsibility of raising money for your churches know all the above facts. You are well acquainted with all those situations. You also realize that in many congregations the amounts raised through the annual pledge and every member canvass must be augmented by other money-raising activities.

Financially strong churches have found that new appeals, new and different ways, obtain new and added funds which otherwise would never have found their way into God's treasury. Here are some proved ones whose results justify their being adopted by many congregations.

1. The Reverend Gerald V. Barry of Christ Church, Riverdale-on-Hudson, in New York, found a source of new financial support by sending each member of the congregation a brand-new dollar bill the first week in June. The parishioners were asked to put "God's dollar" to work during the summer and bring back its fruit to the church three months later. The results were so satisfactory that we give you herewith the complete plan of three mailings:

To the Members of Christ Church: 6/4/51.

Are you surprised to *receive* a brand-new dollar bill

from the Church instead of being asked to *give* one? Well, there's no mistake; here it is!

This is God's dollar. It is being loaned to you. *We want you to invest it.* Invest it to the best of your ability, so it will grow and multiply many times over.

In order words, taking a lesson from the Parable of the Talents (which you will find in the Gospel according to Saint Matthew), here is your opportunity to put your talents to work for Christ Church.

Between now and September 15, let this dollar and the fruit it bears be your link between you and your Church. Whether you vacation in Riverdale . . . or spend your summer away from home . . . put your talent to work.

One dollar may make a cake that will sell for two.

Two dollars may make candy that will sell for four.

Four dollars may buy material that will sell for eight.

Here is a simple way to raise funds that can be practiced by children and adults alike. And as your talent (dollar) grows, and you see its earnings in a milk bottle, an old powder box, or an envelope, see how much satisfaction you will receive in knowing that this dollar you are working with is God's.

Frankly, Christ Church is badly in need of $2,800, with which to liquidate the debt on our Parish House. We don't want to ask you to give more than you can afford. That's why we are sending God's dollar to help.

Bring it back September 15 . . . with the talents it has earned.

Remember . . .

". . . and so he that had received five talents came and brought other five talents, saying, 'Lord, Thou deliveredst unto me five talents: behold, I have gained beside them five talents more.' "

The Rector, Wardens, and Vestry

9/13/51

THE MIRACLE OF THE BILLS
is soon to be revealed!

Sunday, September 23, is the homecoming date for those Talent Dollars entrusted to you during the summer.

Early reports indicate that most of them have been working overtime. How about yours? How many more will you have?

Please to bring or send them back by Sunday, September 23.

Thank you.

The Rector, Wardens, and Vestry

10/8/51

No one likes to be pestered. No one likes to be thought of as a pest—least of all, the senders of this letter!

BUT

—among the 159 Talent Dollars which have not yet come home to roost is the one that was sent to you. Maybe you lost it. Maybe you are using it as a bookmark. Maybe—well, whatever happened, won't you please send it on its way, accompanied by offspring?

The Rector, Wardens and Vestry

While this "God's Dollar" plan was done by Christ Church during the summer, it can be used during any three-month period.

2. *Presbyterian Action* magazine gives the outline for a "Sunday School Rally Day" which includes a special Rally Day offering to make Sunday Schools better:

Before a Church School can have a satisfying Rally Day (September 30), it must have an effective "Rally Month." The following four points are both the *requirements* and the *guarantee* of success in rallying your Church School:

(1) A RESTUDY OF YOUR CHURCH'S TOTAL PROGRAM OF CHRISTIAN EDUCATION—to find its weak points.

(2) A RESTUDY OF YOUR CHURCH'S RESPONSIBILITY LISTS—to find all the persons for whom you are spiritually responsible.

(3) A NEW PROGRAM OF VISITING—to bring into your Church School all the persons who need your Christian teaching.

(4) A NEW PROGRAM OF IMPROVEMENT—to strengthen your Church School for more effective teaching.

Workers' Conference

In carrying out the above fourfold program for "Rally Month," a Workers' Conference early in September will be of key importance. In this meeting the restudy of the Church School program can be begun, with the help of the check list, "Next Steps in Church School Progress." (Order from Presbyterian Bookstores, 10¢ a copy.)

The "Guide"

For a really thorough study of your Church School, the new manual *A Guide for Presbyterian Church Schools* is recommended. (Order from Presbyterian Book Stores, $1 a copy.) This *Guide* also serves as a handbook for the local Church Committee on Religious Education.

Responsibility Lists

During the first two weeks in September, every Church should thoroughly revise its responsibility lists —its list of persons who should be enrolled in the School's activities of study, worship, service, recreation, and fellowship. Every class and group, from the nursery up, should have such a list.

A few energetic leaders should head up the revision and enlargement of these lists, and the job should be completed by the middle of September. During the last two weeks of the month there should be an intensive program of visiting. Representatives of every class and group in the School should visit every inactive member and every prospective member before Rally Day.

The conscious purpose in the minds of the visitors should be to express the genuine friendliness of the class toward the inactive or prospective member, thus to draw him into the fellowship of the group and into active membership. Such visiting will pay rich dividends in Church School enlargement.

3. Every home should have one of the religious trivets made by the Garret Thew Studios, Westport, Connecticut. They read in cut-out metal letters, (1) "Give Us This Day Our Daily Bread," and (2) "Bless This House, O Lord We Pray." In fulfilling this need, one of your church organizations can raise funds in a new and painless way. All it has to do is get samples of these two metal trivets. Display them in the vestibule after church or in the church house at some large church gathering; then take orders from the congregation.

These trivets are ideal gifts for Christmas, Easter, or bridal showers. They can be hung over the front door, in the hall, over the mantel, on the kitchen wall, or used on the dining table. Your group can sell them for the regular price of $2.25 or add on 75¢ as a fair service charge for getting them for the members.

4. One of the most popular methods of raising funds is through church suppers. Yet the *Witness* magazine carried this interesting report:

Suppers a Poor Way to Raise Funds

Pastors generally disapprove church suppers as a way of raising funds, according to a survey made by rural church department of Drew Seminary. Reason: long hours for the women and small returns. The replies from 341 pastors showed that the money return on suppers was very low although the fellowship value was high. Church suppers in a single year netted $49,933 to the churches canvassed, with 7,840 women cooking, waiting on table, and doing dishes.

Perhaps if the church suppers were varied, had a change of pace, they would raise more money for the time and effort involved. One such variation is that used successfully by Trinity Church, Rocky Hill, New Jersey. This parish finds that more people attend when they have a Smörgasbord instead of the usual supper.

5. Just recently a new form of collection envelope has been developed which offers some new advantages for the giver and for the church treasurer. It is called an "Account-O-Lope" and provides a new plan for the every-member canvass. From the following illustration you will see that the "Account-O-Lope" is a completely new and different type of offering envelope.

Account-O-Lopes are put up like a BANK CHECKBOOK. They provide the contributor with a "stub" record of his contributions and a running balance of his PLEDGE just as a bank balance is provided in a checkbook—A CONSTANT REMINDER OF THE PLEDGED OBLIGATION TO THE CHURCH IN DOLLARS.

The Account-O-Lope System does not DEPEND upon "Sunday dates" printed on each envelope to REMIND the contributor of his unpaid pledge. Rather the system emphasizes the PLEDGED BALANCE IN DOLLARS, and provides an excellent record for the contributor's income tax report.

Consequently, "Sunday dates" are not printed on Account-O-Lopes, thus making it possible to use any Account-O-Lope on any Sunday or one for several Sundays. This feature saves the contributor and the treasurer the bother of handling the "several unused" envelopes which accumulate during the absence or vacation periods. After all the important thing is DOLLARS not "dates."

A complete set of 52 is just 2/3 the thickness of sets in cartons, and the Account-O-Lope sets may be mailed to contributors in standard mailing envelopes without getting damaged or crushed in the mail.

Contributed so far this Year - - - $ ....

TODAY'S Offering - $ ....

Balance - - - $ ....

ACCOUNT-O-LOPE SYSTEM
LISBON, OHIO

Name ....
Address ....
Use above lines to notify church of address change

St. Peter's Church
Steubenville, Ohio

FOR

CHURCH SUPPORT

Balance of My Annual Pledge - - - $ ....

TODAY'S Offering - $ ....

Balance - - - $ ....

Date .... 19......

ACCOUNT-O-LOPE SYSTEM
LISBON, OHIO

Name ....
Address ....
Use above lines to notify church of address change

№ 570

St. Peter's Church
Steubenville, Ohio

Balance Due on Annual Pledge - $ ....

Contributed TODAY - - $ ....

Balance Due on Pledge - - - $ ....

Date .... 19......

The Account-O-Lope system does everything the old loose-envelopes-in-cartons can do. They provide a handy container for contributor's offering, a new, fresh approach to the problem of collecting pledges. The first church which used them reported that the new 25¢ Initial-Offering Account-O-Lope produced more than enough to pay for the sets—evidence that the people themselves really like the system. They also report that more people write the amount contributed on the face of the envelop than before, which saves the treasurer the trouble. A survey indicates that most of their contribu-

178

tors are using the "stub" and appreciate the opportunity to keep a record of their contributions and balances of pledge.

The Account-O-Lope was developed by John Taylor of Lisbon, Ohio.

6. For monthly articles on case histories of tested ways to raise money read *Woman's Day*. For example, one of these religious articles told exactly how the First Presbyterian Church of New Rochelle, New York, raised $4,800 on a bazaar. That's a great gift to God's work in any city, especially in a community the size of New Rochelle (population 60,000).

7. A student at Duke University developed a new way to collect money for the American Leprosy Mission. He has a piggy bank in his rooms. Any time a visitor uses profanity, he has to pay the piggy bank. Of course churches couldn't use this very same money-raising method because good members don't swear! But the piggy banks could be distributed to collect fines for losing one's temper.

8. Of course the surest method of balancing a church budget—of being able to carry out an expanding program of church and mission activities—is to follow the Bible's recommended plan for giving. Yes, you guessed it—that is tithing—giving back to the good Lord just one tenth of the monetary blessings he has given you.

One of the best case histories on tithing was written up in the *Presbyterian Survey* by Hugh B. Carter, Pastor of the Sunset Hills Presbyterian Church, Charlotte, North Carolina. Just read this for sheer inspiration and proof that tithing can be carried out even in the smallest of churches.

"Whether it is easier to say to the sick of the palsy, Thy sins be forgiven thee; or to say, Arise, and take up thy bed and walk? But that ye may know that the Son of man hath power on earth to forgive sins (he saith to the sick of the palsy), I say unto thee, Arise . . ."

Jesus raised the palsied man in order that men might know that the Son of Man has power on earth to forgive sins. For the same reason, I believe, He raised the Sunset Hills Presbyterian Church of Charlotte, North Carolina —a church which was as flat on its back as the palsied man.

Therefore, as you read this story of the miracle of grace at Sunset Hills, it should be remembered that these things were done in order that we may know that the Son of Man has power on earth to forgive sins.

Look at the palsied church as it was! Weeds were waist-high in the churchyard. The stairs that led to the choir loft were rotten and broken through. Doors needed replacing, outside and inside. A toilet and lavatory were needed. A new sink and cabinets were needed in the kitchen. These were the more obvious physical needs.

Financially, we had this report—that we had robbed God. The treasurer reported a bank balance of $19.24. This is an incredibly small balance for a church of one hundred members—a church receiving Home Missions aid amounting to more than $100 monthly.

Spiritually, the story is already told. The spiritual languor of the church was reflected not only in poor physical equipment and run-down financial condition, but in poor attendance at Sunday school and church. For six months a weekly average of fifty attended church and about forty-five came to Sunday school. During the same period we received nine new members. We had no evening service, no prayer meeting, and no men's organization. Behold the palsied church!

In the plight of this depressing situation our officers laid hold on the words in Malachi 3:10: "Bring ye all the tithes into the storehouse . . . and prove me now herewith, saith the Lord of hosts, if I will not open you the windows of heaven, and pour you out a blessing, that there shall not be room enough to receive it."

As a means of leading the other members to an active

acceptance of this challenge, ten of our twelve officers made a covenant with God to tithe for three months, October through December. On the last Sunday in September, almost half the congregation made a similar covenant. The next three months were known as "A Venture in Faith."

Now see what happened!

On the very next Sunday, there was an all-time record attendance at church with ninety-nine present. This surpassed even the Easter congregation. Mind you, there had been no campaign or drive for attendance. This just happened! Throughout the remainder of these three months, attendance showed an average increase of more than fifty percent. This was the first evidence of the promised blessing.

The Sunday school began to move along with the church. Attendance and offerings more than doubled. Interest climbed to new heights. As a result of the new emphasis, certain things came to pass, such as: (1) all rooms and floors painted, (2) nursery redecorated, (3) pictures, maps, books added, (4) a piano purchased, (5) a new class formed, (6) new teachers installed, (7) at least $100,000 in benevolences appropriated and disbursed, (8) scholarships provided to send two young people to Presbytery's summer conference with all expenses paid, (9) toilet and lavatory facilities purchased and installed, (10) and other minor improvements too numerous to mention. The Sunday school has pioneered in giving to benevolences, in physical improvements, in increased attendance, and in offerings received.

The church followed with the installation of new front doors, new back stairs, and a completely renovated kitchen. These items were costly, but they were necessary. A long-carriage typewriter was purchased for the church office. Ever since this period the church lawn has been cut regularly and kept in good condition. The entire church—outside and in—was beautifully painted and new light fixtures were installed on the front.

The Men's Club was revived, yea, leaped to its feet.

Regular monthly meetings were begun with splendid attendance and good fellowship. The club was further developed when the men entered a team in the church softball league. While runs batted in were not always sufficient for victory, no game was lost by default! The goal of the club is to include every male member of the church.

Two incidents in connection with the Men's Club are worth noting. In the spring, the men held a housecleaning in the Lord's house. They removed rugs and pews, washed and waxed floors as well as all the furniture in the sanctuary, and made the church shine. (The women washed windows, curtains, and venetian blinds during the same week.) The men put on a church supper for the women, asking only that the ladies be present to help eat.

Needless to say, the Women of the Church have prospered exceedingly, and God has worked through them to raise the church to new levels spiritually and financially. A new circle has been added and another is in view. It is not out of order to state here that the Women of the Church are dependable, responsible, and devoted servants to a gracious risen Lord through His church. During the months when our life was feeble it was the Women of the Church who carried the flickering torch and kept their feet on solid rock. It is the women who now lead us into new avenues through their weekly prayer meetings.

By way of extra blessings, a lady volunteered to do secretarial work at no monetary consideration. She has been as faithful as though she were employed under contract, working five hours a day, five days a week. A church secretary was more than our church was able to ask or think possible before.

The blessings have continued to pour in beyond the three months' "Venture in Faith," perhaps because most of our people did not withdraw their tithes. The covenant with God was continued by nearly all.

Within six months from the date that the church

treasurer announced a balance of $19.24, Sunset Hills had assumed all its obligations and was no longer receiving Home Mission aid. This was not our objective in our venture of faith. It came as a gift from God, poured out as a blessing—a by-product.

Whereas our budget in 1949 was $4,000 and our people pledged only $2,700 (less than half the congregation made any pledge whatsoever), a budget was presented in 1950 for $6,000. The congregation approved this increased budget and gave proper evidence by pledging more than $7,000 on Every-Member-Canvass Day with ninety percent participation, and through the year the offerings went well over the pledged amount.

Gifts have come in almost weekly since we began this "Venture in Faith": a beautiful silver baptismal bowl, a silver flower bowl, linoleum for the Sunday school, indoor games for the Men's Club, a hot-water heater for the kitchen, an electric cooler for cold drinks, and over one hundred dollars in cash as special offerings. There have been others that cannot be named. No gift was solicited; each just happened!

Then we received blessings in adding new members. Since the first day of the period, the church has received an average of more than one person per Sunday, about one-third of whom are making professions of faith.

There is an evening service which is well attended and in which the people engage in studying the Bible, book by book. A midweek prayer service has come into being spontaneously. It is carried on by the Women of the Church, who meet informally during the afternoon in various homes in the community.

Our most thrilling experiences have been in the realm of transformed lives: members becoming interested and devoted to the church who previously were indifferent and cold, officers seriously assuming their responsibilities and keeping their ordination vows, noticeably with regard to church attendance and monthly meetings, broken lives restored and consecrated where previously they had been derelict, families reunited to one another and then to the church, the abatement of physical handicaps as answers to prayer, and the like.

The whole story cannot be told, because our blessings cannot be counted. But this much is plain: Jesus has said to the palsied church, "Arise," and Sunset Hill has heard His voice.

All has not been accomplished. The church does not see itself as a model. We are not independent of God's grace. Our faith is still a frail thing, with all that we have witnessed. We do not say to others to follow us, but we do seek to point all to the Son of God who is able to give exceeding abundantly above all that we ask or think.

We believe that God has done these wonders in our midst, and not we ourselves. We believe that He has manifested Himself in order that we might know that this same Jesus who raised the palsied man is at work today.

Our message is that Jesus Christ came into the world to save sinners. And in order that slothful, disobedient, and selfish children of God might *know* that He has the power to forgive sins, He has worked a miracle of grace among us at Sunset Hills.

We know how the crowds must have felt when they saw the palsied man get up and walk; insomuch that we are all amazed, and glorify God, saying: "We never saw it in this fashion."

10. In the *Commission* magazine Frances McCaw Goldfinch writes about a Baptist church in Asuncion, Paraguay, where they "Tithe with Joy":

Deep spiritual power can be expected in a church when the membership practices Christian stewardship. The Ciudad Nueva Baptist Church, Asuncion, Paraguay, with sixty-nine members, has eighty-five regular contributors.

The church is mission-minded. It maintains eight mission Sunday schools.

The church has a praying membership. Five prayer

groups, divided according to age, meet immediately preceding every service of the church and the Sunday school.

The Ciudad Nueva Baptist Church was organized with fifteen charter members in 1946. It had its beginning earlier when preaching services were begun in an open-air tabernacle on a lot where a Baptist family had lived for many years.

Most of the charter members had been members of the First Baptist Church of Asuncion. The first pastor was Pedro Ruiz Diaz, a young Paraguayan who had been graduated from the Baptist seminary in Buenos Aires. Mr. Goldfinch and I continued as members of the church, helping with the Sunday school and other work.

Some pastors in the River Plate seem to feel that money shouldn't be mentioned from the pulpit because of the fact that they receive their livelihood from the church. But gradually our young pastor came to understand, through Bible study and contact with missionaries, that tithing and stewardship are truly parts of the worship of God and the privilege of every Christian. He began to preach and teach tithing, explaining it very carefully so that the young as well as the old might understand.

The pastor wrote ten suggestions with Bible references for the tither. He also prepared a pledge.

The Ten Commandments were memorized and said in unison from time to time. Each month when the envelopes were distributed, the pastor gave a message on stewardship. For the children, he drew diagrams, with decimals, and asked very simple questions, such as, "If you had ten cents, how much would you tithe?" The people came to feel that giving a tenth is a very natural part of becoming a member of the church.

We did not have canvasses or pledges of any specific amount of money. However, the church studied its budget carefully and accepted recommendations from the finance committee when changes were advisable.

The envelope system of giving was adopted, and immediately many who were not members of the church for various reasons wanted to tithe. The majority of the children in the Sunday school asked for envelopes. Many adult members of the Sunday school and many regular attendants at the worship service who could not be baptized due to irregularities in their civil status, etc., wanted to have a share in the financing of the church. Therefore, the number of tithers grew and became larger than the membership of the church.

11. Joseph C. Good and Dr. Fred V. Poag developed a successful flip-chart presentation which sold the tithing plan first to the canvassers and then to the congregation of the Shandon Presbyterian Church in Columbia, South Carolina. It enabled this church to meet its $44,314 budget.

12. I like the "you" and "shareholder" angle in the following appeal of the Traveler's Aid:

MEMO TO: You, owner of a share in our achievement

FROM: Edward E. Watts, Jr., President, Traveler's Aid Society of New York

Best thanks for your generous support during busy 1951! One hundred twenty-one thousand one hundred one persons found ready help and skilled counsel at the Society's lamps . . . beneficiaries of the friendly interest you displayed.

This is not the anniversary of your last gift, and the enclosed annual report is not an "extra" appeal. We do want you to see this record of how your 1951 contribution was used and how far we were able to s-t-r-e-t-c-h it.

Traveler's Aid counts it a privilege to number you among its members.

Both the you and shareholder appeal can be easily and successfully adapted to church appeals.

13. I simply cannot help but give you another outstanding example of tithing. Why? Because tithing is

God's plan of giving. And tithing makes for a stronger spiritual as well as a stronger physical church.

This example is the Lutheran Laymen's Movement for Stewardship. The members practice tithing, setting aside ten percent of their income for God. When they begin tithing, their faith invariably takes on new meaning. As one Lutheran put it, "Christians give not for special favors or for prestige but out of gratitude. Many believe that the reasonable first step in making offerings is the Christian tithe." No wonder they call these Lutherans "Men with a Mission."

We read recently an interesting item entitled "Church-Giving Rises" which went on to say:

Some 36,000,000 U.S. church members increased their annual contributions by an average of about two dollars apiece—and U.S. church-giving in forty-six Protestant Anglican and Eastern Orthodox communions reached an all-time high, topping the billion-dollar mark for the second year in succession.

Two dollars more apiece a year is an encouraging gain but it doesn't equal the increased cost of doing Christ's work. We must all give more . . . share more. So start raising some of the ideas in your church to increase its capacity for good works.

14. Every month *Woman's Day* magazine runs an article telling all about some proved way to raise church funds. For example, one monthly article explained in detail all the unusual ways through which the First Presbyterian Church of New Rochelle, New York, raised $4,800 at a church bazaar, in that small community. *Christian Herald* magazine also features many money-raising articles. You who have this problem should read both publications *regularly*.

15. One way to insure a better response to any financial appeal is to make sure that the givers or pledgers are adequately thanked. In too many drives, there is no

"thank you" sent to the givers. They never hear from the campaign committee, or the head of the institution, until they are asked to subscribe again. Although gratitude is the most fleeting emotion, there is no excuse for its not showing up in church financial matters.

One of the organizations which does an outstanding job of thanking its supporters is "Boys' Town." They go so far in their appreciation as to make each giver an "Honorary Citizen of Boy's Town," with an attractive card to visualize the recognition.

16. In *Building Up Your Congregation* we spelled out the reasons for . . . advantages of . . . and results from the *"Loyalty Sunday"* method of raising the annual budget. The Reverend Fred C. Wiegman is using a somewhat similar plan, called "Church Day," at the Trinity Lutheran Church in Akron, Ohio. Here is how he highlights their drive:

"Our Church Day, for the past twenty years, has raised eighty percent of our budget. At five Communion Services (preceded by three letters and one issue of the Parish Paper dealing with (a) the stewardship of tithing, (b) the world budget, and (c) the local budget, five laymen give talks on the needs of the church. Pledge cards are passed out and carried to the altar by the members. The twenty percent of the remaining budget is obtained by personal calls."

17. *Guideposts* magazine ran this money-raising idea, which can be duplicated by thousands of churches—try yours, perhaps.

"How can a church raise $10,000 for needed equipment? This problem faced the Reverend Harleigh Mood Rosenberger, Minister of the Baptist Church, Lockport, New York. Then he recalled an article in the November 1947 *Guideposts*. Adapting the project described in this article, Mr. Rosenberger distributed 230 ten-dollar bills to his congregation last May and told them to put the money to work. They accepted the challenge enthusiastically—sold baked goods at the church, hot dogs at the county fair; washed cars, mended clothes, and found other profitable turnovers."

18. The First Christian Church of Portland, Oregon, has developed an interesting and successful way of raising scholarship funds to help theological students. Once a year the church has a $25 plate Scholarship-Aid Banquet. The money from the project goes to help support students preparing for full-time Christian service. The need for more clergymen is so great, so many seminary students need help . . . that this is one of the most important activities mentioned in the entire book. How long since your church has raised money or sent a check to one of the theological seminaries of your denomination? This banquet idea is one proven way to do it!

As promised in the chapter heading, we have listed many ways in which various churches are raising funds. Most of these are in addition to the regular every-member canvass of the Loyalty Sunday pledging. As in many church matters like fund raising, there is another side of the coin. There are those churches and individuals who believe in and practice the plan of having only one financial drive and pledge per year. For example, Harry Bunge of the St. Paul Evangelical Lutheran Church of Auburn, Nebraska, writes us on his questionnaire:

"Personally I feel all churches would be strengthened if the raising of money for the work of the church—both locally and at large—would be on a voluntary and proportionate basis; not by sales, bazaars, cake sales, and 'what have you'! God's goodness to us should be the compelling factor of our stewardship of time, talents, and money—a voluntary compelling force of gratitude from within, rather than compulsion and pressure from without. The same difference we have in a spring which gives freely of its water as compared to an ordinary well which must be pumped to produce the water."

Frederick G. Erb, President of the Citizens National Bank and Trust Company of Pottstown, Pennsylvania, puts the same basic idea this way:

"I personally feel that many of the congregations ask their people for too many such appeals. We have found in our church—and it has been working for the past fifteen years—that if we ask our people once a year for a special offering we are a lot more successful. When we have our Every-Member Visitation in the fall of the year, we explain to our people the needs of the church for both current and benevolent expenses. We have found out that they respond, and we meet our quotas a hundred percent.

"I, of course, am a tither and believe that we should work toward the idea of getting all our church people to tithe. We must get them conscious-minded that they must put their giving for their Christ first and not last as so many do."

Chapter 15

PROVED
DIRECT-MAIL PLANS
FOR ANNUAL
CANVASS

O NE OF THE BEST WAYS to remind people to support the church more regularly and more adequately is to send them some *useful* reminder. For example, this can be done with a blotter or a calendar. A blotter is good because it is used when people are writing out checks. It reminds them to write a check for the church.

Calendars remind parishioners of their needed financial support day after day, month after month. Trinity Church, Columbus, Georgia, sends out a handy calendar which costs only $6.50 per hundred.

1. One of the most attractive and effective money-raising calendars is that put out by the Henry Street Settlement House in New York City. Mrs. Stella A. Koenig, secretary of this outstanding settlement house, has written a most helpful book on raising funds. Entitled *How to Raise Funds by Mail,* her book contains dozens of tested ideas for increasing the returns from your mailings.

2. Blotters—A Constant Reminder

Do you have many executives and office workers in your parish? Here is a way to help them keep Christ's message at their fingertips.

Put out an ink blotter of a size suitable for mailing, with pictures or art work on one side. There are many ways of doing this and the cost should be small. Someone in your parish might possibly have contact with the advertising-novelties field and could offer sound advice as to style and cost, or perhaps could get a business firm to donate them.

Religious pictures or drawings, or a short biblical quotation applicable in the day-to-day pressures of the business world, would serve to remind the user of the church and the comfort of His ways.

To Raise Funds by Direct Mail

"Satisfactory results in the mail campaign are much more difficult to achieve today than a decade ago. There is widespread competition from the most expensive and well-planned advertising of all types of business. Nearly every individual who is able to contribute receives too much mail to give serious consideration to any project that does not instantly capture his interest." (From *How to Raise Money* by William K. Gamble.)

Here are the questions to be considered *and answered* before organizing an Every-Member Canvass by mail.

1. Can it be done?

a. Is there an adequate and sufficiently accurate mailing list?

b. Is there a potentially high enough percentage of return to warrant such a type of canvass?

c. Do your parishioners have a normal interest in and concern for the adequate support of the parish program?

d. Have you allowed sufficient time to create such an interest and concern before you require a reply from a contributor?

e. Will the necessary costs of a mail campaign be so prohibitive that the net results are too small to meet the need?

As a general axiom the most valuable function of a direct-mail canvass is to reach parishioners that cannot be reached personally.

2. *How much expert* experience and advice in preparing and distributing of the materials is available in the parish?

a. Can your literature and material be expertly pre-pared?

b. Do you have the office help and equipment to handle the job?

Three stages of a direct-mail canvass.

1. Planning and producing the materials to be used and establishing an adequate mailing schedule. (Three mailings, each building up to a climax, is usually con-sidered the minimum.)

This planning to include:

a. Selection of the type of appeal most likely to be successful. Appeal should be vivid, dramatic and im-portant enough to stir the imagination. It should point up a specific need and be a "natural."

b. Literature and supporting materials should be highly readable, suited to the receiver, and emphasize the basic appeal selected. All materials should carry a demand for action.

c. Most direct-mail canvasses use a letter or a series of letters. These should be carefully written, follow well-recognized rules for obtaining a reading, and be signed by those who carry the most confidence.

2. Mailing

a. Follow a specific, well thought-out mailing sched-ule.

b. The timing of your mailing to reach receivers at the period of highest susceptibility is important.

c. Accuracy in enclosures and addressing is a must.

3. Tabulation of returns and follow-up.

a. A definite set-up to handle replies promptly and to check off returns is an essential.

b. A committee and the necessary equipment to lo-cate and re-address non-deliveries is important in order that mailings will not be wasted uselessly.

3. Keeping in mind that the number of follow-ups directly affects the extent of the returns, it is advisable

to "stay with them" until sure that additional effort will not produce justifiable returns.

> Lord, grant us so to desire the things
> Which belong to our peace,
> That we may accept with quietness
> And with confidence the disciplines
> Which are their cost. Amen.

4. The Reverend Raymond L. Scofield, rector of St. Mark's Church, Jackson Heights, New York, with Walter Tibbals mapped out a direct-mail program to bring in new members, revive the interest of old members, and better the financial structure of his church. It worked out very well and the samples of the various mailing pieces are reprinted to aid you in planning a similar campaign.

Money-Saver for Churches

Third-class mail rating is a money-saving device for non-profit organizations and a time-saving one for their office staffs. It is a boon to churches, church organizations, diocese, and missionary districts, in mailing such material as bulletins and Every-Member Canvass material. A rate increase on third-class mail became effective on July 1, 1952, but churches and other religious organizations may be excused from the increase by making proper application.

This is how to get a third-class permit for bulk mailing, which is such an important part of a church's business, and also how to avoid the rate increase, as explained by Mr. R. C. Daffer, Senior Assistant Superintendent of Mails, U.S. Post Office, Washington, D. C.

First, apply to the local postmaster for a "bulk mailing permit for third-class mail." Be sure to specify "third class" since there are bulk mailing permits for other classes of mail.

There are three ways of mailing in the third class category (turn to page 204) :

RECTORY
33-40 81st STREET
NEWTOWN 9-7845

February
21
1951

PARISH HOUSE
33-50 82nd STREET
NEWTOWN 9-8893

My dear Neighbor:

Saint Mark's Church welcomes you to Jackson Heights!

We are a group of people who like the way the Episcopal
Church presents and interprets the Christian religion.
Some of us value its traditions, its history and the dignity of its Services. We pray together and play together.
Our aim is to adopt into our family all who will come to
us - regardless of their Church affiliation. We are an
Episcopal Church for ALL PEOPLE. We are a very friendly,
happy society standing for the best in Christian morality
and in American democracy.

You may have noticed our beautiful Church building and
the large well-equipped Parish House. The Parish House
is the center of our social activities for every age group
and for many interests . . .in fact there is something going on every day of the week. We believe the Christian
Church should be friendly . . . we try to be. If you are
unacquainted in this community and are not already connected with any Church, we shall be most happy if you will come
to us - make yourself known - and become a part of our busy
life.

Why not take a minute to fill out the enclosed card and drop
it in the nearest mail box?

Sincerely,

Raymond L. Scofield

Rector

P.S. Our Church is on 34th Avenue, between 81st and 82nd
Streets. The entrance to our Parish House is 3350 - 82nd
Street, adjoining the Church.

RECTORY
33-40 81st STREET
NEWTOWN 9-7845

March 14, 1951

PARISH HOUSE
33-50 82nd STREET
NEWTOWN 9-8893

Dear Neighbor:

A short time ago we wrote to you about Saint Mark's Church.

This letter is to tell you a little bit more about what goes
on in our busy life . . .because we think there is something
to appeal to every one.

Saint Mark's Church, while Episcopal in denomination is open
to ALL. We have lots of people coming to Church every day
who have been raised in other Faiths. It is an Episcopal
Church for EVERY ONE.

Some of these folks came to know us through the Cub Scouts,
the Boy Scouts, Brownies or Girl Scouts, the Boys' Choir,
the Girls' Choir, the Young People's Fellowships (two groups,
one from 12 to 15 years of age and the other from 15 to 21).
We think children need the training and association built by
these Christian organizations.

If you have ever lived in a small town you know how nice it
is to know your neighbors . . .well, we have sort of a small
town here in Jackson Heights - it is a small town in a big
city and you can meet your neighbors here at Saint Mark's.
For instance, at the "Coffee Hour" which is held in the Parish
House following the 11 o'clock Service. Here you may talk to
those in charge of the various Church Committees, such as:
Women's Guild - Sewing Guild (for St. Barnabas, St. John's
Hospital, the Missions and the Annual Bazaar) - Young Married
Couples Group (21-35) - Evening Branch of the Women's Guild -
Altar Guild - Garden Group - Men's Fellowship Group.

The "coffee hour" also affords me the opportunity to personally meet and talk with my friends and neighbors - both old
and new.

For your information and convenience we list our Services for
Holy Week:

```
Palm Sunday - Holy Communion ...................8:00 A.M.
              Church School ...................9:30 A.M.
              Morning Prayer, Sermon, Process-11:00 A.M.
              ion of Palms (Boys' & Girls' Choir)
```

196

```
Monday........... Holy Communion ..............10:00 A.M.

Tuesday ......... Holy Communion ..............10:00 A.M.

Wednesday ....... Holy Communion .............. 7:00 A.M.
                                               10:00 A.M.

Maundy Thursday . Holy Communion .............. 7:00 A.M.
                                               10:00 A.M.
                                                8:00 P.M.

Good Friday ..... The Three Hours.....Noon to.. 3:00 P.M.
                  Evening Service ............. 8:00 P.M.

Easter Sunday ... Holy Communion .............. 7:00 A.M.
                            (Choral) 8:00 A.M.
                                     9:30 A.M.
                  Morning Prayer, Sermon, Holy 11:00 A.M.
                  Communion
                  Children's Service .......... 3:00 P.M.
                  Presentation of Mite Boxes
```

If you plan on coming to the 11 o'clock Service on Easter Sunday we suggest you fill out the enclosed card for tickets which will assure you of seating in the Church.

I extend to you a personal invitation to attend at least one of our Services during Holy Week to get acquainted with Saint Mark's.

                    Sincerely,

                    Raymond L. Scofield
                    Rector

P.S. Don't forget . . .we have a Nursery School (free "sitter's service") for your young children during the 11 o'clock Service every Sunday. Call us at NEwtown 9-8893 for details.

Easter

1951

My dear Members and Friends of St. Mark's:-

"And the third day He rose again from the dead"

Either we believe that statement as fact or we don't. If we believe it, we must believe it all of the time. It is not a pretty little fetish to be coddled on Easter and put away in the hall closet the rest of the year. On it rests our alignment, either with Christians who believe in the continuation of this life, with its demand in the sanctity of the individual, and a purpose for life, or with those who hold that 'this life is all there is; therefore, let's make the most of it, forgetful of any higher law' There is no middle course; there is no neutrality.

Some say 'What difference does it make'? Too many vital questions are answered by that evasive reply. To believe that I am undergoing a spiritual evolution in this world, 'a factory where persons are made', steered by a God-given free will, inspires me to value righteousness, not motivated by fear of punishment or hope of reward for goodness. It instils a purpose in my existence, otherwise purposeless. It makes me long to be reunited with those whom I love and who have 'flown over the hump' before me. It enfolds me in the rebirth of Spring, the symbol of the Resurrection, and makes me certain of the victory of goodness. It shows me the way to attain. It inspires me to do good and to be good. It assures me that all men are the temples of God. It raises me from the slave of man's economic and political systems to be a Child of God.

So, we are a part of the Easter fact, on which our faith is built. Jesus rose from the dead. His goodness is indestructible. By the same means we will continue our lives through eternity.

I wish you a very happy, certain and joyful Easter.

Faithfully,

R. L. Scofield
Rector

P. S. Enclosed is a copy of a letter sent to new residents of Jackson Heights.

Costs of materials and operation have gone up for the Church as well as in other things. Please increase your Easter offering.

.... - R. L. S.

Saint Mark's Church

RAYMOND L. SCOFIELD, Rector

34th AVE., 81st TO 82nd STS., JACKSON HEIGHTS, N. Y.

RECTORY
40 81st STREET
WTOWN 9-7845

PARISH HOUSE
33-50 82nd STREET
NEWTOWN 9-8893

June 23, 1951

Dear Parishioner:

Now that the warm weather is here . . . we hope
you are going to take a vacation. Everyone needs
a rest.

Before you go away and while you're enjoying yourself will you give a thought to St. Mark's Church?

Over the summer, expenses at St. Mark's keep going.
They are just about the same as in winter . . minus
heat and coffee, but during each of the summer months
the Church revenues are less than half of what they
are during each of the other months of the year.

Here's where you can help. Won't you bring your
pledges up to date if they are behind, and further,
won't you keep them up to date if you are absent
from the Church. That way your Church won't have
to borrow from the Bank.

God's work is never done and we must function at full
strength, 52 weeks a year.

May you have a happy, pleasant and healthful summer,
and may the blessings of God Almighty be with you and
remain with you always.

Sincerely yours,

Raymond L. Scofield

Rector

RAYMOND L. SCOFIELD, Rector
33-40 81st STREET, JACKSON HEIGHTS
RECTORY- NEWTOWN 9-7845

PARISH HOUSE
33-50 82nd STREET
Tel. NE 9-8893

November 5, 1951

Dear Friend:

Every year at this time your Church - Saint Mark's - starts its drive for yearly pledges and new members.

This year we are trying a slightly different type of canvass. . . we will not call on you at this time unless you ask us to, nor will we pester you with telephone calls - or pop out from behind the hedges and bushes while you are on your way to church.

In a few days we will send you the facts; you be the judge of what to do.

May the blessing of God guide you and be with you in considering your pledge for 1952.

Sincerely,

R. L. Scofield

Rector

200

Saint Mark's Church

8101-17 34th AVENUE, JACKSON HEIGHTS, N. Y.
NEWTOWN 9-8893

RAYMOND L. SCOFIELD, Rector
33-40 81st STREET, JACKSON HEIGHTS
RECTORY: NEWTOWN 9-7845

PARISH HOUSE
33-50 82nd STREET
Tel. NE 9-8893

November 26, 1951

Dear Friend:

Recently we sent you the facts on Saint Mark's
Church. Did you read them? They are most
interesting and important!

So far we have not heard from you. Will you
please return your pledge card filled out or
the enclosed card so that we may know you are
still a member of the Saint Mark's family?

Just check the card and mail it - no postage
is required.

Sincerely,

R. L. Scofield

Rector

P.S. Don't forget to attend Saint Mark's Annual
Parish Meeting on December 3, at 8:00 P. M. in
the Parish House.

HOW DO YOU VOTE? IT'S YOUR CHOICE- YOUR RIGHT TO

DECIDE

(FRONT COVER)

Dɪʀᴇᴄᴛ ᴜꜱ, *O Lord, in all our doings, with thy most gracious favour, and further us with thy continual help; that in all our works begun, continued, and ended in thee, we may glorify thy holy Name, and finally, by thy mercy, obtain everlasting life; through Jesus Christ our Lord. Amen.*

(BACK COVER)

Do you want GOD and this country the way you have built it?

HERE'S WHAT YOU DO

(PAGE 2)

Will you double your pledge to St. Mark's?

———

It would be great if you would— but we don't want you to!

———

Look at the table on the next page and

HELP ST. MARK'S

(PAGE 3)

if your weekly pledge in 1951 WAS	then please give IN 1952
$ .50	$ .75
1.00	1.50
1.50	2.00
2.00	2.50
2.50	3.00
3.00	4.00
4.00	5.00
5.00	6.00

THAT'S NOT TOO MUCH TO ASK TO...

(PAGE 4)

KEEP...

1 God in our homes

2 Peace in our hearts

3 The strength of Christianity in all of us

AND

4 ST. MARK'S CHURCH GROWING

(PAGE 5)

Proposed Budget for 1952
Estimated Receipts

COLLECTIONS	$ 4,900
Open offerings on Sunday mornings and other services, Easter, Christmas, etc.	
CHURCH SCHOOL PLEDGES	2,400
CONTRIBUTIONS AND GIFTS	5,100
From Church Guilds and Organizations, Bazaar, and from individuals for specific purposes.	
FOR WORK OUTSIDE PARISH	2,800
Gifts and subscriptions for Diocesan and General Church Missions Program, including Episcopal Charities Appeal, Church Charities Foundation, etc.	
RECEIPTS FROM PLEDGES	24,300
Owing to deaths, removals, etc., experience indicates that total pledges of $27,000 will be required to produce receipts of this amount	
Total estimated receipts	$39,500

Estimated Expenses

SALARIES	$15,300
Salaries and pension assessments of the Rector and Clergy assistance, salaries of office staff and Sexton	
MUSIC	1,900
Salaries of organist and choir, choir supplies, vestments, music, care of organ and pianos	
OPERATING EXPENSE	10,600
General expenses of maintaining Church and Parish House, including insurance, heat, light, gas, telephone, stationery & printing, postage, repairs and improvements, etc.	
CHURCH SCHOOL	400
Church School books and supplies (but not including permanent equipment and overhead items)	
INTEREST	2,500
Interest on Mortgage and Debentures	
DIOCESAN AND GENERAL CHURCH PROGRAM	4,600
For missionary, educational, social service and religious work of the Parish, Diocese and General Church	
ADDITIONS & BETTERMENTS TO PROPERTY	1,100
Purchase of Furniture & Fixtures, Extraordinary repairs	
REDUCTION OF DEBT	3,100
Amortization of Mortgage, Redemption of Debentures	
Total estimated expenses	$39,500

FILL OUT THE PLEDGE CARD ENCLOSED AND MAIL IT NOW OR

Drop it in the collection plate Sunday

(PAGE 7)

```
_____ ENVELOPE NO._____

_____


                    ST. MARK'S CHURCH (EPISCOPAL)
                          JACKSON HEIGHTS, N. Y.

        I PLEDGE FOR THIS YEAR          MY LAST YEAR'S PLEDGE WAS

    PARISH                 ☐ WEEKLY    PARISH               ☐ WEEKLY
    SUPPORT    $_____   ☐ MONTHLY   SUPPORT   $_____  ☐ MONTHLY

    CHURCH                 ☐ QUARTERLY CHURCH               ☐ QUARTERLY
    MISSION    $_____   ☐ YEARLY    MISSION   $_____  ☐ YEARLY

                        Signature:_____
```

Dear Mr. Scofield:

☐   I am not at present connected with
    any church in Jackson Heights.

☐   I would like to learn more about
    Saint Mark's Church.

Mr.
Mrs.
Miss_____

Address_____

_____ Apt. #_____

1. With uncanceled stamps (ordinary uncanceled stamps cannot be used).

2. Postal meter.

3. Without stamps.

These conditions apply to all three of the methods that have just been listed:

1. Material to be mailed must be printed matter or form letters either in folder form or enclosed in unsealed envelopes. A folded church paper will be ac-

cepted without an envelope, saving not only the expense of the envelopes, but the time required to stuff them.

2. There must be at least 200 or more identical pieces of mail (or mail weighing 20 pounds or more) tied in bundles of about 50 for mailing.

The fee for a third-class bulk mailing permit is $10 and is only good for the calendar year or any portion of the calendar year remaining. In other words, if a church applied for such a permit in October or November, it would be required to pay another $10 at the beginning of the next year to renew its permit. The permit must be renewed before any mailings in each new year.

All third-class mail must have this endorsement: "Section 34.66 P.L. & R." This tells the postmaster that the publisher or sender of material agrees to comply with the postal regulations. Literally, the endorsement means: section 34, paragraph 66 of the postal laws and regulations.

The permit is good for all types of third-class mail at the rate of 14 cents a pound weighed in bulk with a minimum rate of one cent a piece. As much as eight sheets of mimeographed paper stapled together can be mailed third class.

Bulk lots of books and catalogs having 24 pages or more (including covers), 22 or more of which are printed, may be mailed for ten cents a pound weighed in bulk, with a minimum rate of one cent a piece.

Individual pieces—printed matter, circulars, pamphlets—may be mailed third class by authorized religious organizations for one and one half cents an ounce or each fraction thereof.

Effective July 1, 1952, the rate for third-class mailings were increased to one cent and a half of mailing. This applies to all except religious, fraternal, labor, philanthropic, and veterans' organizations. To avoid this increase a church must write a letter to the postmaster asking for exemption under the new law. Unless this letter is written the church will have to pay the increased rate.

The method of mailing without stamps under the third-class rates requires an additional $10 just for the privilege of not using stamps. This extra $10 (besides the annual fee) need not be paid every year but only once, and the privilege of mailing without stamps is effective always after payment of that initial fee.

The church may deposit with the post office at the time of mailing, or before, the money to cover postage cost, if stamps are not used.

Permits, but no fees, are required for use of pre-canceled stamps and metered mail.

The upper right-hand corner of a piece of mail requires this information which may be mimeographed, printed (might be done by hand), or metered:

Section 34.66 P.L. & R.
U.S. Postage
Paid
Name of city the post office used is in.
Permit number of church.

DETERMINING THE AMOUNT OF PLEDGE

One of the most difficult, yet important, pieces of writing in any annual-appeal literature is that which advises the member on how much he or she should pledge for the year . . . month . . . or week. One excellent way of solving this problem is found in the attractive and effective brochure which Robert Colwell (of Sullivan, Stauffer, Colwell & Bayles, Advertising Agency) developed for the Hugenot Memorial Church in Pelham, New York. It reads as follows:

"How to Determine Your Own Responsibility"

Many people ask how much they should contribute to Church Support and Benevolences.

There is no single answer. Each should give as the Lord has prospered him. A pledge of a thousand dollars a year might represent a heart-felt gift from one Christian. $78 a year—$1 a week for Church support and 50¢ a week for Benevolence—might be an equally sacrificial offering from another.

The Bible teaches us that all things belong to God. We are stewards, not owners, of his bounty. Some devout Christians give one-tenth of all their income, the Biblical tithe, for the Kingdom of Christ—the most important work in the world.

"Many cannot choose this percentage. However, your Church does urge you to plan your gift in terms of come definite percentage of your income. Above all, we ask that every member pledge something both to Church Support and Benevolence. We hope each Church member in your family will make his own individual pledge."

Mr. Colwell added a fine public relations note through this sentence on the back cover: "This booklet was printed without expense to the church."

The introductory page in this brochure is also worthy of being used by other churches in their annual appeals. Notice how the following sets a sincere religious tone or mood:

ACTS: II, 45-47

(A description of the early Christian Church)

"And sold their possessions and goods, and parted them to all men, as every man had need.

"And they, continuing daily with one accord in the temple, and breaking bread from house to house, did eat their meat with gladness and singleness of heart.

"Praising God, and having favor with all the people. And the Lord added to the church daily such as should be saved."

Chapter 16

DETAILED TRAINING AND PLAN FOR EVERY-MEMBER CANVASS

By Ted Gannaway and Edwin Yowell

I<small>T IS THE AUTHOR'S GREAT PRIVILEGE</small> to bring you a tested and proven plan for an Every-Member Canvass which is used annually with success by a growing number of churches in New York State. This laymen's training program is the result of outstanding work done by Ted Gannaway, Director of Laymen's Work for the Diocese of New York, and Edwin Yowell of Christ Church, Tarrytown, New York.

We are sure that even the experienced organizers and workers on the Annual Canvass will get one or two new ideas or techniques from this outline. Messrs. Gannaway and Yowell also developed a successful plan for conducting an Every-Member Canvass by direct mail, and a plan for direct mail and visitation. You can get a copy by writing to either of them. Ted Gannaway's address is Synod House, Amsterdam Avenue, at 110th Street, New York 25, N. Y.

WHY EVERY-MEMBER CANVASS?

1. The plan is fifty years old with fifty years of successful history.

2. The plan deals constructively, simultaneously, and effectively with the three besetting problems of every parish:

a. Perennial waning of spiritual enthusiasm.

b. Constant lessening of a sense of corporateness and Christian fellowship.

c. Increasing cost of religious essentials.

3. The plan has the unqualified endorsement of all major communions in the United States.

4. The plan has successfully met parish crises such as:

a. A desperate need to extricate a parish from an accumulated deficit.

b. An awakened realization of the value of the parish to the community and dissatisfaction with the present status situation.

c. A conviction that the future security of the parish calls for an immediate attempt to broaden its basis of support from a few large gifts to financial participation by a majority of its membership.

d. A determination by the parish to go on a sound financial basis, i.e., full missionary quota and operating expenses covered by pledges using the duplex envelope and Every-Member Canvass.

e. Decreasing endowment income demanding wider membership participation in financial support.

f. Shifting population movements requiring rediscovery of parish manpower and new courses of financial support.

g. Parish recognition that the lifeblood of its growth and expansion is the missionary zeal of its membership, culminating in a decision to insist on active participation by all parishioners in the missionary program.

h. Physical condition of the parish properties requiring raising additional funds to maintain present plant and program of activities.

i. Unexpected emergencies that cannot be met with methods of raising funds previously employed.

TYPES COMMONLY USED

1. Personal Visitation

A personal call by a trained canvasser on every communicant family (unit) for the purpose of:

Explaining the Church's program and plans.

Obtaining a valid pledge of payment of money toward the support of that program and those plans.

2. By Direct Mail

A series of mailings designed to carry the story of the Church's program and plans into every home and including a pledge card and envelope for pledge or payment of contributions.

3. Direct Mail and Personal Visitation

Loyalty Sunday

A combination of the 1 and 2 above in which as many contributions and pledges are obtained by mail, and those *not* so responding are called upon by trained canvassers.

4. Experimental Donor Days

A plan whereby the communicants are prepared by the minister through instructions from the pulpit on the plans and program of the Church, the missionary imperative of the Christian faith, and the necessity for adequate support. The minister then sets aside certain days to meet the families of his parish at the chancel and together personally present their gifts at the altar.

A Suggested Outline of the Basic Essentials
for a Successful

EVERY-MEMBER CANVASS

To Raise Funds by Personal Visitation

Personnel
   (*For each 100 communicant units*)
   One lay chairman
   Committee on special gifts

SUGGESTED ORGANIZATION FOR 100 COMMUNICANTS

CHAIRMAN
(Group)
Commander

VICE CHAIRMAN
(Squadron Leader)

SPECIAL GIFTS COMMITTEE
(Bomber Squadron)

VICE CHAIRMAN
(Squadron Leader)

Team Chairman
Flight Leader

Workers
Pilot   Pilot
Co-pilots

TRAINING AND SUPPLY

TRAINING AND SUPPLY

| Literature and Mail | Parish Secretary | Rector and Clergy | Treasury and Audit | Arrangements | Publicity and Display |

RECRUITING

General Chairman obtains — { Two Vice-Chairmen / Special Gifts Committee

Vice-Chairman obtains — Three Team Leaders

Team Leader obtains — Two Workers

Each Worker obtains — One Co-worker

Six team leaders
Twelve teams of two each
(*For each additional 50 communicant units, add*) :
One vice-chairman
Three team leaders
Six teams of two each

CONFERENCES

1. Planning (Minister presides).... .. ..

INVITE: Minister and associate clergy, vestry and canvass chairman.

AGENDA (Allow two full hours) :
a. Establish campaign theme.
b. Determine objectives and dates.
c. Explain budget items.
d. Fix number calls to be made.
e. Appoint pre-campaign special gift committee and assign calls.
f. Develop potential worker list and allot names.
g. Nominate vice-chairman and team leaders and make recruiting assignments.
h. Set date for recruiting report meeting.

2. Recruiting Report Meeting (Canvass chairman presides)

INVITE: Same group as above plus vice-chairmen.

AGENDA (Allow 30 minutes) :
a. Install vice-chairmen.
b. Install team leaders.
c. Distribute worker lists to vice-chairmen and then to team leaders for team selection (As appointments are made, fill organization chart by phone call from team leaders) .

3. Workers' Rally (canvass chairman presides)

INVITE: Minister, associate clergy, vestry, general

chairman, special gifts committee, vice-chairmen, team leaders, workers and special guests.

AGENDA (Allow 3 hours if supper meeting; 2½ if not) :

a. Devotional service and prayers (in chapel). Commissioning of workers.

b. Invocation and supper. (See table set-up attached.)

c. (2 min.). Minister introduces canvass chairman

d. (5 min.). Canvass chairman declares objectives and theme, welcomes workers and exposes organization chart

e. (8 min.). Parish treasurer (or senior warden) covers budget items

f. Team leaders given call cards and report envelopes for assignment to teams at tables. (Pause 10 min. for distribution, discussion and questions).

g. (15 min.). Chairman briefs workers on campaign plans and procedures

h. (30 min.). Vice-Chairman conducts training conference on techniques

i. (30 min.) Inspirational address on parish and missionary program

j. Prayers and adjournment

4. Workers' Report Meeting (Canvass chairman presides)

INVITE: Minister, associate clergy, wardens, treasurer, and all Canvass personnel.

AGENDA (Allow one hour) :

a. Report of special gifts chairman and committee. (Team leaders should collect and tabulate returns during report of special gifts.)

b. Roll call by team leaders giving results.

c. Treasurer records results to date on organization chart.

d. Question and answer period.

e. Announce time and date of final report meeting.

f. Prayers and adjournment.

5. *Workers' Final Report Meeting* (Canvass chairman presides)

INVITE: As above in 4

AGENDA:
a. Prayers.
b. Team leaders report roll call.
c. Distribution of citations.
d. Treasurer gives final tabulation of results.
e. Service of thanksgiving.
f. Workers thanked and adjournment.

DIRECT MAIL

1. *Minister's Letter* (to be mailed immediately following Planning Conference)

FORMAT—for readability—four paragraphs of 5 to 9 sentences each. Sentences to consist of 17-21 words each. Words to average 1.8 syllables. All on one page, parish letterhead, personalized as much as practicable. For impact—a simple direct statement of the minister's expectations from each parishioner. (No apologies, budget explanation, pleading for attention, nor false optimism.)

For memory retention—start paragraphs with the pronoun "you" where possible. Speak in terms of the readers' interests, not the warden's, vestry's or minister's. Use simple non-ecclesiastical wording. Select sincere, colorful phrases that carry a punch.

2. *The Parish Folder* (to be included with the above). A four-page printed (where possible) illustrated folder. Suggestions: one page may be the simplified budget; one page, a carefully worded, short statement from the canvass chairman; one page carry the major items of the present parish and missionary program and essentials of the program plans for the coming year. Cover page, a picture of the church, the campaign slogan, and dates.

3. *Diocesan Missionary Folder* (to be mailed the day of the Workers' Rally).

4. *The National Church Folder* (to be mailed the day before the campaign opens). To be mimeographed or imprinted with a direct appeal and endorsement by the minister and the Canvass Chairman.

DUTIES AND RESPONSIBILITIES OF CAMPAIGN SERVICE PERSONNEL

The Minister

Call and preside at Canvass Planning Conference. Aid in selection of general chairman.

Meet with and assist the special gifts committee.

Assist in the assignment of call cards to vice-chairman.

Act as chaplain at all meetings.

Conduct worship services in support of campaign.

Assist the special service committees.

The Treasurer.

Prepare call cards for all communicant units.

Assist in selection of calls assigned to special gifts committee.

Receive all contributions and pledges.

Supervise audit and prepare campaign-progress reports.

The Chairman and Committee on Arrangements.

Arrange details of all workers' meetings, including meals, table arrangements, and decorations, etc.

The Literature and Mailing Committee.

Order, collate, and mail all literature, letters, and campaign materials on schedule agreed upon at the planning conference.

The Publicity and Display Director.

Prepare and send out press releases, set up displays at meetings. Arrange for photographs. Operate training equipment.

The Parish Secretary.

Prepare call cards for all communicant units.

Address and mail all literature, letters, and materials.

Operate a general information service for all workers.

Accept and record properly reports on workers recuited.

Notify or remind team leaders, vice-chairmen, and special committees of all meetings.

The Continuing Canvass Director.

TERM: Usually three to five years consecutively.

PURPOSE: To conserve the experience gained in each canvass; To know and use the best worker talent in the parish; To know and arrange the mechanics of conducting a canvass; To insure continual high standards.

QUALIFICATIONS: Young in spirit, tactful and capable of drawing out workers, thoroughly familiar with the parish and its budget, meticulous as to detail, ingenious in overcoming obstacles, alert to meet changing conditions and sharing the rector's or vicar's complete confidence.

SOURCES: Last year's successful canvass chairman, parish treasurer, parish keyman in laymen's movement, junior warden, vestry, advisory board, etc.

DUTIES: To recruit the annual canvass chairman; To organize the canvass preliminaries; To conserve the records of workers and evaluate them; To recruit possible new workers during the year; and such other duties as shall carry out the purpose of the position.

The General Chairman

Call and preside at all conferences and workers' meetings except the planning conference.

Recruit the vice-chairmen and brief them on duties.

Recruit qualified members of a special gifts committee and assist them in making the pre-canvass calls.

Confer with the minister, parish treasurer, and wardens on literature, posters, publicity, direct mail, displays, carding, meeting arrangements. Appoint chairmen to cover each above phase of the campaign.

Make five solicitation calls for contributions.

Conduct workers' training conference.

Supervise all phases of campaign.

Assign replacements when workers are unable to function.

Special Gifts Committee.

In cooperation with the minister and parish treasurer obtain the names and address of potential larger givers prior to the opening of the Canvass. Call upon each or enlist the aid of qualified people to assist in such a call and obtain as generous a contribution as possible prior to the Canvass.

Report such gifts at the meeting of the workers at the opening of the Canvass in such fashion as to provide the maximum stimulus to the campaign.

The Vice Chairman.

Recruit three well-qualified team leaders to serve as head of two workers' teams each.

Guarantee attendance of team leaders at all campaign meetings.

Divide call cards into packets of five according to address.

Issue call cards to team leaders.

Make five solicitation calls for contributions.

Collate reports of team leaders at workers' report meetings.

See that team leaders complete assignments as rapidly as possible.

Assist the general chairman in carrying out his duties, particularly in the conduct of the Workers' Training Conference.

Team Leaders.

Attend workers' rally and report meetings.

Recruit two teams of workers from workers' listings assigned.

Issue call cards to teams. Five calls to each team.

Guarantee attendance of workers at rally and report meetings.

Collate reports of team workers recruited by him.

See that team workers assignments are completed as rapidly as possible.

Workers.

Select and recruit a co-worker to assist in making calls.

Accept assignment of five calls, complete these calls and report results to team leaders.

Attend workers' rally, training conference, and report meetings.

PERSONNEL RECRUITING PLANS

In addition to the plan for recruiting canvassers given in the previous pages, the following have been used with success.

1. *The Area Plan*

The Parish is divided into geographical areas. A team leader is obtained for each area by the minister, the canvass director, or the annual canvass chairman. Each team leader obtains as many workers from his area as the number of calls to be made in his area requires. (For average canvassers no more than five or six calls per worker should be required. An exceptionally good canvasser can be given ten to fifteen calls to complete.)

2. *The Vestry Plan*

Each vestryman is automatically considered a team leader and given a quota of canvass workers to recruit.

3. *The Parish Organization Plan*

A varying quota of adult canvass workers is assigned to each major parish organization, and the organization recruits workers from their membership. (This includes team leaders and canvass officers if assigned.)

4. *The Men's Club Plan*

The organized men's group of the parish takes over the recruiting and furnishes the necessary personnel from among its own membership.

5. *The Open Selection Plan*

The minister and the canvass director cover the parish rolls and select six to twelve men to be team leaders. Selection is based on the proven ability of the men, and the number selected is dependent upon the size of the parish.

TRAINING OF CANVASSERS

By Edwin Yowell

Christ Church, Tarrytown, New York

The Training of Every-Member Canvasser

Any conversation regarding the *training of a canvasser* for the Every-Member Canvass presupposes three important factors:

1. A competent *general chairman* has been selected well in advance of the time the actual canvass begins.

2. A *general program* has been settled upon by this general chairman *and* the people he is responsible to.

3. *Accurate church records* are available. It is particularly important that the church roll be corrected prior to the time of the canvass.

Selecting the Candidate

In the past, many churches have had the unfortunate tendency to let the same old gang run all the church functions year after year. This is *not efficient, not smart, and not good* churchmanship. The general chairman and the minister should go over the church rolls and select, depending on the size of the parish, from six to twelve men to be *team captains.* The church's best team captains will generally come from people who have experience in dealing with people in their business lives. Lawyers, salesmen, engineers are always particularly adept in handling small groups such as a canvass team would comprise. After a man has obtained a certain maturity, necessary for effectiveness, of twenty odd years of living he has become, *potentially*, the greatest asset the Church has as an active worker. All that is necessary is effectively to direct his energy into the proper channels by the training we shall undertake today, and the Church will have a worker of far greater merit than the older man who has done the Church's chores for years through habit and what is sometimes called a "sense of duty." If the truth were known it would probably reveal that a great many of these men who have been asked year after year to make the annual Every-Member Canvass would be pleased if they were excused from their duties.

We are not selling the older men short; however, it is a well established fact that the young men of our churches are not asked to participate in many church functions because of what *Willard Pleuthner* so aptly called "Dangerous Dignity."

Religion is a living, vital thing. It is not necessary to be ninety-five, or even sixty-five, to properly appreciate its importance in everyday living.

Once the minister and the general chairman have selected the list of men they wish to ask to become team captains, the general chairman should personally contact each man and ask him to serve. The chairman should explain why it is important and why this particular person has been asked to head a team. The younger the person is who is asked the more honored he will feel for having been asked. This is the sort of captain we are looking for. The man who has worked on the canvass for twenty-five years will scarcely feel honored if he is asked again. He will more likely approach it with the "oh well" sort of attitude.

Training the Team Captains

Once a complement of captains has been arranged for (with one or two alternates, just in case), a meeting of the minister, the general chairman, and these team captains should be held in some appropriate church building for a general meeting. At this meeting the minister should formally turn the project of the yearly Every-Member Canvass over to the general chairman and from that point on exercise only what restrained control his own good judgment tells him is necessary.

At this general meeting the church secretary should be present, or whoever is responsible for the actual church budget. This functionary should attend all future meetings so that accurate, factual information will be available to the general chairman, the team captains and the workers. After the general program has been explained to the team captains and thoroughly discussed, the parish roll should be gone over and potential workers picked. Each captain should be given a free hand in picking the men who are going to work under him. Enough workers should be picked so that the captains will not have over six workers, and each worker will not have over eight or ten addresses to call upon.

As soon as the team captain is settled with his workers the actual training of the individual worker begins. This can be done either of two ways, depending on how many training meetings are to be held.

1. A general meeting, at which time a selected speaker could give a talk that would be generally related to the problem at hand, to be followed a few days later by a team meeting, which should be held at the team captain's home. Or (2) to reverse the above and have the team meeting first, followed by a general meeting, of the same type as mentioned before.

At the individual team meetings to be held in the home of the captain, the captain should explain in a give-and-take session just what, when, and how he expects his team to operate. I say "give-and-take" advisedly, however. Let the team captain be reminded that *he is* the captain and is responsible for the efficient function of his team and should not be stampeded or pressured into actions or methods which he does not approve.

The Actual Training of the Canvass Worker

The first and great problem of any representative, regardless of whether he is representing his church, some commercial organization, or simply himself in a discussion with his neighbor is to *know what he is talking about*. All sales managers maintain that there are three absolutes that the embryonic salesman must know. They are (1) know your product, (2) know your product, and (3) know your product. It is the responsibility of the team captain to see that each of his workers has a *workable knowledge* of the current budget and has an *intimate knowledge of the church organizations as they exist in his particular church*.

Do not try to make too many calls in one evening. It is better to make a single good call then ten poor ones. Before you get to the prospect's address, have everything in hand. Get out of your car and walk *purposefully* up to the door. *In front of the prospect's house is not the time to do your bookkeeping. Wear a hat.* It gives you something to take off in a show of courtesy (which all women like), and after you have it off, it gives you something to do with your hands. *Read the name off the card.* Ask the question: "Are you Mrs. Smith?" This gets the prospect into the conversation. Most people can't think and talk at the same time. If the prospect is talking to you she can't get her guard up and start to think of the different ways of saying "no." *Speak up.* Say: "I'm Ed Yowell, of Christ Church." Associate yourself with the church. To you, she can say "no," but it isn't quite so likely that she will cut you off if you mention the church. Remember when you introduce yourself to leave off the title. Your name is not "mister." It is Ed, Sam, Bill, or Joe—who knows, it may even be Clarence. *This is a friendly call. Be friendly.* You are not going to make much headway with the average American by giving yourself a lot of titles—especially when you are standing on his doorstep with your hat in your hand. Smile—establish yourself in that instant you have as a good fellow. *Those first twenty seconds are the most crucial part of your interview!*

If the prospect has a difficult name to pronounce, try saying it out loud before making the call. Most names are easy to pronounce if you give your ear a chance to hear them. *Stand on the side of the door that makes it necessary for her to open the door to talk with you.* If the prospect is talking with you from behind a partially opened door she is much more likely to tell you "no" before you get a chance to explain *who* you are and *what* you are. *Do not spill the beans on the doorsteps.* Ask the prospect: "May I come in?" Few, if any, people will tell you "no" to such a direct question.

Don't run over the prospect like a Mack truck with your sales story. There is always the business routine of your hat and coat. It must be placed aside. This normal routine places your prospect ever more at ease. After you are seated ask the prospect if she went to church today (assuming that it is Sunday). If it is not Sunday ask her if she went to church this past Sunday. This is your normal opening to discuss the business at hand. Lead easily into it by stating that "As you know, this is Loyalty Sunday." If she still looks expectant, continue: *"This is the one day of the year when the church solicits your financial support for its activities for the coming year."* Now the cat is out of the bag. At this point the individual canvasser must operate according to the ability, or the limitations, of his own personality. No amount of "canned sales talk" will make a person who is by nature tongue-tied into a glib, smooth talker.

The inexperienced should remember that his greatest asset is to be sincere, straightforward, and not to make the first call until he has all his basic facts down pat. You can cover up many things if you are clever but you can never cover up lack of knowledge when you are selling a product—and, gentlemen, *we are most assuredly selling our Church with its many blessings each time we ring a doorbell!*

When you get to the actual size of the pledge many people will ask you what *you* think. *Have a ready answer.* This should not be an off-hand answer. The general chairman of the canvass should furnish this information. Your average pledge must be the number of people divided into the amount of money you must raise on the canvass. This does not necessarily mean the total figure of the budget, as many churches have other sources of income. The only figure that the canvasser is concerned with is the figure arrived at by dividing the amount to be raised by the canvass by the number of people to be called on. Obviously you would not talk in terms of the average pledge with a couple with an income of twenty thousand a year any more than you would talk of an average pledge to the pensioner trying to get by on two thousand a year. *Discretion must be used.* It is the individual discretion used by the canvasser that will govern his effectiveness.

A great many people will want to make pledges much smaller than the church has a right to expect them to make. When talking to these people do not belittle the amount they have offered but dwell on the positive reasons why the church is essential in the community. If they talk in terms of a dollar a week, break it down to a daily pledge . . . this is only fourteen cents a day. A dollar may buy a lunch, but with current prices, fourteen cents will buy very little.

When the prospect says that he can't afford to pledge as much as he did last year or that the same pledge as last year is the best he can do, explain that the church's dollar too is buying less and less. *Do not passively accept the same old pledge.* Keep the conversation on the positive side. Don't sit around and agree that everything is going to pot. *Offer a solution, the church!* Tell the prospect this is something positive you can do! In describing the church do not use "soft" words. *Use words with positive meanings.* Do not say that it is *good* to have the church in the community. Say it is *vital* . . . say it is *essential* to have the church in the community. Since you are there to say something *get the most into what you have to say* so that your prospect *will get the most out of what you are saying.*

In discussing money there are two prime factors to be remembered: (1) be factual and (2) be relaxed.

Don't fluster, don't look away. Look directly at whom you are talking. Use the same tone you would use if you were talking about how blue the sky is. Do not apologize for what you are saying. It is a privilege to do God's work, and you have been honored by being asked to help. Do not be self-conscious, your embarrassment can easily be transferred to your prospect, and then you are really in a mess. Keep the canvass card in your hand. Tell the prospect that it is your only record. Don't let her put you off by saying that she will mail it in. You have two strikes against you if you do. If she tells you that she has not had a chance to talk it over with her husband, and you are not able to overcome this objection by explaining that he would probably leave it up to her good judgment anyway, tell the prospect that you will be working on other calls later in the week in this neighborhood and that you will call back. Don't let her put you off if it is at all possible, but let her know that you are perfectly willing to return at her convenience. On this score it is perfectly possible not to take "no" for an answer. If you state flatly that you *will* return there will be little she can do to try to stop you.

REMEMBER: Make all contacts personally. Do not use the phone. If you wish to pave the way by sending some literature and a short personal note saying that you will call at such and such a time it will be fine, provided that you actually follow up as you have promised. If you do not, you will have put yourself in a bad light to start with and everything you say will be properly discounted when you wish most urgently to make a point. Do not phone as a substitute for a letter. Some folks get very brave over the phone and will tell you anything just to get rid of you. Regardless of the attitude of your prospect, if you have him face to face you have a chance, but over the phone you haven't if he has really made up his mind that he doesn't want to see you. Remember: *Don't give him this chance.* Work for maximum results, not for time saved. Since you are not

placing a value on your time, don't act as if you were
on a piece-work basis.

Do not let the Worker take the canvass cards of his
FRIENDS. *You simply cannot do business with your
friends.* You will get a far more favorable relationship
with someone you do not know. Your friends tend to
take you for granted—either that or they will not take
you seriously. A stranger will be sincere with you automatically, whereas a friend or neighbor can much more
easily put you off.

A definite time limit should be placed on the time
the canvass is going to take. There may be a few cards
that are uncollectable by the time the canvass is over,
and these few should be turned over to the church
secretary for proper follow-up. In most cases the canvass
should not exceed two weeks or three weekends.

In conclusion bear in mind the following facts.

When considering the qualifications of the individual
worker watch out for the "know it all." The man who
has stopped learning is going to be very hard to control.
A man who will not take directions will hardly ever
justify his existence in an organization. *This is essentially an organizational function.* There is *no place* for
the *non-conformist,* the *rugged individualist,* or *the
man who will not take directions.*

A *simple yet comprehensive plan* must be agreed on
at the outset as to *responsibility, methods, and personnel.*

A *feeling of organization* will be achieved if the
general chairman will make it a point to contact each
of his *team captains* by phone at *least twice* during the
actual canvass, and the *team captains* will contact their
workers at least twice during the actual canvass and
each time offer to help with any special problems. Remember, the captain who just goes along for the ride
on the routine calls is wasting his time and is probably
robbing his worker of a feeling of competence which is
absolutely necessary for anyone calling on the public.

You do not want to work a man who feels he needs a crutch every time he makes a call.

The captain should give to the general chairman a record of every pledge card given his worker and the worker should be specifically instructed not to give the card to the prospective pledge-giver. A record of any additional pertinent information should be made on the back of the pledge card at the time the call is made. Later on there is a tendency either to let it go altogether or to put the information down in an inaccurate manner.

The captain should make it clear to his workers that he *expects* them to contact him if any special problems should arise. The general chairman should make it specifically clear at the first joint meeting of the minister, the general chairman, the team captains, and the workers that the lines of responsibility lie in this sequence and that for the sake of simplicity or organization they should not lightly be ignored.

A record should be kept by the general chairman of the effectiveness of each of his captains and he should require of his captains that they mark their workers at the end of the canvass as to degree of effectiveness and potential. This record should be kept confidential by the general chairman and the minister and should be used as a help in lining up the next year's canvass personnel when that time comes. After this has been done one or two years, the canvass personnel problem will be licked except for replacements of those who drop out or move away.

CAMPAIGN MATERIALS

1. An oilcloth streamer banner carrying the "Theme." To be displayed in parish house or meeting place during campaign.

2. A large flat of the canvass organization carrying the names of the workers and all personnel. Should also

provide space for writing in quotas and amounts reported if parish desires.

3. (Optional) A spectacular display portraying graphically the progress of the campaign (i.e., a detached model airplane on runway to be moved along as pledges are reported until minimum objectives are reached, then airborne as campaign totals are recorded).

4. Lapel name cards for workers—in colors to designate rank and to furnish an automatic attendance check at rallies and report meetings.

5. Parish activity and missionary exhibits around the sides of the meeting room.

6. Center pieces for card tables carrying team name and workers' designation as place cards. (See model table arrangement using model aircraft.)

7. Citations or awards for workers achieving goals. (Can be small silver "wings" in form of pins.)

8. National Council Missionary Posters and Every-Member Canvass posters. (Use in church vestibule and parish hall.)

9. Program film strips or motion pictures showing Church at work.

10. Workers' instruction sheets.

CAMPAIGN OFFICERS' MATERIALS

1. Recruiting report forms. (Used by vice-chairman and team leaders in reporting workers as they are lined up.)

2. Sample packets of all literature and campaign aids going out to all parishioners. (To be distributed to workers as recruited.)

3. Calendar of meetings showing time, date, place and purpose. (To be given to workers as recruited.)

4. Workers' registry for campaign officers giving name, address (home and business), telephone num-

bers, and special information on each, one copy to be retained by each officer to permit close contact with workers.

5. Report envelopes to collate and transmit cash and pledges.

WORKERS' MATERIALS

1. *Canvassers' Call Card.* Name, address, telephone number, and unit strength of each communicant unit to be called on. Grouped by fives by address; workers' card on top. Coded to indicate previous year's gift.

1A. *Workers' Code Card and Instruction Folder.* (Facts for canvassers.)

2. *Pledge Card and Envelope.* To be signed and, if requested, sealed in envelope provided.

3. *Report Envelopes.*
     Team Report.
     Workers' report.
     Vice-chairman's report.

4. *Treasurer's Tabulation Sheets.*

5. *Duplex Envelopes.* To include treasurer's card of thanks and indicating expected amount and serving as original reminder of pledge.

A new Every-Member Canvass plan has been promulgated by the Baptists. They have been getting unbelievable results with it. For full details I suggest that you write The Council on Missionary Cooperation, American Baptist Convention, 152 Madison Avenue, New York 16, New York, and ask for their manual entitled, *A Manual for the Every-Member Canvass Sector Project.* It may cost you a dollar or so.

Chapter 17

A TESTED METHOD FOR MODERN TITHING

CONFESSION TO THE READER: We originally intended to have only three chapters in this book on ways to secure church funds. That number seemed sufficient and covered the main financial campaign, plus extra ways of raising money for the church's work.

Yet when we tabulated the findings from the questionnaires sent out to 2,600 clergymen, we found that many people asked for a discussion of tithing—the oldest and surest way of raising money for our churches' and God's work. In fact, we consider tithing so important that it was made a key chapter in our first book, *Building Up Your Congregation*.

We were so encouraged by the "write-in-vote" of request for tithing by so many of the clergy and laymen that we decided to add this chapter. We hope you find it includes new material on tithing—new to you.

One of the most complete explanations and "sales talks" on this original method for supporting God's work which we found, was a talk given by Bishop Richard S. Emrich of Michigan. Here are the key thoughts from this Detroiter's outstanding address.

Note: If you would like the full and complete discussion, just write the Bishop at 63 East Hancock Avenue, Detroit 1, Michigan. Ask for a copy of the "1952 Reinecker Lectures," which includes talks on missions and the ministry of the laity. The cost is $1 per printed set of lectures.

THE PRACTICE OF
PROPORTIONATE GIVING

One of the tasks of a bishop is to form a policy and to make universal in a diocese those practices which are sound religiously and will help to overcome financial problems. There is one policy which I believe should be adopted by our whole Church because in many, many dioceses now people have gratefully adopted it, that is proportionate giving. It is not, of course, really new: it was tried and tested for many years by one of the larger parishes of Michigan, a parish which has the best record proportionately of any in the Diocese.

Many minds in many parishes, facing the same problem and the difficulties which we have been discussing, have arrived independently at the necessity of a standard—the necessity for the teaching of proportionate giving. This has the tradition of Scripture and of some of the Early Church behind it. It was the practice, as we all know, in the Old Testament to tithe—to give 10 percent of one's income to the Lord. This practice was undoubtedly supported by our Lord.

Let's list some of the reasons for this proportionate giving, or the Modern Tithe.

Let us sketch again the need for a standard and a guide. We tell people about the needs of the Church and of the community (and that's good), but we give them no guidance whatever in *how* to give. The results of this are clear—a giving, by the vast majority of our people, that bears little relation to their ability to give. There is a serious giving on the part of a small inner circle, but a wandering, confused ignorance on the part of most others. But if the law is a guide and is necessary to Christians, you do not think that we should show people what the love of God and man means as far as our pocketbooks are concerned? *Now*, when a sincere canvasser approaches a sincere new churchman, and the latter asks, "What would you suggest that I give? What does the Church say?" The Church usually weakly answers, "Give what you can"—and that is no answer.

Since I have been in the ministry I have never gone to any man and asked him for a specific amount. There are rich men in my diocese but I have never said, "Give $3 a week." I don't know enough definitely about any man's personal affairs to ask him for a specific amount. But I do not have the slightest hesitation in asking every man to be responsible to God, grateful to God, to remember his soul and his Maker, and to be fully serious. I have not the slightest hesitation in asking a man to give remembering what he has received. The time has come to say with definiteness, and to suggest without prying into details, what seriousness and gratitude mean. They mean 5 percent to the church and 5 percent to community charities.

Now, someone will say, "too much"; and here I can only repeat something taught me by a layman. How can any man say that 5 percent of his *net* income is too high a standard when the government permits him to deduct 15 percent of his *gross* income? If the men in Washington say 15 percent of gross income, you would not respect the Church or its estate of the Gospel it wants to preach if, apart from the traditional tithe, it suggested a lower figure than 5 percent of net income. There will be some people who will say that this is too little, and I know some now; and there are more people than you imagine who are already giving this, when you think of building funds, special gifts, pledges, and so forth. But this is a standard, a guide, and the real sacrifices of the few will continue to go beyond it. And the result of teaching this is an immediate raising of pledges, as people turn and look at the percentage they now give.

Once last year I talked with a man who tithes. He is a fine person, admired by everyone, and I asked him this question: "Why do people who tithe look with such confidence at the future?" And he replied, "Because they are the kind of people who tithe. They live for the right things, and they know that tomorrow, no matter what happens, love for the Lord will see them through." The practice of tithing does bring spiritual rewards, and, springing from the spiritual, leads to a stability which brings material rewards. I believe this is true. The only thing is that we must be very careful to keep the thought of reward on a high Christian plane.

It is true to say that giving springs from faith: it is just as true to say that faith is strengthened by giving. And since this is so, we do our people a real injustice when we do not hold before them a serious standard which could lead them to deeper things. If you teach this, you will find that people discuss it, that it becomes common knowledge in a congregation, and that a new seriousness comes to the people. Is not one of the problems of the Church that we have not asked really serious things of men, specifically, which reveal to them the full seriousness of the Faith and the necessity for important decisions? This is certainly only part of what we should suggest to men, but its full seriousness should be welcomed by a Church that often plays with Christianity.

Tithing is democratic, and fair. There are rich men and poor men in the Church, and before God within His Church they should stand on an equal footing. The rich man should not feel that he is taking over; and the rich man should not feel that he is the only one responsible, which sometimes happens. They should stand side by side as friends, knowing that both are trying to be responsible and that both are responsibly using the talents God has given them. When a man dies and his casket lies before the altar, God asks chiefly whether with his particular talents he was a grateful and responsible man. There should, therefore, be equal and fair standards for all men: a tithe—5 percent to the Church and 5 percent to community charities.

And, speaking of fairness—and here, I believe, is where the laymen have arrived at this theory independently—doesn't the fact of inflation drive us to the theory of proportionate giving? In a day when the value of the dollar fluctuates, how can you finance a church unless when there are more dollars in circulation, the church receives more dollars, and when there are fewer we receive fewer? It would seem to me that proportionate giving is the only thing that will meet inflation.

The way to begin it is, of course, with ourselves. Revivals in the Church begin with groups of men who believe deeply and, because they know a thing to be true, can speak of it with power. The best teaching is not to exhort others to tithe, but to share with them your own experience and to give them the deepest religious reasons why *you* tithe. I can bear witness that it means much in my family and affords us, as we budget, an opportunity to show ourselves and our children that we are really trying *to put the Lord first*.

Two things I am afraid of, and I will close with these: 1. I am afraid of self-righteousness—the tithers may some day be looking down on the non-tithers. This is a possibility, I suppose, just as church attendance could lead to self-righteousness—anything can. I think the best thing is to teach the principle in all seriousness, and have laymen bear witness to its meaning, but leave to the Lord the final figures of those who tithe. In the last analysis it's between a man and his God. I have seen no self-righteousness at all, but this would do away with any danger of it. 2. My greatest fear is that men who do not understand the great motive of tithing—gratitude to God—will look upon it as a "money-raising scheme." It is not. It is, rather, a way of teaching all of us, a means to bring us to God, a result of serious faith. It teaches us what is important in life, brings home to our budgets the claims of God and the awareness of His Presence, teaches us gratitude, teaches us how to worship by giving ourselves.

The man who knows that God is the central fact of his life, who feels the daily nearness of God, who sees around him the evidences of God's love, and who gives himself to God in gratitude, is a transformed man. The purpose of tithing is to secure, not just the tithe, but the tither; not just the gift, but the giver; not just the possession, but the possessor; not the money, but each of us in a new way and a great way for the Lord.

NOTE: If you are interested in this Detroit plan of tithing, write Bishop Richard S. Emrich for copies of the booklets: *What Shall I Give for What God Has Given Me?* and *Don't Miss the Point.*

Being the general chairman of a canvassing program is not an easy job. If it were an easy job, you would not have been asked to do it. The same is true of your canvassers, for if theirs were an easy job, you and the general chairman could have handled the entire canvass by yourselves.

Because of the importance of the training work you are to do, we have asked a professional organization to write this training section for you.

Read it carefully and often between now and your Fall Canvass.

MEETING GUIDE FOR
EDUCATIONAL CHAIRMEN
1952 EVERY-MEMBER CANVASS
DIOCESE OF MICHIGAN

THE CANVASSER TRAINING MEETING

You must have ready for your canvass workers the following props and people to help you expertly to stage the training sessions. You will need a strip film projector, a suitable screen, a lectern, piano, tables, chairs, blackboard, canvassers' packages, the new tithing poster and the new tithing leaflet, and the slidefilm used in this meeting. (Also the motion picture on tithing if you need it.) Group the canvassers so that they can all see the screen and the lectern. You should have on display a copy of the poster, tithing literature, pledge cards, parish record cards. Provide pencils, scratch paper, ash trays.

You will need a projectionist, a pianist, and a man to handle lights. You should be at the door to greet all canvassers as they come in.

Before the meeting, be sure your projector is properly set up and tested—have the lectern and the screen in place—and arrange that the light on the lectern and projector do not go out when the house lights are dimmed. Run a trial meeting with the pianist and projectionist before the meeting is held.

The general chairman has arranged the meeting. Present at this meeting will be the general chairman, the rector, and the senior warden.

THE MEETING

At the exact moment which the meeting has been called for, call the canvassers to order. Seat them by teams. Lead them in singing a hymn—we suggest verses 1 and 3 of Hymn 535. Then, the rector should read two short collects—for the Church, on page 37 of the Book of Common Prayer, and then the fourth collect on page 49.

Let the rector talk—*three minutes*—on the Christian experience to be gained from Modern Tithing. The general chairman should talk—*three minutes*—telling the canvassers why they have been chosen and what a tough but satisfying job they have ahead of them.

LEADER—NOW YOU BEGIN YOUR ACTUAL TRAINING. WHAT FOLLOWS IS WHAT YOU TELL YOUR WORKERS. TRY NOT TO GIVE THE IMPRESSION OF READING IT.

"A man once asked this question of his friends, 'What do you consider the most satisfying human relationship in your experience?' The replies ranged all the way from religion to childhood. The happy smile of a child, the understanding nod of a friend, the firm handshake of another, the effect of prayer—all seemed to bring a deeper understanding of humanness.

"As canvassers you have the particular privilege of being able to meet with people who make up this parish, of getting from them an acceptance of their responsibility to God, to their church, and to themselves. To some of you this will be difficult, to others it will be an easy, pleasant job. To those of you who will find this work difficult, I can only say that the reward for doing good thorough jobs will be well worth the effort you put into it. And for those of you who will find easy enjoyment from the work, I urge that you spare nothing in your drive to bring into our parish the finest results that any canvass has ever made in the history of (name your church).

"As a canvasser you must do the following: One. Examine with us here at this meeting a list of those persons on whom you are to call. And select from that list those that you feel will be the most difficult to sign up on the Every-Member Canvass, and plan to call on them *after* you have called on those that you feel will be more easily persuaded by you. When you have had a chance to pick your tough prospects, discuss with the other people on your team, including, of course, your captain, the ways in which they would approach the difficult parishioner. We will at this time turn the meeting over to you individually at your tables. In front of you, at your place, is a list of those on whom you are to call. You are being asked to call on no more than ten parishioners, usually not more than five. Talk it over; there will be a limit of ten minutes on this discussion."

LEADER: DURING THIS TABLE DISCUSSION YOU SHOULD VISIT EACH TABLE AND DETERMINE IF THE VARIOUS GROUPS ARE HANDLING THE DISCUSSION CORRECTLY. HELP THEM IF THEY ARE NOT. THIS IS WHAT THEY

SHOULD BE DOING: EACH PERSON SHOULD BE QUIZZING
ANOTHER AT THE TABLE ABOUT ANY PARTICULAR FRIEND
THEY MIGHT HAVE. THEY SHOULD BE DETERMINING WAYS
AND MEANS TO GET TO THESE INDIVIDUALS AND FAM-
ILIES.

IN EXACTLY TEN MINUTES, CALL THE MEETING TO ORDER
AGAIN.

CHECK EACH MAN AT EACH TABLE. ASK HIM IF HE HAS
GONE THROUGH HIS LIST. ASK HIM IF HE HAS ANY PAR-
TICULAR QUESTIONS HE WOULD LIKE ANSWERED REGARD-
ING THE LIST OF PEOPLE ON WHOM HE IS TO CALL. THEN
GO ON AS FOLLOWS):

"We have gone over our list of parishioners, and they
have been segregated and discussed so that we are now
prepared to go out and talk to them as *individuals*. But
now we have to find out what we are going to talk to
them about. Your job as a canvasser poses a physical
problem of completing this canvass on 'C-Day,' or at
least within a week after 'C-Day.' And it also requires
that you know completely the subject you are going to
discuss with our parishioners. You must understand
that you have been selected to do an extremely important job for your church. It is as much the Lord's
work as kneeling in your pew on Sunday. As a canvasser today, you are the middleman in a revolution.
We are not launching the old type of canvass predicated
on underwriting a fixed operating budget. This is
rather the missionary work of spreading the basically
religious concept of Modern Tithing.

"A pamphlet has been prepared that tells the story of
Modern Tithing. We are not asking you to take my
word, the Bishop's word, but rather the word of hundreds of men like you: your neighbors. Today, we can
talk about what tithing *has done* and is doing for other
people, not what it could do nor what it might do. Let
me quote directly from the survey made by your diocese called 'What Tithing Has Meant to Me.' Before

we go into this survey, however, let's be sure we all
agree on what Modern Tithing means.

"Modern Tithing means that the truly serious member of the church designates a definite portion of his
income to church and charity—that five percent of his
income goes for the support of his parish, the Diocese
and the National Church. It represents the true realization that all we have has been gained through Another,
and it results in a closer, more personal relationship between a man and his God.

"Maybe this sounds like a batch of fine-sounding
generalities. Well then, let's read how your friends and
neighbors say it. You have a copy of their statements
before you. Let us take the next five minutes to read it."

EXACTLY FIVE MINUTES LATER, CALL THE MEETING TO
ORDER.

"Let's read just this one introductory page again—

(LEADER READ):

" 'NOW WE KNOW.'

"During the past two years, the Diocese of Michigan
—the Bishops, the Department of Promotion, and many
of the clergy and laity—have talked about tithing in
terms of what it would do for anyone who seriously
gave it a try.

"The tone, up to this point, was, 'If you will try tithing, we *believe* this is what will happen to you.'

"Now, as we begin the third of our seven-year educational program, we come to a new phase of the discussion. No one need conjecture any longer. We can say,
'This is *what happened*.' Many people, in parishes all
across the Diocese have tried it. We have seen tithing
in action.

"We are on solid ground.

"No influence in life is more powerful than the influence of other people's actual experiences. No evidence
is more conclusive.

"Here in this leaflet are verbatim quotations from people who have themselves been tithing long enough to tell you, first hand, how a tither feels—about Church, about life, about himself.

"The quotations printed here are taken from the results of a questionnaire sent to people in all kinds of parishes, and in 'all walks of life.' Here all sorts and conditions—mechanics, executives, housewives, lawyers, salesmen, teachers—tell you what has exactly happened to them as they practice tithing.

"We aren't talking theory any more.

"NOW WE KNOW!

"Now let's run through a few of the things these people said.

"One thing they said was that they no longer feel they are giving, but that now they are returning. What they mean is that they will remember that two years ago we started this whole tithing program with a pamphlet, the title of which was 'What Shall I Give for What God Has Given Me?' We are beginning to get results. People are realizing now that all they have has been given to them. It came from God—it belong to God. They are only *using* it.

"What I want to call to your attention is what it does to a man when he realizes that. It changes his whole outlook on life. He stops thinking of himself as sustaining himself by his own efforts, and as being a 'self-made man.' He's started to think of himself as what the Bible used to call a 'steward.' He has now become in his own mind the custodian of God's property, which is very different from being the frantic preserver of his OWN projects. An outstanding example of this is the Reformed Church of Spring Valley, New York. The congregation had to finance a new Sunday school building. But like most churches it did not have any money for it. One of the leading businessmen suggested that the members tithe for the new building. With the Reverend A. L. Wyckoff, the executive developed a most appealing and impressive bond certificate, to visualize and dramatize this proved form of giving. It was called a "Tither's Trust Bond."

As we cannot show the inside of the Bond, we give you herewith the wording which appeared at the top of the inside page:

THE TITHERS TRUST COUPON BOND

No._____   The Tithe

Taking Stock in your Religion

The Guarantee

Know ye all by these presents: "Bring ye all the tithes into the storehouse . . . and prove me now herewith, saith the Lord of hosts, if I will not open you the windows of heaven, and pour you out a blessing, that there shall not be room enough to receive it." MAL: 3:10.

This Is Not a Speculation: It Is an Investment.

Interest Payable Monthly: Principle Due at Death.

Do Not Expect To Draw Interest, Unless You Have Invested Your Principle.

This Bond Is Preferred as Assets, and Participates in Dividends.

Not Transferable

A UNIQUE AND UNPARALLELED FEATURE
OF THIS BOND

You, yourself, each month fill in the amount of interest you wish to take.

DIVIDENDS

There is also guaranteed to bearer, upon satisfactory fulfillment of the original conditions prescribed, which are: Bring ye all the *tithes*, bring ye *all* the tithes, bring *ye* all the tithes; an equal share in the undistributed surplus of benefits which have accrued, together with an equal share in those which have been accumulated by the Tithers Trust, also a blessing so great that there shall not be room enough to receive it—without our new building, also in the due process of time the New Sunday School and Recreational Building.

No limit is placed upon the amount of benefit allowed to one person, either in this life, or the life which is to come.

The consideration for this most unusual and remarkable bond is "The Tithe," that is, one-tenth of your income. It

is offered on this sliding scale of cost so that it is within
the reach of all. Five cents will buy it, if that is your tithe,
five million dollars cannot buy it, if it is not a tithe.

Did the Tithers Trust Bonds pay off for the Church?
You bet they did! They raised $50,000 for a church that
had no money for the badly needed Sunday school
building. Why? Because the unusual appeal and the
Tithers Bonds reduced the irritation and embarrassment which some people in the congregation suffer
when they start tithing.

If you have a similar problem and want to use
Tithers Bonds, why not write the Reverend Mr. Wyckoff for a sample of the bond certificate?

We conclude this important *requested* chapter by re-
producing the proven method which the Diocese of
Michigan has developed for getting more members to
make an annual pledge based on the biblical plan of
tithing—but in a modern way. The following page
reproduces the Tip Sheet which is followed by the
mimeographed and printed material used by the general chairman and workers.

Now we reproduce for you the calendar used by the
clergy and general chairman to schedule the various
activities—all in relation to "C-Day" or Canvass Day.

THIS IS THE EDUCATIONAL
CHAIRMAN'S GUIDE

Your job as educational chairman is to train canvassers, so that they make good calls, tell a convincing
story, and bring back to the church results: modern
tithing pledges.

This Meeting Guide will help you do this. Use it
next fall with your canvassers as you see it used here
today.

Two years ago the idea of modern tithing was to most
of us a new idea. Some of us made progress the first
year. More of us the second year. This year most of us

TIP SHEET

Your Job as General Chairman

1. You must first convince yourself of the importance to your parish, the Diocese and the National Church of the Every-Member Canvass. They form a spiritual as well as a physical viewpoint.

2. You must select, convince, and inspire a good group of captains and canvassers.

3. You must continually keep the prod under every one—minister, vestry, guild, team captains, and canvassers, until you are convinced that the canvass is complete. You must, in fact, be obnoxious in your pressure for the work of the Lord.

4. You must insist on and get reports and commitments when they are due.

5. You must help your fellow parishioners to enjoy a new experience in Christianity: MODERN TITHING.

will go out well prepared, especially if we follow the plan set forth in this guide. In the material supplied you for your canvasser instructions, you will find answers as to why people tithe and what we now know about the tithing situation in the Diocese. We have made a survey, and you will see it later in this meeting.

October

			1	2	3	4
5	6	7	8	9	10	11
12	13	14	15	16	17	18
19	20	21	22	23	24	25
26	27	28	29	30	31	

November

						1
2	3	4	5	6	7	8
9	10	11	12	13	14	15
16	17	18	19	20	21	22
23	24	25	26	27	28	29
30						

Steps

1 Determine C-Day (write it in)

2 C-Day minus 30 Start your organization

3 C-Day minus 12 Personnel complete

4 C-Day minus 5 training sessions
C minus 3 - Make-up training session

5 C-Day plus 7 Report day

6 C-Day plus 14 End of canvass

7 C-Day plus 15 Start the clean-up

(THIS SCHEDULE GIVEN TO ALL PARISH CANVASS CHAIRMEN FOR THEIR OWN USE)

You have the job of taking men and women who have property.

"How would you like to help a man to change that way? How would you like to be the agent through which a man gets such a new outlook on life? Well, that's what you are! That's what this canvass is all about.

"Think what it will mean if you can plant this seed in the lives of the people in our parish!

"And do you see how different this is from the old-style canvass call, where you just went out and asked a man to underwrite a budget?

"A second thing they said was that they were relieved to be out of the hit-or-miss pattern in their pledging to church and charity. This is a valuable service you will be rendering as you go out on these calls. How many times have canvassers been asked the direct question: 'What shall *I* give?' and they have been unable to answer. Now you *can* answer: 'Five percent of income or as near as you can come to that percentage.' You can be definite, and at the same time impersonal.

"I think it will mean something to you if you can help take the confusion about giving out of the minds of some of the people of the parish.

"Do you see how different this is from the old budget calls?

"A third point: people said that tithing makes them feel that they are really IN the Church. Now they can call it OUR Church.

LEADER: SLOWLY, WITH EMPHASIS:

" *This is the biggest thing you will ever get a chance to do as a canvasser or in any other capacity.*

"For fundamentally, what is Christianity? Christianity itself is being a member—belonging, participating, being in a relationship—being in a Christian family.

"It isn't the clergy who 'save' people. People save each other—by *accepting* each other—by *belonging* to each other. Here in this survey are people telling us that this belonging—this 'salvation,' really—has come to them through tithing.

"There is nothing more important in anyone's life than that. Think what it will mean to you if you as a canvasser can bring that to some of the people in this parish.

"So you see how different that is from the old budget call?

"Fourthly: they told us they want their children to be taught to tithe. That they feel that it is unfair to the children *not* to teach them.

"Do *you* know how important this is?

"Ask a man what he wants for his children. Not what he wants them to have; not what he wants them to do— but what he wants them to *be*. If you ask him that, what he'll tell you will always in the end come down to the kind of relationship and the kind of inner living he wants for them.

"Here are people telling us that they have found such new relationships and such great inner change that *that* is what they want for their children.

"How would you like to be the agent through which that comes to some of the people in this parish?

"Do you see how different your job is from the old talking about a budget?

"Five. Some of them told us that since they began to tithe, they no longer feel some of the old inequalities that they used to feel in their relationship with other members of the church family. They have found that they are doing their fair share and the richest man in the parish can do no more. Do you see what this means? It pulls the parish together. It gives the parish family a chance to be a *real* family. Do you want to bring that to some of the people in this parish?

"Six. And in the survey, we found some things that indicate that we still have an information job to do. We found that people are not too clear on what the tithe really is. Some of them think it's duty; some of them think it's a device for raising money; some of them think it includes only the Church. They don't realize that charities are God's work, too. These are things that still remain for you to tell them. Minor things, perhaps, but part of the general education with which real tithing is to be undergirded.

"In all these things, certainly, you will see that your job has a dignity and a value that no canvasser could claim in the old days, when he went around asking people to support a budget. You are no longer a money-raiser. You are an agent of God with the wonderful job of helping people to a new richness of life.

"I don't believe a man here can help but feel the urgency behind Modern Tithing. And this brings us to another vital point of this session. Just what does tithing mean to you? Have you *personally* ever tried it? I charge you at this time to pick out your own canvass card and call first upon yourself. Think about this, because until you are convinced, you will have a hard job convincing others, and that is the great job the Church has asked you to do. If you can convince one person that they should enjoy the complete personal satisfaction of tithing, even though it be but yourself, you have performed a great missionary work for the Lord.

"We have asked you to make the first call on yourself. This should not be too difficult for you, as you are always available to yourself and probably enjoy talking to yourself. However, we have prepared for you a tip sheet and a number of suggestions on how most readily to handle calls on the other families assigned to you.

LEADER: HAVE A QUANTITY OF THESE TIP SHEETS AVAILABLE—ONE FOR EACH WORKER.

TIP SHEET

"To assure a successful canvass, *you should plan to leave the better part of your next two weeks free.* It is important that you clear these arrangements with your family, so that they are not making appointments for you at the time when you wish to be out canvassing. On Sunday, immediately following church service, you will have a luncheon meeting with your general chairman and will receive your entire package of material. Having previously planned the order in which you intend to call on your people, you will be ready to start at the close of this luncheon meeting.

"To assure a brief and satisfactory call, first *contact the parishioner by telephone* and make sure that he and his wife will both be available to talk to you. In this way you can organize your time so that you are not contacting people while they are at dinner or have company. Before making the call you should study the family's church-record card. This will be available to you from the parish record card.

"With their record in your mind, you can *organize your call* and be prepared in advance for the points you can stress that will meet with a favorable reception.

"*Get there on time.* The very act of arriving at the time you stated you would be there is flattering to the person you call on. It also has the effect of giving you a good organization of your afternoon and evening.

"*Get acquainted with the family* if you do not know them. A few moments spent at this time can make the call easier, and you should have some familiarity with their interests from parish records.

"When you feel that you are on a friendly basis, you should *give them the tithing pamphlet to read.* It is a good idea to have the pamphlets available for all people who may be present. Being familiar with the pamphlet yourself, you can start a tithing discussion by mentioning certain statements which particularly appeal to you, or which you think might appeal to them.

"*It is important at this point that you endorse the tithing idea.* You can do this by explaining your stand on tithing. If you like the idea, but haven't yet reached the full goal, say so.

"Then be sure to ask the parishioner on whom you are calling if he has any questions to ask. Don't be afraid to say that you do not know the answer, but ask the parishioner if you can use his telephone to get him a true answer from someone who can, namely, his rector.

"*Then ask for immediate action.* Be sure you have a pen with you. Hand the man his pledge card, ask him if he wants one card for the entire family or separate cards for each member of the family. Also tell him that you have plain envelopes in which he may seal the pledge card if he so desires.

"If he says, 'I would like some time to think this over,' thank him and tell him you will *call back the same day,* and set a time. This procedure will very often result in his signing immediately or agreeing to have a signed card ready for you at a definite time later on.

"*Report every call.* This is extremely important. Immediately after completing a call you should spend the few moments required in recording on your parish card all comments made by any member of the family, whether these comments relate to tithing or are simply new items of interest about the family. It is through this important record that the clergy and the vestry can find out about points they are not now covering.

"If you have found it impossible—after repeated attempts—to see some person on your list, turn his card back to your captain, so that the clean-up squad can complete the call for you.

"We have here a film strip which we feel will tell the stoy of a not-so-good canvasser and another canvasser who had the right idea."

LEADER: AT THIS POINT HAVE THE LIGHTS TURNED OUT, AND AS YOU READ THE SCRIPT, SIGNAL THE PROJECTION-IST EITHER BY TELLING HIM TO ADVANCE THE PICTURE TO THE NEXT FRAME, OR BY RAPPING ON THE EDGE OF THE LECTERN WITH A PENCIL.

SHOW FILM

TIP SHEET FOR CANVASSERS

1. Clear the decks with your family.
2. Make dates with parishioners by phone.
3. Study the family's record.
4. Organize your call.
5. Get there on time.
6. Get acquainted with the family.
7. Give them the tithing pamphlet to read.
8. Endorse the tithing idea.
9. Ask for immediate action.
10. Call back the same day on slow signers.
11. Report every call.

MAKE YOUR FIRST CALL ON YOURSELF

WHY DO PEOPLE DECIDE TO TITHE?

There is apparently no single answer to the question of what leads a man or woman to try this way of giving. The incentives are many and various. Here are some of the reasons people gave when we asked them what made them decide to tithe:

"The way it was explained in church."
"Our Rector talked to us about it."
"We felt we were not getting as much out of life as we should."
"I heard another woman tell why she tithes."
"The Bishop told us about it."
"A Methodist friend told me about it."

"We want to express our gratitude to God."

"We realize that in not tithing we are not trusting God implicitly."

"I heard a sermon on the radio."

"As a lay reader, I couldn't urge others to tithe without trying it myself."

"The Diocesan literature convinced me."

"I heard a story about God's Acre on the radio."

"We talked about it in our discussion group."

THERE WERE PROBLEMS

No one goes into tithing casually. A profound reorganization of living habits is involved—for the individual and for the family.

Here is what people told us—about their apprehensions, and how it all worked out.

"I was afraid I couldn't afford it, but we manage to pay our bills and get along with plenty, thanks to God's generosity. We had a new home and many previous commitments, but as time goes on we are getting out of the woods."

"It solved all our problems in regard to budget, commitments, and—best of all—Church."

"The switch to a definite percentage was easy."

"Some luxuries had to be given up."

"One must cut other expenses."

"We don't give in order to receive, but actually the more we give the more we are blessed with."

"I don't feel as if I had given up anything. At first I did not know if I could work it—now it's easy."

"I just plunged in on faith, and reasoned about it afterwards. The only problem was that of giving up some of the 'things' which in the long run are of no importance anyway."

"A problem? Not when it's given freely from the heart, and to our best Friend. Since it all comes from God in the first place, tithing is the least we can do."

BUT HAVING TRIED IT THEY LIKE IT

Maybe it wasn't always easy, but when asked if they

now believe tithing to be a sound approach to Christian giving, here is what people said:

"It makes me feel I've been able to do a little for the One who gave me life."

"It takes the hit-and-miss out of giving."

"Yes—it helps to cultivate an attitude of mind in which giving is always present."

"It's the *only* way. No more doubts and worries about 'How much?' or 'Can we afford it?' Now we face only the positive question: 'Where can we do the most good with what we have to give?' "

"It gives one firm ground to stand on before God and man."

"It is a fair way. Everyone gives his fair share."

"It answers the all-important question: 'How much does the Church expect?' "

"It's systematic."

IT CHANGED THEIR RELATIONSHIP TO THE CHURCH

The tither sees things differently. That has been a constant claim of those who have been working with our parishes on the tithing concept.

One big difference in his outlook is in how he sees his church. Here is what people said about how that had been changed:

"It stimulated my interest in the Church's welfare."

"It has renewed my interest in working in and for the Church."

"The Church means more to me now. The Holy Spirit is always close to me."

"It makes me really a part of the Church."

"It makes it 'our' Church."

"It increases our interest in the Church, which automatically brings the Church into the center of our home."

"Your heart follows even one-tenth of your treasure."

"It has strengthened our relationship to the Church. There seems to be a more personal touch."

"There is a stronger bond."

"It helps us understand the Church's problems."

"Sure thing! Where you invest your money you want it put to good use. I find myself impatient with ineffective leadership."

"We have the satisfaction of doing this part of our job in the right way."

"It has made the Church a part of us."

IT CHANGED THEIR RELATIONSHIPS WITH OTHER PEOPLE

When God's world looks different, the people in it look different, too.

Tithers tell us they find friendships and family ties strengthened. Here is what they said:

"I have a personal responsibility now for bringing and training more people for God's family."

"There's a feeling of *belonging* you can't describe."

"It leads toward the Christ-centered family."

"It brings the whole family closer."

"You get real friendship out of your church."

AND IT CHANGED THEM INSIDE

The chief claim that has been made for two years has been that tithing will transform the tither. As first-hand evidence that this claim is true, here is what people said about how tithing affected them:

"Since we started we have never had a feeling of financial insecurity."

"I used to be distracted sometimes by the clothes of the obviously wealthy people of the parish. This no longer bothers me, because I know we are now supporting our church as well as they."

"The real fun is in the joy of being a 'rich man.' I find we can now give $50 where $5 was 'all we could afford' before we started tithing."

"It has brought us the warm feeling of satisfaction and accomplishment that comes of doing a job just right."

"Makes you feel much better."

"It is a good way of life."

"I realize now that to be the right kind of Christian I must give thanks to God in a practical way."

"It showed me the joy of knowing God."

"We grow in faith."

"I am much happier now."

SOME MATTERS WE MISSED

It never occurred to us to ask whether tithing was fun, or whether 10 percent seemed to be enough for a man to give. Enthusiastic tithers, however, told us all we wanted to know and a good deal more. Here are some of the "extras," the unsolicited information that came in:

"Giving does not need to be *limited* to tithing."

"I believe children should be taught to tithe when they are very young."

"Do start teaching tithing in the youngest Sunday school classes. Let the children grow up to responsibility."

"We are not giving—we are only returning that which we have custody of."

"It makes giving so very easy."

"The 90 percent now goes farther with us than the 99 percent did before we began to tithe."

"We would prefer to give more than 5 percent to the Church and less to charities. Our confidence in what the Church does with the money is greater than the confidence we have in some of the community things."

"If the one-tenth were followed by all professing Christians, Christianity would soon convert the world."

"Giving by tithing is fun."

Chapter 18

BLESS YOUR CHURCH WITH A "GARDEN FOR GOD"

The kiss of the sun for pardon
The song of the bird for mirth
One is nearer God's heart in a garden
Than anywhere else on earth.

CHRIST KNEW THE LOVELY LANGUAGE of flowers, so He talked frequently about flowers, trees, plants, and growing things. No one realized more fully than the Master, that God's goodness to His people is perfectly exemplified in the world of nature. That is one reason why Christ loved gardens.

Most of us churchgoers love flowers and gardens, but in glorifying God we stop with flowers on the altar. Yes, we forget that our own churchyard should also *witness* with a "Garden for God."

In growing a church garden God's language of flowers speaks to us more forcibly, giving us a greater inspiration. For example, in that old favorite hymn that we sing, "In the beauty of the lilies Christ was born across the sea." Potted Easter lilies help visualize that thought. Yet, how much more vividly these same lilies remind us of Christ's Resurrection and His love when they are growing *naturally* . . . growing outside under God's blue sky . . . in a church garden.

Has your church a "Garden for God"? If it is like the majority of churches, it *can* have one if you and your fellow church workers arrange it. You say your church property is not big enough for a generous-sized garden. Then you can at least have a cross-shaped bed. You can still let the language of flowers add its charm to your church. How? By planting rows of bulbs along the path leading up to the church door. You will be surprised how a spring showing of tulips, hyacinths, and daffodils will inspire your members and the passers-by.

If for some reason you cannot line the walk, you can usually put in beds all around the church building's foundation. These can be filled with bulbs.

Now that we have discussed some solutions for small churchyards, let us think about a "Garden for God" on ample church grounds. Here we have an expert to help and guide us. She is Katharine M. McClinton. Her book entitled *Flower Arrangements in the Church* has a section on "Church Gardens" that will give you a wide variety of inspiring, practical suggestions. If your local bookstores do not have a copy, they can order one for you from the publishers, Morehouse & Gorham, 14 East 41 Street, New York City. Do get a copy and let it be the start of your plans for a church garden.

Right about now some thrifty soul is thinking, "It is all very well to discuss the glory of the church garden, but where is all the money coming from?" That's a natural question. The solution is found in mankind's almost universal love of nature. You will be surprised how the congregation will respond to requests for contributions of time, money, and plants for your church garden. Some family may want to pay for the entire garden as a memorial to some loved one. What a fitting memorial is a growing, blooming, inspiring "Garden for God."

At a special Garden Sunday Service, each class in your Sunday school can contribute a rose bush, plants, or six to twelve bulbs. The choir may want to take over furnishing flowers for one section of the garden. The ladies' organization and the men's club could easily donate the rest of the required plants.

Speaking of men, a "Garden for God" is one of the

surest ways to get more men interested in church work. So many men love gardens and flowers that your call for volunteers on Saturdays will strike a responsive note in many a male's heart. You will discover that some men with no gardens of their own will literally jump at the opportunity of doing gardening in the churchyard.

Even in the heart of New York City a gardenless apartment dweller from Greenwich Village individually took over the neglected garden at a well-known downtown church. In a short time, this young man restored it to its original charm. He made it a joy for the congregation and passers-by. Care of a garden is one church activity where men and women can work together with equal effectiveness and mutual satisfaction.

One of the best ways to start your church's "Garden for God" is to form a church garden committee, composed of men and women. Before drawing up a plan, they will consult with local growers, nurserymen, outstanding gardeners, and local representatives of state horticultural schools. In fact, one of these experts may volunteer to draw up your plan or be a major factor in designing the over-all plan.

These cooperative people will help you plan a church garden which will require a minimum of care and attention. For a properly planted garden can add to the charm and inspiration of a church *without* adding any extra upkeep. You simply concentrate on bushes, plants, and bulbs which require little or no care. Perennials are best! You go in for azaleas and boxwood where weather permits. Rhododendron, laurel, and andromeda are also excellent. When a family wants to plant a memorial in the church garden, they can put in a yew tree, or, where the climate is right, a pink or a white dogwood tree.

A good time to have your garden-planting services is some Sunday in October. Most families are home then; planting and transplanting conditions are good then. The week before "Garden Sunday," have someone from the committee explain the basic idea, and show the plan for your "Garden for God." He or she will ask for cooperation and contributions of plants, bulbs, trees, etc. A detailed map of the plan can be mounted on a board and placed in the vestibule. There each family or organization can sign their names or initials over the tree, plant, shrub, or bulbs they will bring next Sunday. This signing up prevents duplication. You may not get all your needed material the first year. Yet that adds interest and value to subsequent Garden Sundays.

Christian Herald magazine is very much interested in this subject. In fact, they would have run this chapter in their fine publication if it had been available earlier. However, *Christian Herald* ran an article entitled "Church Gardening with a Purpose." With their permission I bring you interesting excerpts from it.

"Is there a part of your church property that is crying out to be beautified? Here are some ideas on gardening, with definite plans for specific areas.

"If you have space at the side or the rear of your church building, it can be developed into an attractive picnic grove or outdoor meeting place. Such an area should be level and covered with good turf. Shade is needed, but it should not be so dense as to spoil the growth of grass or to keep the ground too moist. A scattered planting of fine shade trees, such as red oaks, maples, or elms, is all that is necessary. To secure the partial privacy that makes such a grove most valuable, use hedges or border plantings of shrubbery. This need not constitute an outlay of money. See for yourselves how many suitable shrubs and trees you can find in nearby woods that may be had for the trouble of transplanting.

"Picnics, long socials, pageants, and entertainments can be held in such a spot—even church services, in warm weather.

"A 'Garden of Memory' can be made out of a small space adjoining the church sanctuary. This gives people a lovely place for strolling quietly after church, renewing acquaintances, and greeting the minister. If it adjoins a city church with symmetrical lines and paths of flagstone or cement, the garden may be formal. Or, if it is a country church, it may be given an informal treatment, with flowers simply banked on either side of a grassy path. A rose bush in memory of the sweet life of someone's mother, a bed of pansies for thought of a friend who passed on, an evergreen tree, as enduring as the influence of the former minister in whose honor it is planted—these would be appropriate features.

"Individuals and groups within the church will be interested in taking part in such a garden and contributing to it. But do observe these cautions: 1. See that every new plant conforms to your original plan, so that there will be no crazy-quilt effect about the garden. 2. Locate and develop the garden in such a way that it will not compete with the picture the church building presents, nor interfere with the appearance of the church as a dignified house of worship.

"Instead of buying and discarding an expensive evergreen, every year, many churches are acquiring growing Christmas trees. Practically every church property can have such a tree. A conical-shaped evergreen with rich, dark foliage, one that will grow vigorously, will be best. Place it in the corner of the lawn, or at the side of the building but never in the center of the front lawn. At Christmas time it may be decorated with tinsel and lights, drawing attention to the church and adding beauty to the community."

In conclusion the writer sincerely prays that these few words will inspire the creation of thousands of "Gardens for God" all over this beautiful country. God gave us all the beauties of this flowery rich world. Isn't it only fair and our Christian opportunity and duty to plant and cultivate some flowers to the glory of God? Let us remember that after the Crucifixion Our Lord's body was taken to its resting place in the Garden of Arimathea. Let us take ourselves to our churchyards and commemorate that resting place by developing a "Garden for God."

Chapter 19

INEXPENSIVE WAYS TO MAKE
YOUR CHURCH MORE INSPIRING
—MORE USEFUL

THOUSANDS OF CONGREGATIONS would like to make their churches a more beautiful, more inspirational place in which to worship but do not have funds to build a new sanctuary. Or higher construction costs have forced them to file away their lovely new building plans for future consideration. This common situation is far from hopeless.

1. Several solutions have been worked out by Dr. John R. Scotford, President of the North American Conference on Church Architecture. This Congregational minister described them in a talk before a two-day conference on church architecture in Chicago. As reported in the fine religious section of *Pathfinder* magazine, Dr. Scotford's suggestions include the following:

To beautify the small church, Scotford advises creating a strong center of interest at the front. Put the Communion table at the back of the platform with a velvet or silk hanging (usually scarlet) behind it, and shift the pulpit to one side.

If there's a chancel window, cover it up, Scotford says. It lets light into the eyes of the congregation and distracts from the Communion table. Take out some of those useless chairs in the chancel. Move the choir to one side.

Unclutter and get rid of those fancy balconies and gaudy pipe organs of yesterday, Scotford urges.

Many of the unattractive features in a church can be eliminated with paint, he adds. It helps to paint doors and window frames the same color as the walls.

2. We like the way the problem of keeping a church building *inspiring* is answered in *101 Things a Layman Can Do*. Here is what it says under "Sprucing":

"An historic parish with a beautiful early American church had insufficient funds for repainting the white exterior. Something must be done! But, what? With temerity the rector suggested that perhaps the men of the parish might donate their services. The idea took hold and a committee was appointed to lay out a plan, procure the paint and ladders, and supervise the work. At eight o'clock on a Saturday morning twenty-five laymen and the rector appeared in overalls, armed with brushes. The work was completed that day.

"This type of thing is going on increasingly in the Church. There is more involved than the saving of money. There is a pride in accomplishment, a satisfaction in using one's talents for the Church, and there is fun and fellowship. It is one thing for a man to say, 'See what we had done.' It is another thing for a man to say, 'See what we did.' The choice between a twenty-five dollar contribution and a few hours' labor may be the choice between nominal interest and sincere interest. Church property is in constant need of maintenance, repair, and improvement. Its condition may bespeak the spirit of its people. Its appearance may well be a most effective means of advertising. When we entertain guests in our home, we ascertain that the house is in perfect order. We are proud of the home in which we live. Should we not have the same pride in God's House? In our desire to bring others into the church we must not overlook the impression the church will make upon them. A rusty iron fence, bare spots in a lawn, creaky pews, or scaling walls do not give the impression of progress or real interest.

"Laymen, with their concern for their community and the institutions of the community, must carry this concern into the church. Although the vestry is charged with responsibility for the property of a parish, this does not mean that they will refuse suggestions or offers of help. Nor will a board fail to see that the upkeep of the property affords a real opportunity to utilize the manpower of the parish. Let us see a few things that the men can do:

"CLEANING PEW CUSHIONS, kneeling cushions, and rugs is not only an annual job, it is tedious and rather expensive. Turn twenty or thirty men loose on this undertaking, and it will be accomplished in short order.

"THE GROUNDS AROUND the church, despite wear and tear by children, should demand the best possible attention and beautification. Many men enjoy gardening and are amateur horiculturists. Utilize their hobbies and interest.

"THE PARISH HOUSE is always a good topic of conversation. If it is used constantly, as it should be, touching up and repairs are a perennial problem. This is a job that men enjoy. Look around your parish house. Is it dark and dismal? Is the equipment in good repair? Is it attractive to children and the Church School teachers? Want a job?"

3. The Baptist Church in Little Falls, New York, made its services more inspiring by eliminating that usually unavoidable "baby static." They built a soundproof room, with large glass panels facing the front of the church, where parents with young children can watch and hear the services without having to disturb the rest of the congregation. Many churches have usually unoccupied balconies or rear pews, where this same arrangement would solve the problem of families who cannot find Sunday baby-sitters.

4. Another way to help worshipers (in large cities)

get more out of the service is to solve their pre- and post-service parking problem. When parishioners have to worry and bother about finding a place to park the car, when they walk blocks to find the family car, it often takes away from the effect of the service. Sometimes there is property near the church which can be purchased at a reasonable amount and turned into a parking lot.

For new churches the problem is easier to solve. Albert F. Heino, Chicago architect, recommends that parking space be provided for 25 percent of the membership. He believes that churches of 500 or more members should have at least two acres.

5. Particularly helpful for anyone interested in upkeep of a church is the remarkably practical book *Church Maintenance Manual* by Roger C. Whitman (Doubleday and Company, Inc., 1951). Mr. Whitman is well known for his column, "First Aids for the Ailing House," which appears regularly in many newspapers across the country. The book gives detailed instructions for the care of such inspiring factors in church services as the following: Altar flowers, altarware, vestments, hymnals and prayer books. Every church should have a copy of *Church Maintenance Manual* and use it *constantly*.

Through the courtesy of the author, Roger C. Whitman, and publishers Doubleday and Company, we are privileged to reprint herewith a key section of the book:

CHURCH MAINTENANCE CALENDAR

SPRING: With the approach of spring and warmer
weather it is suggested that:

Vestments, linen, and altarware be examined for possible cleaning, laundering, and repair.

Vestment storage places be mothproofed.

The heating system be inspected and put in condition for the next twelve months. The furnace should be cleaned; the motor for the oil burner or hot-air fan or hot-water pump may need servicing.

Chimney be cleaned, if necessary.

Outside masonry be inspected, particularly around the chimney, to correct cracks or loose joints caused by freezing weather conditions.

Flashings be inspected around chimney, windows, and doors so that leaks and breaks can be repaired.

Storm windows and doors be repaired and painted after removal so that they will be ready for use the following winter. They should be stored in a dry place and covered to keep off dust.

Outside electrical connections and fixtures be inspected by a licensed electrician to correct possible weaknesses caused by winter storms.

Cellar walls and floors be inspected for new cracks, faults, and damp areas.

Damaged trees with limbs weakened by winter storms be promptly attended to by a tree surgeon.

Outside steps, walks, and driveways severely damaged by freezing weather conditions be repaired.

Lawns be seeded, fertilized, and rolled to assure handsome growth. Clear away loose branches and twigs. Apply correct insecticides to lawn, trees, and flowering plants.

Snow-removal equipment be repaired and stored in a dry place.

SUMMER: Except at resorts, summer is usually a less active season for most churches, with fewer services, lowered attendance owing to vacation absences, and closed Sunday schools. This is the ideal season to effect repairs:

Check altarware, vestments, and linen for needed cleaning, laundering, and repair.

Assure mothproofing of vestment storage spaces.

Inspect carpets, hassocks, and cushions for necessary cleaning and repairs.

Examine hymnals, prayer books, and Bibles for needed repairs and replacements.

Paint and repair inside and outside of church where necessary.

Inspect for insect damage by termites, carpenter ants, powder-post beetles, etc.

Eradicate lawn weeds and fertilize if necessary. Apply correct insecticides to trees and flowering plants.

FALL: Fall is the time to batten down for snug winter security. Here are the recommended steps:

Inspect altarware, vestments, and linen for necessary cleaning, laundering, and mending.

Mothproof vestment storage spaces.

Screen doors and windows should have frames painted and mesh varnished upon removal so that they will be ready for use the following spring. They should be stored in a dry place and covered to keep off dust.

Drain outside pipes and faucets. Empty garden hoses, repair joints and nozzles where necessary and store.

Clean gutters and leaders of accumulated rubbish.

Check weather stripping on windows and doors and replace where necessary.

Have lawn mower serviced so that it will be ready for use the following spring. Repair garden tools where necessary and store in a dry place.

Rake lawn free of leaves. Apply seed and fertilizer to assure good, early growth the following spring.

WINTER: With the coming of cold weather, here are normal precautions to take:

Examine altarware, vestments, and linen for needed cleaning, laundering, and repairs.

Assure mothproofing of vestment storage spaces.

Repair storm damage as soon as possible. Watch for new leaks around windows, doors, and masonry.

Heavy icicles should not be allowed to form where they may fall and injure someone below.

Free outside steps, walks, driveways, and parking lots of ice and snow.

Check tightness of insulation by examing roof after a snowstorm. If snow melts slowly and fairly evenly, insulation is good; if it melts rapidly, insulation is faulty.

ALL SEASONS: Always guard against fire hazards; piles of oily rags; inadequate storage of inflammables, such as painting and cleaning materials; defective electric lines and connections; overloaded electric lines and overfused switch boxes.

Naturally the use of these suggestions will vary with the size and organization of the church. Architecture and climatic conditions will also be factors. But remember that here are a lot of useful jobs which can be given to men and women who will benefit by the *opportunity* to do something *for* their church instead of just *getting* from their church.

Chapter 20

HOW TO
GIVE YOUR CHURCH
A "LORD'S DAY LOOK"

Successful stores discovered that during "business hours" their building . . . their entrance and windows all say, "We're Open for Business."

On Sundays, God's houses of worship should look different from the way they do during the week. For Sunday is the Lord's Day. And churches should have an inviting, come-in-and-worship appearance.

This Lord's Day Look is neither costly nor difficult to develop. Here are some of the things you can do so easily and quickly:

1. Have the ushers greet people on the outside steps instead of inside in the vestibule. This impresses the passers-by that a friendly welcome awaits them at your church. Yes, people respond to such action!

2. Fly a church flag over the doorway. A flag is one of the oldest and surest methods of attracting attention. It is so revered that a church flag can be flown alone, even without the American flag.

A beautiful church flag reminds all who see it of God's love . . . the brotherhood of man . . . the many blessings a church offers and provides worshipers. Waving in the breeze, a church flag makes the entire front of a church look different on Sunday.

No, the cost of a flag and pole doesn't have to come out of the regular budget or finances. In nearly every church there is at least one family which will be glad to give a church flag as a memorial to a loved one.

3. Why not have vases of cut flowers at either side of the main doorway? Flowers are one of God's greatest gifts to his children. Two bunches of flowers add beauty to the doorway. They remind all that God gave us Nature's beauties to enjoy.

4. Some churches give their Sanctuary a Lord's Day Look *all* through the week. This is right because we also want and need Divine Help all through the week. Most churches are located on busy streets and intersections. Therefore they should use their location to influence all who pass by. These churches light up their windows and steeple at night. Others flood-light the front of the church. All these are religious reminders of God's love and help, and bring more people into church on Sundays.

5. Not only should a church look different on Sunday, it should sound different. If possible, the church bell should be rung every hour from 9 A.M. through noon. Hardly anything goes deeper into one's religious heart than the mellow sound of a church bell. The message of the bells has been going on for centuries. Why not use it more frequently on Sundays in your churches?

6. One of my good friends and associates, Bill Gardner, wonders why more churches don't put a loudspeaker outside, so that the congregational singing can be heard by all who pass the church during the service. This reminds them of their Sunday school days, their own church attendance, and is the strongest possible suggestion to attend next Sunday.

7. During warm weather have your choir gather at

the front steps and form their procession outside the front door. This is another religious reminder which can help all churches increase their attendance.

As mentioned previously, we should be concerned with making our church sound differently, as well as look differently on the Lord's Day. Here is a way your congregation can do this to the inspiration of neighbors, passersby, and members. That is to install one of those inexpensive systems which play *recorded* church-bell music from your church steeple or tower. A loud-speaker at the top, plus a sturdy record-playing device, bring your congregation and neighborhood the joy and inspiration of bell-played hymns.

Chapter 21

LET YOUR CHURCH GROW BY STARTING ITS OWN MISSION

By Bishop Richard S. Emrich, of Michigan*

INTRODUCTORY NOTE: When the questionnaires mailed to 2,600 clergymen and lay workers were tabulated, it was found that one of five most wanted chapters was on the above subject. Therefore we looked for the most experienced person to discuss this important factor in the growth and expansion of the church. Several clergymen in different denominations are doing outstanding work in this outreach of larger congregations. Among these we selected the Rt. Rev. Richard S. Emrich, S. T. D., Bishop of Michigan. Below follows the stimulating story of Bishop Emrich's experience in his own words:

Let me begin by making several general observations before turning more particularly to the subject of Missions and our Faith.

First, it is clear that the vitality of a movement can always be gauged by its missionary zeal. If people believe that something is true, they want to spread it. This point does not demonstrate the truth of a movement (Mohammedanism, Communism, and Christianity have all displayed missionary zeal); it merely reveals

* Bishop for the Diocese of Michigan.

its vitality, that its followers *believe* it is true. And, under this point, the immediate future of the world of course lies in the hands of vital movements. We should remember that no faith is sure unless it is enthusiastic, and that any group of people that loses its sense of destiny is dying.

When, therefore, we come upon clergy and laity with little missionary interest, we should remind them of what they are really saying. They do not believe in a vital Church, and they are willing to give the souls of men over to any dark faith that comes along. The lack of missionary zeal has been due to a watered-down version of Christianity which did not know the Gospel. It was not the liberal theologians who were the fathers of the missionary movement, but rather the old-time Evangelicals, with their insight into the plight of man and the great facts of sin and redemption.

It is sobering to realize that the profundity of the faith of our parishes can be judged by the manner in which they grasp the missionary task. A vital Church is a missionary Church. A believing Church is a missionary Church. And yet, in the words of P. T. Forsyth, there are clergy and congregations who have such small understanding of the Faith that "they think missions are a kind of hobby carried on by the Church instead of their belonging to the very being and fidelity of the Church."

Secondly, I sincerely believe that the future of the missionary enterprise—because of our dominant political and economic positions—depends upon the United States and the growing power of Canada. English and Continental missionary work has received a serious setback, and, with our world leadership, there falls to us great responsibility. We can no longer sit as children in the reflected light of the great English missionary societies; we are now, by our position, the leaders of the world, and we've got to grow up rather rapidly.

All of us know that religious apathy is a sin, but we should know also that religious apathy is being displaced by something worse. In its place there has come the sin of hopelessness. There are many people who are saying that the Church is weak, that it is like the lone light of an isolated farmhouse in a great blizzard. And, with that hopelessness, there goes, of course, the failure of nerve in the great task of the Church.

Let me bear witness that the Church is not weak: it is a tremendous body with a very great immediate future. On just one trip, for example, I met with the Bishop of Minnesota in Minneapolis and the Bishop of Olympia in Seattle; preached in our Cathedral in Honolulu and in many vital missions and parishes; visited schools, parishes, and missions in the Philippines; preached to thousands of people in nine dioceses in Japan; visited with the Bishop of Hong Kong; preached in Westminster Abbey and in St. Paul's Cathedral, London. *Weak!* Suppose you had in Virginia and Washington a Communist party the size of the Episcopal Church alone, with tens of thousands of members, with classes, weekly meetings, magazines, radio programs, paid leadership, and so forth. We are not weak. The only thing weak is our failure to see the great destiny God has for His Church—that's the only thing that's weak about us. The only thing that's weak is right in the middle of us. I believe that we are in the midst of a great religious revival, and that we must keep people from hiding God in the hole of hopelessness. We must preach hope—and one of the ways to preach hope is to preach missions.

I learned abroad that you cannot give what you do not possess yourself, that the present spawns the future; and I saw the deep cause in ourselves of whatever weaknesses there are abroad. Let me illustrate.

We raise up a young man in a comfortable parish at home, where in his church life he comes upon no missionary plan or even great concern for the area in which he lives. He is a member of a typical, rather static, middle-class church, whose vestry is satisfied if it raises an inadequate budget. They send some missionary money abroad, but carry on no evangelism in their own area, and don't intend to. They send money to Liberia and the Philippines, but would not dream of reaching out to the racial and national groups in their own community. This young fellow goes off to seminary, where he spends a considerable amount of his spare time arguing about churchmanship. And then he is sent abroad to the mission field by a home Church which has given him little or no training in missionary endeavor, but hopes for the best. (Some of you may think that description is harsh: I don't think it's harsh at all.) Then, of course, when that fellow gets abroad, he is a reflection of the church *at home*. I found, mixed in with superb work, men like that, and I blame in justice the Church *at home*. We cry for missionary money, but we need some things more than money.

One of the most tragic mistakes by our Church is its continued teaching that the word "missions" means work carried on *somewhere else*, and its failure to show people that if you can't evangelize in your own community at home, you won't be able to evangelize when you get overseas. Part and parcel, therefore, of the whole missionary enterprise is the waking up of the Church *at home*, so that we reveal to the whole Church how to win people here and to establish missions in our own growing country. If we can't do that here, and if we have no real plan for America, how can we expect the product of the home Church as it is reflected abroad to be very startling. This inference that "missions" means work carried on somewhere else has even led some people to express a kind of resentment when an American diocese makes real plans for its own area.

Let me suggest at least the beginnings of a missionary policy which could lead our Church to rapid growth— and this should begin at home:

Every Christian Shall Be Taught To Evangelize. It is the duty of every Christian to bring others to the Lord. That great missionary bishop, Azariah of Dornakal, taught this, and built a vital and effective diocese in a few years. *Each one reach one.* In a city of 400,000 souls in Japan I found an Episcopal church, the only one in the city, which had fifty communicants, and yet was fifty-five years old! And I preached this principle in Japan as I do in my own diocese: evangelism misses the boat unless it is built on the basic unit of the Church—which is the working, witnessesing *individual*.

An analysis of several congregations has convinced me that the majority of people who are brought into the Church are brought in by the laity. The initial contact and the introduction to the fellowship comes through laymen, even though the greater part of the instruction may come from the clergy. The goal is a *working, witnessing fellowship*, in which every person who is confirmed, and every person who is baptized, is taught, "It is your duty to bring people to the Lord." Some words of Bishop Nygren, recently written, are relevant. He says:

"In actual fact, there is no difference between us ministers and other Christians. Whatever is true of us, is true of all. Or better said, only that which is true of all Christians is true also of us. Of all Christians, without exception, is the word true, 'Ye are a royal priesthood, a holy people, a peculiar people, in order that ye might preach the wondrous works of Him who has called you out of darkness into His marvelous light.' Of all the members of Christ it is said that they are priests. . . . When we now set about to reflect upon the minister's call and task, it is of importance that it first be said, with all emphasis, that all Christians in the deepest and innermost sense have one and the same call and election of God."

Every Christian is to bear witness and every Christian is to win souls for Christ. *Each one reach one.*

Every Parish Shall Form a Mission. This is the way the Church does grow, as can be illustrated by the study of many dioceses. What we need to do is to take this great *fact* and teach it as a *policy*. In the history of the diocese of Michigan there are nineteen churches which were begun by three parishes, and this year we have already begun six without adding any real amount to the diocesan budget. Just as the basic unit of a congregation is the individual, so the basic unit of a diocese is the parish. If this were taught as a policy of church expansion, we would slowly end the picture of large parishes waiting for someone else to be a missionary while great fields lie right at their own doorsteps. And if this were practiced here, it would be practiced abroad.

Every Christian Shall Be Taught To Work for the Church with His Hands. If we do not have the funds to hire someone to paint, clean, build, repair, then let Christians (the follower of the Carpenter) do it themselves. What Bishop Yashiro, the presiding bishop of Japan, does as a carpenter, with a group of some forty young people, actually *building* churches with his laity, should be taught as policy. Instead, because of human sin, young men who are trained as priests sometimes come to think that they are "gentlemen" and that manual work is below them—which is an Aristotelian-Greek idea, not a Christian idea.

There Shall Be Developed a Ministry of the Laity. In such a ministry laymen shall teach, visit, and take part in every service of the Church. The task before us is too great for the clergy, and the great untapped reservoir of manpower is the laity. We have, without knowing it, drifted into "clergy religion," in which the clergyman is not the leader of a working, witnessing congregation, but rather the man who works *for* the congregation.

The great task of the Church today is by a deepening of fellowship to raise the laity from a preoccupation with finance to the level of religious witness. It was not weakness but strength, and a witness of which we are proud (particularly those of us whose states are close to Canada), when the Duke of Edinburgh in his recent visit stepped forward from his pew three Sundays to read the lessons. That was a witness more powerful than any clergyman in Canada could make. And if we set out to develop this ministry of the laity in visiting, in giving baptisimal instruction, in the conduct of Bible reading groups, we would have enough men to conduct more of our parish functions and many of our services in these parochial missions I was talking about.

DOCUMENTARY NOTE. After reading this talk, originally given at the Theological Seminary in Alexandria, Virginia, you wonder how Bishop Emrich's plan of church growth through establishing missions is working out. The answer is in this newspaper report, headlined, "Mission Fever Spreads in Diocese":

"Once before, earlier in the spring, we used the above headline to describe the several parochial missions which had sprung up here and there since four new missions had been formally admitted at Convention. What was a fever has now become an epidemic. If the various missions that are now in the talk and survey stage really develop, it will bring the year's total to 12.

"Already underway is a new mission in the city of Livonia, a fast developing area west of Detroit. Sponsored by Christ Church, Dearborn, things got underway on Sunday, May 25, in the George Bentley High School. The Rev. G. Paul Musselman was the first preacher, and succeeding services will see a distinguished roster of guest clergy.

"The women in the Lake Orion—Oxford area have organized into two guilds preparatory to the establishment of a mission there. It will be under the sponsorship of All Saints', Pontiac.

"St. Andrew's, Ann Arbor, expects, at a future time, to establish a mission using the beautiful chapel of St. Francis already erected.

"Spade work and preliminary surveys are under way at Holly under the direction of St. Jude's, Fenton, and at the west-side Wyandotte, in which St. Stephen's in downtown Wyandotte is interested.

"We hear, too, that a chapel at Sand Point in the

Thumb area is now building. The Rev. E. Caldwell of Forester will conduct services for vacationers."

CLOSING NOTE: We would like to close this chapter with a challenging thought from the Baptists regarding missions. The great and growing Baptist Church has a record of missionary work which is admired throughout Christendom. In this folder, "Let the Facts Speak," the Council on Missionary Cooperation of the American Baptist Convention gives us these startling statistics:

"Missions are cheaper than war. The cost of making the first two atomic bombs was $2,000,000,000. This amount would have put 10,000 missionaries in the field for a period of 100 years at $2,000 each a year.

"The total cost of the war to America was about $300,000,000,000. This amount would put 1,500,000 missionaries in the field for 100 years at $2,000 each a year.

"Why will man spend his resources to destroy lives and property, when he could use them to do so much good?"

Chapter 22

JOINT ACTION
BRINGS MORE SOULS,
MORE DOLLARS

By Joseph E. Boyle*

Hᴏᴡ ᴄᴀɴ ᴛʜᴇ ʟᴏᴄᴀʟ ᴘᴀʀɪsʜ or church compete these days with the multitude of claims for the time, interest, and money of laymen? That is a question which has troubled clergy and laity alike. It is a problem which many churches have had difficulty in solving, even with worthy efforts.

It is unlikely that the pressure for the time, interest, and money of the laity is going to decrease in the days ahead; instead, it is more likely to increase and the problem will therefore become more acute rather than less.

What can be done about it?

More than 2,000 communities of the nation have in the last four years found a new and at least partial solution to the problem. It is called the Religion in American Life campaign, nationally; locally, it goes by numerous titles. But whatever it is called, this new approach to the community represents joint action on the parts of churches and synagogues of many faiths and denominations. Let me add quickly that "joint action" in this case has nothing to do with basic creeds and tenets; it concerns itself only with emphasis on the importance of religion to our American way of life and the importance

---

* Vice President in charge of public relations at J. Walter Thompson Co. Formerly Associated Press Correspondent and Director of Promotion, National Council of Episcopal Church.

of support—both personal and financial—for our institutions of religion.

The Religion in American Life effort has long passed the stage where it is mere theory; again and again communities which have used the plan for joint action have recorded these results:

—increased church attendance

—increased church membership

—greatly increased financial support

Here are a few sample reports:

Helena, Montana: "Many churches had the largest average attendance in the history of the community."

Crowley, Louisiana: "An average increased attendance of about 15 percent was reported, with many new members."

Worcester, Massachusetts: "Sixty-five churches secured $165,189 in new and increased budgets over the previous year."

One clergyman wrote: "It is like Easter every Sunday now," after the Religion in American Life plan had been carried out in his community.

What is it about this plan which makes it new and effective? It is simply the use of modern methods of mass communication on behalf of the Church. These modern methods can be employed to reach the people; the whole community. They include the newspapers, the radio, television, magazines, and outdoor posters. And the simple fact is that these media of communication cannot be used with the greatest possible effect by one local church or even one denomination or faith; they must be used on an inter-church, an inter-faith basis if they are to be used the way they can and should —and now have been used.

There is nothing particularly new about this method of approaching and influencing masses of the people. Ample proof has been provided by the Community Chests, the Red Cross, the Heritage Foundation, and other movements and "causes." But admittedly, organized religion has been slow to use a similar approach, because of the great differences in fundamental beliefs, terminology, methods of worship, and methods of finance. Religion in American Life compromises none of these individual characteristics: it merely provides a means for all the churches to talk to and influence whole communities, leaving to the individual to choose the faith or parish which he prefers to support.

Except for unusual events and occasions, the media of mass communication (newspapers, radio, magazines, etc.) long ago discovered that they could not give continuous time and space to the Church's message. At the same time, these media of communication realized that they should give continuous time and space to a limited number of efforts (limited primarily because of their own limitations of time and space) and, as a result, they organized what is called the Advertising Council. This Council is merely the joint agency of all major media of communication which screens and selects the causes to which these media will give concentrated attention during certain periods of the year.

The Religion in American Life campaign was organized to take advantage of these facilities, through the Advertising Council. A national committee of laymen, headed by Mr. Charles E. Wilson, supervises the campaign. This committee does not buy space and time in your local newspapers, on radio, television, outdoor posters, and in magazines. It pays only the mechanical cost of producing the advertisements and messages; the mass media *give* the space and time for the advertisements and messages.

But of course a local or community committee is essential to take full advantage of the materials and facilities which the national committee, through the Advertising Council, provides. Hence, in hundreds and hundreds of communities in all parts of the nation, local committees are organized to hold meetings, provide speakers and materials for attendance or financial campaigns. November is the period selected for this joint-action program on behalf of all the churches and synagogues. During November, on radio and television, in the newspapers and magazines and on outdoor posters, messages telling of the importance of religion; the importance of church attendance; the importance of taking the children to church or synagogue will be appearing.

If there is a community committee in your town or city, the individual pastor can get much help from it. If there is no community-wide organization, he still can use this period of religious emphasis to organize his laymen for calling on those in his neighborhood to interest them in church attendance and support.

No longer can there be any doubt that joint action by the churches brings more souls and more dollars. Again and again, the Religion in American Life effort applied to the local community has brought renewed interest on the part of the laity and increased pledges and contributions.

Religion in American Life is supported by this distinguished list of organizations:

The American Baptist Convention
The American Bible Society
The American Unitarian Association
The African Methodist Episcopal Church
The Augustana Evangelical Lutheran Church
The Church of the Brethren
The Congregational Christian Churches
The Disciples of Christ
The Evangelical and Reformed Church
The Evangelical United Brethren Church
The Laymen's Movement for a Christian World
The Methodist Church
The National Board of the Y.W.C.A.
The Presbyterian Church in the U.S.A.
The Episcopal Church
The Reformed Church in America
The Seventh Day Baptist Conference
The Synagogue Council of America

The United Church Men

The United Church Women

American business and the advertising industry provide nation-wide advertising during November through their public-service organization, the Advertising Council. The Volunteer Agency for the years of RIAL campaigns is J. Walter Thompson Co., New York, N. Y.

SEVEN STEPS
TO ORGANIZE YOUR COMMUNITY
FOR AN EFFECTIVE
RELIGION IN AMERICAN LIFE
PROGRAM

This brief guide outlines the SEVEN STEPS basic to a successful local Religion In American Life program. The guide is intended to provide tested methods for effective organization by a community in support of its churches and synagogues. It may be adapted or used only in part to meet local circumstances.

1. *Help "Spark" the Program*

RIAL can start in your community when one layman, one clergyman or the chairman of a "spiritual aims" committee of a service club believes that local action is needed to obtain full advantage of the RIAL advertising and publicity. Many successful local RIAL programs stem from the energy of one enthusiastic person. Will you start it?

2. *Enlist Every Interested Group*

After consulting with key clergymen, call a meeting by inviting one representative each from all cooperating churches and synagogue, *plus* the Y.M. and Y.W.C.A. Y.M. and Y.W.H.A., P.T.A., leaders of Boy Scouts and Girl Scouts, Boys' Clubs, Camp Fire Girls and other youth groups, General Federation of Women's Clubs, Business and Professional Women's Clubs, Chamber of Commerce, Junior Chamber of Commerce, American Legion, Knights of Columbus, Grange, Farm Bureau, and any other community groups with a religious interest who might desire to participate.

3. *Decide to Organize*

At this exploratory meeting, present the full story of RIAL—What it is. How it works. Who supports it. Its value and ways to get maximum results. (The RIAL story is contained in the theme folder, "SHOW THEM THE WAY—THIS WEEK.") Then, organize immediate action by getting commitments from delegates present to set up a General Committee. This is the over-all policy-making group and should consist of a key representative from each interested community group.

4. *Elect Officers*

From the General Committee choose the following officers: general chairman (preferably a layman active in religious and civic affairs) ; vice-chairman (a clergyman) ; vice-chairman (a layman who might become next year's chairman) ; secretary and treasurer. Also, select four able and experienced lay people to serve as chairmen of the following committees:

a. *General Publicity*— (For chairman, enlist the services of the person who directed publicity for your Community Chest, Red Cross, or similar efforts.) This committee will promote the use of RIAL advertising by local newspapers, television, radio and billboards; also, press coverage, window displays, and special events. Every newspaper will be offered free advertisement mats, every television station will receive two film strips, every radio station will be provided with a supply of spot announcements. The committee should encourage generous use of all this material.

b. *Promotional Literature*—for reviewing, purchasing, and distributing stimulating material to build up attendance in each of the *participating congregations*. Write to RIAL headquarters for samples, especially the RIAL kit.

c. *Telephone Invitations*—with an outstanding woman as chairman, to organize the women of the community to invite every family to religious services during November. This plan allocates the names of one page, or less, of the local phone directory to be telephoned by each woman. Example: In Marion, Ohio, every home-telephone subscriber received a personal invitation to attend worship services.

d. *Statistics and Records*—for setting up machinery to keep an accurate record of attendance each week in every cooperating unit during the month of November. Records might be tabulated and published in the newspaper each week or at the close of the campaign. Attendance-record reports are available from the national RIAL office for use in reporting (a) local church and synagogue attendance and (b) total community attendance.

5. *Set Up Time Table for Pre-Campaign Activities*

Establish a schedule of events timed to build up momentum during the fall months. Careful planning in advance will set up a timetable for a strong program of local promotion, simultaneous community events, and joint emphasis by participating groups. A full calendar of activities for November, or some other month, will increase the results of the local program.

PRECEDING MONTH

Publicity Committee plans local radio, TV, and newspaper coverage for November. Makes personal visits to radio and TV program directors and to newspaper editors to encourage consistent support. Example: In Paterson, New Jersey, daily sermonettes by layman and lay women on subjects like "What I Believe" were broadcast by the local radio station during the entire month; and both local newspapers carried front-page "boxed" sermonettes or talks by laymen every day of the month.

Have each cooperating church or synagogue send out first letter (second week) announcing plans. Enclose an attendance-builder leaflet such as "The Empty Pew" or "The Filled Pew."

Set up plan for weekly mention of RIAL in bulletins or calendars of each church or synagogue.

Arrange for special religious display in some centrally located business-house window.

Organize "telephone invitation plan."

Distribute posters to cooperating religious groups, business houses, and all others concerned with the effort for placement in windows or on bulletin boards.

Have each local church or synagogue set up a "welcome committee" for newcomers to services during November.

Appoint "attendance-record takers" in each local religious group.

LAST WEEK—place first newspaper advertisement.

Have each cooperating group send out attendance-reminder cards showing campaign theme—"SHOW THEM THE WAY—THIS WEEK."

Make sure every home has a RIAL sticker on the front door or window and that each car also carries one.

6. MONTH OF CAMPAIGN

Suggested outline, for each week in November, of special program, emphases, events, and other plans. Throughout the month it is especially important that all participating groups repeat each week the aim of the local program—to increase attendance and support for churches and synagogues. Constant repetition will spread the news of your RIAL program, and enhance its effectiveness.

FIRST WEEK Each clergyman of all participating bodies should announce through bulletin or pulpit the opening of the campaign as an intensive, month-long effort to increase attendance and support. Use the specially prepared RIAL bulletin or calendar from the national office.

Start telephone-invitation plan with a friendly invitation extended to every family in the community. Encourage everyone to "come to worship" every week during the month.

Place second newspaper advertisement.

Place notice in weekly calendars or bulletins.

Campaign chairman should check to see that all aspects of program are properly underway.

Mail Attendance Builder No. 1—"Your Spiritual Vote." Each church, synagogue, or group should mail these cards to every prospective newcomer to religious services.

SECOND WEEK   Complete plans for a community-wide all (three) faiths "Thanksgiving-to-God" service. Where it is not possible for all groups to meet jointly, it is recommended that separate programs be set up for simultaneous observances. Suggested program: Two- or three-act play dramatizing the Thanksgiving period by local high-school or college drama group. This might be implemented by a community chorus or glee club using all Thanksgiving numbers.

Cooperate with United Church Canvass where such operates as a community project. Otherwise, conduct a campaign for attendance at worship services—a "go-to-church" emphasis.

Mail Attendance Builder No. 2—"By Proxy."

THIRD WEEK   "Thanksgiving-to-God" community-wide service or program.

Designate this Sabbath or Sunday as "Service Club Day," "Youth Day," "Grange," "Legion," "Lodge," etc., and extend special invitations to all members of these groups and others in the community to attend.

Send letters of appreciation to local or national business groups who have contributed time (on radio or TV) or space (outdoor posters, bus cards, newspapers, etc.) for the RIAL campaign. *This is important!*

Mail Attendance Builder No. 3—"The Pattern You Set."

FOURTH WEEK   Collect attendance records from each cooperating group, summarize totals and publicize.

Have newspapers, radio, television, and local clergymen announce results and general effects of campaign
with a forecast of expanded efforts throughout the year
leading to a greater campaign the following fall.

Mail Attendance Builder No. 4—"Real Security."

7. POST-CAMPAIGN SCHEDULE

A. Prepare and send complete record of local results
to national RIAL office. Report full details of local
RIAL campaign, showing statistics of attendance, week
by week and for each church and synagogue for the
month. Please use the RIAL attendance record form
which will be sent to you. Also, please send to RIAL
a complete set of newspaper ads, radio spot announcements, pictures of window displays, and other forms of
local publicity. As a suggestion, a scrapbook with these
various pieces of publicity is usually the best form of
telling your local RIAL story.

B. Organize an "expression of thanks" letter-writing
plan in appreciation of free advertising contributed during campaign. Encourage individually written letters to
the radio and TV network presidents, your local newspaper advertising manager, your local outdoor-poster
firms, local bus advertising companies and others who
donated time or space. More specific details can be secured by writing the national office.

Although the annual RIAL campaign concentrates
on November of each year, the work and activities of
Religion in American Life goes on throughout all
twelve months. At all times you, your church, or your
local committee can secure from RIAL the following
material for increasing church attendance . . . increasing church membership . . . and for increasing financial
support:

ITEM	Rate Each
1952 RIAL PROGRAM KIT (includes samples of most items on this page). One copy free to a community. Extra copies	$ .10

SEVEN STEPS (A simplified manual outlining the basic seven steps which have been tested and found successful in the organization of an effective local RIAL program) 10

"SHOW THEM THE WAY—THIS WEEK" (Illustrated leaflet describing RIAL program, for distribution to clubs, societies, community groups). Limited quantities free. Extra copies...........   .02

RIAL WORSHIP FOLDERS (Four-page folder, 8½" x 5½", with colored illustration on front cover, and inside pages left blank for local mimeographing or imprinting. Designed for use in local Sabbath worship or a community-wide union program or service)..........................   .02

RIAL THEME POSTCARD (Postcard, 5½" x 3¼", carrying 1952 RIAL illustration and theme. For mailing to call local attention to your RIAL program effort to increase attendance and support) 01

RIAL ATTENDANCE PROMOTION POST-CARDS (A series of four postcards, 5½" x 3¼", each set in the series a different color, carrying RIAL illustration and messages urging worship attendance. To be mailed on each of four weeks in November or any other month, as a continuous direct-mail project) :
No. 1. "Your Spiritual Vote" 01
No. 2 "By Proxy" 01
No. 3 "The Pattern You Set".................   .01
No. 4 "Find Real Security"...................   .01

RIAL WINDOW DISPLAY POSTERS (16" x 28", heavy cardboard, in four colors, carrying RIAL illustration and theme. Designed for bulletin boards and store windows). Not included in kit..   .15
(Quantity prices: 25-99 copies—10¢ each; 100-499—9¢ each; 500 or more—8¢ each)

RIAL GUMMED STICKERS (3½" x 6" with RIAL theme and illustration in two colors, gummed on one side. Can be effectively used on auto, home, and business windows...........   .01

THE EMPTY PEW (Successful leaflet for increasing worship attendance. Excellent for letter enclosure) 02

THE FILLED PEW (Campaign leaflet to "Empty Pew" with positive appeal. Good attendance booster for RIAL year-round emphasis).........   .02

Detailed information on radio, television, posters and other similar items relating to the localizing of the RIAL program will be found in one or more of the Confidential Bulletins issued periodically.

Note: Postage is extra on all orders. Material ordered cannot be returned for credit. Please allow at least 15 days for delivery.

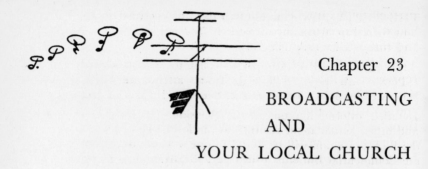

Chapter 23

BROADCASTING AND YOUR LOCAL CHURCH

By Charles H. Schmitz*

"**M**Y DADDY'S GONE TO THE RADIO STATION to make a *transgression*." A certain clergyman's little daughter said that to someone who called him on the phone. Her father had previously told the family that he was going to the radio station to make a transcription. But the youngster misunderstood. Maybe she hit the truth more exactly than she realized. There have been local religious broadcasts that may also be thought of as a "transgression." Nevertheless, it is our deep conviction that the local broadcaster, fully understanding his privilege, opportunity, and responsibility can be the most important person in the whole broadcasting field.

The local broadcaster is most important.

The local religious broadcaster knows his community and is known by it, whereas the network broadcaster is usually a highly remote and imaginative figure to the listener. The local broadcaster possesses a native quality and understanding, whereas the network broadcaster cannot help but be under the influence of the metropolitan mind. The local broadcaster may easily be

---

* Educational Director of Broadcasting and Film Commission of the National Council of Churches of Christ.

reached by his listeners, whereas the only contact to be had with a network broadcaster is by correspondence— and that is very unsatisfactory.

Most important of all, the local religious broadcaster represents a local group of believers known as Christians. This local church is the heart and basis of life and growth in the Kingdom of God. There is such a thing as "the Church Universal" just as there is such a thing as the "World Bank," but we can do Kingdom business only with the church on the corner, just as we can have financial transactions only with the bank on the corner, not with the "World Bank." The listener with no sense of belonging may come to know the high meaning of belonging, not to an elusive "Church Universal" but to a matter-of-fact church down the street. The local broadcaster alone, not the network personality, may bring the listener and the local church together in a happy, fruitful relationship for both.

Local radio and television stations are coming more and more to see that their program schedules must be community-centered, must reflect the community "public interest, convenience, and necessity," not that of a city a thousand miles away. In some years that have gone by, broadcasting has judged itself by looking at itself in the larger cities with their peculiar metropolitan slants. Radio and television may be at their best there, but *only* at their best for the particular cities from which they originate. Local stations are becoming wiser, they are more and more reflecting the local area, rather than simply copying the schedules of New York stations. Note well the area difference in religious music. Area tastes vary. A religious program succeeding in one locality may be an utter failure in another. The local leader in broadcasting is aware of his community and has the power to key his thinking and broadcasting to it. The target for the network broadcaster is too, too far away for his work to be ultimately effective. His programs have value in creating a spiritual climate, in supplementing local broadcasts, but no network program can ever become a worthy substitute for programs initiated at the local level by local religious leaders. Only the local person possesses the broadcaster's "hook" which can make him the truly effective "fisher of men."

The local broadcaster is most important. I have yet to discover a local church which has grown any appreciable, continuing way as the result of any network broadcast, whether that of its own denomination or communion, or that of an inter-denominational agency. But I can point out to you local church after local church that has grown in a continuing appreciable way as the result of its radio ministry to its own community.

There is always a temptation to let the other fellow do it. We like to think that the great names of religious leaders the network offers as good bait are the all-sufficient answers. Big names do not necessarily make for good radio. A good pulpiteer may be a poor radio personality. There are too many sermons born out of big cities and popular books rather than out of life and the very heart of America. The religious leaders who have lived in our big cities for years have forgotten how the rest of the people in this country live. Do not yield to the temptation to let the other fellow, who lives and thinks far away, do the job that you need to do in your own home town.

The broadcaster's targets

"That which distinguishes this day from all others is that today both orators and artillerymen shoot blank cartridges." John Burroughs, the naturalist, said that on July 4, 1859.

Religious broadcasting lends itself to orators and artillerymen and blank cartridges. Blank cartridges provide noise, smoke, and fire. BUT even if the gun is aimed at a target, the target is never affected. In broadcasting there is oratory that is fluffy and noisy; there are words that are like empty shells. Much of this comes about because there is no sound reasoning behind our broadcasting. There is no attempt from the top down and the bottom up truly to understand radio and television. There is little understanding of the audience, the available targets.

We need not make a blank cartridge of our deepest faith in God, in Jesus, in the Bible, in the Church. We can take our most profound convictions and literally aim them at the targets. Radio and television are the great home-missions media of the Church. Through these we may go with the Master through doors that are shut. Through broadcasting we may go with His Way, His Truth, His Life, to minds that are closed.

What then are the targets behind the shut doors?

1. To key programs to the *shut-outs* as well as the *shut-ins*.

The shut-outs are those who have had no contact with the contemporary life, language, and meaning of the Church.

The shut-ins are those with church-related backgrounds but now in confinement because of illness or age.

(Note: the population of the United States has doubled in the past fifty years, resulting in more people being outside the Church (as well as inside) than ever before. Over 3,925,000 babies were born in 1951, breaking all previous records.)

2. To break through the shell of the *hardened churchgoers*.

There are those for whom church-going has become a casual duty apart from everyday life, a substitute for Christian living.

There is a kind of self-righteousness and self-satisfaction among some church people that makes the Church offensive to many. The attitude referred to is that which says, "How can you be more like me?"

3. To reach the people for whom life has become a meaningless blur.

Life no longer makes sense for some people.

Life has become a kind of skillfully prepared confusion.

Life is like an atomic bomb, subject to much effort, study, research and expense, ultimately (after careful tests) resulting in an explosion that appears like a white *cloud* in the desert.

4. To find people who have *no promises to live by*.

Broken promises seem to be a part of the life of every man.

5. To discover the *fearful* and the *insecure*.

There is a great hunger for peace of mind.

6. To discover also those who are *embalmed in security*.

The individuals who have money in the bank, good jobs, lovely homes, little trouble.

To discover those who "have need of clothing" (Rev. 3:17) and who, like dead men, are embalmed in security.

7. To seek the *lonely*, the *forsaken*, the *friendless*.

There are many individuals who have no sense of belonging to anyone.

8. To reach those who are *on the move*.

According to the Census Bureau, 1 out of every 5 of the population changed residence every year from April 1947 to the Spring of 1950. Twenty-eight million persons a year were involved.

From 1940-47 a total of 70,000,000 persons, or about half the population settled in different homes. (This does not include the armed forces.)

Those who are on the move may become lost to the Church.

9. To enlighten the *misinformed* with factual information about Christian life today.

People know little about the full ministry of the local church.

10. To stimulate *thoughtless Christians* to rediscover their Faith.

Some Christians have stopped thinking and no longer know what it is they believe.

11. To win *young people* to Christ's way, truth, life. There are 15,000,000 teen-agers in this country.

After thirty years of broadcasting we do not yet have a continuing program for young people of high-school and/or college age.

All of these are our broadcasting program targets. They are the very human reasons why we should broadcast. They are the people we may love with our deepest faith in God as the present interested, merciful Father of us all; in Jesus as the once-upon-a-time and as the continuing Saviour; in the Bible as the Book with relevance and meaning for today; in the Church as the fellowship of believers around the world. Radio and television are God-given miracles of communication for *just* such a time as this. They are far-reaching in their possibilities for good. They suggest that we understand their peculiar disciplines. They ask that we accept their high privileges. They expect that we will use them as responsible disciples of Jesus.

Why hasn't broadcasting affected the targets?

Broadcasting has not affected the targets because we have confused HEARING WITH LISTENING. There is a decided difference between hearing and listening. The woman pointed it out when she said, "I hear my husband getting up in the morning, but I don't listen. If I did listen, I would have to get up and get his breakfast!" Hearing requires no response, listening does. Hearing is never the criterion of the success of any program, but we have so assumed.

Another error of judgment that has been ours is that we have *equated loyalty to a broadcaster with Christian service*. Many religious broadcasters have had loyal audiences for years. But loyalty to that person does not constitute loyalty to the cause for which he stands.

There is something else that may issue in a blank cartridge, and that is when we infer that *good script-*

writing, production, and air time equal good results.
Some of our religious broadcasts are about as foolish as
having Marian Anderson sing in a cemetery—no response expected. Just a good show! We may have the
best program in class "A" time and still it can be only
a blank cartridge. Our aim is not to have hearers say,
"What a lovely broadcast," but to have them say,
"That's good, now I'll *do* something about it."
How may the targets be affected?

We may affect the target by recognizing that we can
make leaders in religious broadcasting without necessarily making microphone personalities. Sometimes in
our workshops the participants suppose that we are trying to make microphone personalities out of all of
them. That is impossibile. One may be a leader in
broadcasting without ever using the microphone.

There were two brothers in Old Testament times—
Moses and Aaron. Moses was not what we would call
a microphone personality—he was a stutterer, a stam-
merer, a man "slow of speech and slow of tongue." But
Moses could THINK, he could lead. Aaron, his brother,
was a microphone personality. Aaron could talk on any
subject, anytime, anywhere—but Aaron couldn't think.
He had all the rules of good speech mastered, but he
had no sense of right and wrong. He could persuade
people, but it didn't make any difference to him
whether he persuaded them about worshiping a golden
calf or the Living God. Aaron needed Moses. And
Moses needed Aaron.

We are seeking, finding, training men who, like
Moses, will do some honest forthright thinking and
ultimately bring the Aarons to task. We are training
men and women to become chairmen of local radio and
television committees, script-writers, builders of variety
in programming to reach hearers allergic to present programming.

We may affect the targets by having these local leaders in religious broadcasting see to it that we have the
best in programming, PLUS planned listening along with

planned broadcasting. We need prepared listening along with prepared publicity and promotion. We need listening with purpose behind it. The Maine Council of Churches has a program called the Church School of the Air. It has been on for years, and they have *enrolled listeners*. This is precisely what we mean. We need this guided response so that hearers will not just "turn off the lights and go to sleep" after every program. The ultimate goal of all our religious programming should be to make the hearers become listeners who will attach themselves to the local fellowship of believers—the Church.

The Rev. R. H. W. Falconer has written a booklet called "Success and Failure of a Radio Mission" in which he tells the story of how the Church of Scotland used radio broadcasts to build the local church. It is recommended to you for your reading.

The targets may also be affected by working together to *stimulate interest and attendance in religious radio and television institutes and workshops*. The institutes have been interesting ventures. We have been in some institutes where the participants ask, "What is the National Council of Churches?" This is the first contact they have ever had. In the institutes we distribute literature that provides some answers. Ideas are exchanged. In many cases the radio station managers and the religious leaders meet each other for the first time. This is good. Slowly but surely they come to understand each other. This is service at the grass roots.

The workshops provide opportunity to learn by doing. The participants face their own peculiar community radio and TV needs and work through them toward a solution under guided leadership. Work groups on radio writing, production, newscasting, speech, devotional programming, etc., are held. We point out to them that broadcasting represents the great HOME MISSIONS opportunity, the way to reach the unreached. We suggest they make their programming simple and plain. Rufus Jones, the Quaker, was interrupted in an address by a woman who rose and said, "Rufus, Jesus said 'Feed my lambs!' he did not say 'Feed my giraffes.' " To make it simple and to make it plain is important.

Blank cartridges—how guilty all of us have been in using them. We have tried to reach the common people with anthems that might as well be given in an unknown tongue—they are not understood. We have immersed ourselves in the peculiar language of the church, reflecting the language of many of our theologians who often misunderstand each other, and themselves.

Blank cartridges, like so many broadcast prayers that one person described as being "read with a divine disinterest." Blank cartridges, like scripture so read that it sounds like audible print, and as if the reader himself had no opinions about it. Blank cartridges because we are so afraid to oversimplify. Let's read the Bible again and note well the Genesis Story of Creation, note the 23rd Psalm, and the sayings of Jesus. They are all oversimplified. *Yet*, these are not blank cartridges! Still, through the centuries they hit us hard.

Every responsible venture, even religious broadcasting, requires that we "study to show ourselves approved unto God, workmen that need not be ashamed." That applies to the top brass as well as to the rural minister. We want to affect the targets with the Gospel in a way in which they have never been affected before. We want hearers to become listeners and listeners to become servants of the living God until the local fellowship of believers grows and grows and grows.

Note: For information about workshops write:

The Broadcasting and Film Commission,
220 Fifth Avenue,
New York 1, N. Y.

LAY READER USES SERMON SERVICE ON REGULAR WEEKLY BROADCAST

The Presiding Bishop's Committee on Laymen's Work provides a sermon for each Sunday of the church year for almost two thousand lay readers of the Church at home and overseas. These sermons are used in churches and chapels great and small and are an honest attempt to meet the needs of the lay readers and their congregations. It is not an easy thing for a lay reader to lay his hand on just the right sermon for a particular Sunday.

A recent letter from Victor J. Leonardi, lay reader of the Church of Our Saviour, Placerville, California, tells how he uses the sermons over Station KDIA. On a program called "A Layman Speaks," this churchman uses the sermons as they come along each week. It seems that KDIA is located some eighteen miles—air miles— from his home in Placerville, or twenty miles over a rugged mountain road, or forty-five miles by a good highway. Does this daunt this lay reader? Not at all. He has overcome the traveling situation by establishing a leased line from the telephone company to the radio station. At the proper moment he throws the switch and the lay reader's sermon is on the air. All kinds of ways of telling the Good News!

BROADCASTING DO'S AND DON'TS

Your Preparation

Do

Remember that TV is a different means of communication.

Make friends of the station personnel.

Prepare carefully—understandingly.

Have enough mimeographed copies of the script.

Check and double-check on all props.

Keep introduction and announcements short.

Time yourself and your total program.

Time closing remarks carefully.

Don't

Assume TV is like radio or anything else.

Forget that it takes from fourteen to twenty men and more to put your program on the air.

Assume anything or omit any details.

Consider that carbon copies are always completely legible.

Ignore proper placement of each prop.

Give lengthy, meaningless announcements.

Guess at how long your part of the program is.

Lose final punch through careless timing.

Your Attitude

Do

Be cheerful—the Gospel is good news.

Be sincere and informal.

Be humble.

Be alert.

Be friendly.

Be yourself.

Be personal.

Use person-to-person psychology.

Have purpose and conviction.

Don't

Be funereal.

Be superficial.

Be a "know-it-all."

Be blind to what's going on.

Be starchy and stilted.

Be unnatural.

Be distant or impersonal.

Use crowd psychology.

Be unconcerned.

Your Talk

Do

Talk simply.

Talk clearly.

Talk pointedly and logically.

Talk frankly.

Talk conversationally as if to camera man.

Talk convincingly, persuasively.

Talk from memory—or a posted prompter's outline.

Talk primarily to the home.

Remember you must compete for attention.

Be interesting throughout.

Satisfy the eye and ear.

Combine words with pleasing action.

End with a real conclusion.

Don't

Use difficult words when simple words will do.

Lift viewers into a wordy fog.

Assume you have points when there are none.

Hedge or use double-talk.

Try to project your voice to the back pew when there is no back pew in TV.

Talk apologetically.

Read with a divine disinterest.

Direct your remarks to a sanctuary audience.

Think you are the viewer's only choice.

Allow lags or dull spots in your talk.

Just satisfy the ear.

Assume your talk can get by on itself.

Leave audience hanging in space.

Your Microphone Presence

Do

Know where the microphone is placed.

Make agreed-upon changes in position slowly and smoothly.

Understand that rattling notepaper is easily picked up.

Make sure your notes do not come between you and the mike.

Read (if you must) in thoughts not words.

Have variety in your voice pattern.

Remain silent close to "on air" and "off air" time.

Don't

Suddenly move away from the mike.

Assume that the microphone is attached to you and rises or moves automatically with you.

Touch the microphone.

Muffle the mike with papers or hands.

Bob your head up and down while reading.

Have a dull ministerial monotone.

Whisper just before or just after air time.

Your Camera Presence

Do

Be at ease.

Look into the camera when light is on.

Avoid mannerisms.

Use close to the body gestures.

Lift up your head.

Be a human being.

Be aware of change from camera to camera.

Look above camera lens and avoid shifting your eyes.

Stay in position as agreed upon in rehearsal.

Watch floor manager for time and camera cues.

Don't

Be tense.

Hide your face or get your hands between your face and camera.

Fidget, roll your eyes, bite your nails.

Use gestures at arm's length (it may double the size of your hands).

Bury your head in your notes.

Be an "out of this world" clergyman.

Assume one camera is on you all the time.

Look below camera lens or your eyelids will seem enlarged on the screen.

Move to new, unrehearsed position where camera men cannot follow you.

Let the viewer see you acknowledge a cue.

Your Personal Appearance

Do

Stay within middle range of contrasts in clothing you wear. Avoid extremes—wear shirt of pastel shades of blue, gray, tan, or green.

Sit up straight and tilt head back slightly.
Read (if you must) with script plainly before you.
Sit on the edge of the chair.
Accept make-up if it helps.
Dress modestly.

Don't
Wear a white shirt against a black suit. (Never wear black and white next to each other—a white turned-around collar may become a misplaced halo on the screen.
Lean forward and show your bald spot.
Try to conceal script.
Sit back lazily.
Use make-up if it makes you look bad.
Wear glittering jewelry.

ACCEPT THE ADVICE OF THE TELEVISION STATION PERSONNEL . . .

DON'T ASSUME COMPLETE KNOWLEDGE

FOLLOW ALL DIRECTIONS OF TV DIRECTOR

In your own home town, here are some things you can do:

1. Carefully look over the daily radio and television program listings in your local newspaper, check the religious programs, and then listen to them to see what they are like. Note the concentration of religious programs on Sunday morning and the lack of religious programs during the week (especially evenings).

2. Go to your minister, your local or state Council of Churches or Ministerial Association, and find out what programs they have and what they are doing in broadcasting. Check these with the newspaper listings.

3. Now think of the ways in which you can lift the level of local religious programming, providing more

quality programs in terms of the radio and television criterion of quality, and also providing more variety (religious newscasts, interviews, drama, etc.) in programming. It may be your own church has talent that would make interesting program material. Look for program ideas, script-writers, musicians, dramatic talent, etc.

4. If there is no radio and television committee, initiate one. Everybody's business is nobody's business. The committee becomes the assigned group to watch, think, plan in terms of broadcasting. Get members of the committee to attend the workshops of the Broadcasting and Film Commission or of your own Communion.

5. Meet informally with the manager and/or program director of the local broadcasting station. Tell them you listen to their religious programs. Tell them you appreciate the time the station makes available. Tell them you have some ideas on how new and better programs may be built. Don't lecture or scold or appear to be a "know-it-all." Remember they are beset by many pressure groups. They welcome, too, your willingness to build up the listening audience for the quality religious programs they may carry. They welcome ways and means of making programs now on the air more useful.

6. Try to find good Christian church men in your local broadcasting stations. Tell your local Council of Churches or Ministerial Association about them. Try to get them on your local broadcasting committee. The Red Cross, the Community Chest, and similar groups have enlisted broadcasting volunteers. Why can't the Church do likewise? A radio and television committee made up exclusively of ministers is an inefficient, unbalanced committee.

7. Your church is wider than the distance between its walls. Your church can reach more people than it can seat in its pews. Your church can extend its minis-

try through the miracles of radio and television to contact many, many times the number of people it is now able to reach.

Remember that one broadcast on a local station may reach more people than are present in all the churches of the community at Sunday worship services. You will not *see* the host of listeners because broadcasting is a "blind" means of communication—the audience is never seen. There is a saying of Jesus that is very pertinent to this matter. Said Jesus, "Blessed are they that have not seen and yet have believed." (*John 20:29*)

Chapter 24

PUBLIC RELATIONS FOR YOUR CHURCH

By Frederick H. Sontag*

IT IS USUALLY GRATIFYING to see one's picture in the paper, or a story about one's organization. To be of interest to others beside yourself it should say something, it should say something good, something newsworthy, and should reflect well on you and your church. It is generally agreed and understood that you are against sin, but what are you for? Good publicity tells what you are for and what you are doing about it.

Most city editors are pleasant chaps and most are family men and churchgoers. They are willing to be helpful and it is worth while to visit them and let them know who you are. Meet the religious and other editors. Visit them after their daily deadlines have been met and the paper "put to bed." They are relieved of tension and will have time to chat. Call them on the phone to find out the best time. It varies from paper to paper and depends on whether it is a morning or evening newspaper.

Make friends with the working press and you will learn about the material they can best use to your mutual advantage. Newspaper men work very hard and

* Public relations director and author, has extensive experience and an outstanding record for business, civic and church organizations.

are exposed to many pressures. Don't be another burden or pressure; be a friend. Even if the publisher is in your congregation, don't depend on a note from him to get space. Get to know the working newsman.

Publicity is a major tool in any public-relations program. It is a two-edged tool, however, and can hurt, no matter how many column-inches you get, if you don't get it right. Learn to look at it from the newsman's viewpoint, and the best way to learn that viewpoint is from a working newsman.

Send in parish notices and announcements as such, not as the news scoops of the year. Some events qualify as news items and others as feature stories. IF THERE IS MORE THAN ONE PAPER IN YOUR COMMUNITY, SEND MATERIAL TO BOTH AND AT THE SAME TIME. Get to know their deadline for various types of material. Using common sense and an honest approach, you won't have to ask for news breaks. They have a paper to fill daily and they will come to you when they know you are a reliable and constant source of good news.

Good public relations for churches often mean making them more effective to serve our Lord. This means making a good impression in the community that you are doing a worth-while job for your area and its people.

Giving to the press and other thought leaders the kind of reputation a church should have, that is the aim of many sound church public-relations leaders.

Many churches have poor public relations. Mostly this is caused by unfriendliness, keeping strangers away, being aloof. But also, some churches that could serve people in need are often country-club organizations for the chosen few of wealth, and that drives away both worth-while clergy and lay people. Many churches have large and expensive plants. They stand empty most of the week, and are used only occasionally on weekdays in addition to Sunday services. With young people needing a wholesome place to play, an empty parish house causes bad public relations. A parish house used by the community's children and adults, on the one hand, brings new people to the church, new faces to worship at its altar, and, on the other, shows non-churchgoers and secular local organizations that the church cares for the problems of everyday life.

Some churches have friendly phone service. So when strangers or others in town call, they feel warm and interested in the church. A hard, brush-off parish phone operator, be it clergyman, secretary, or sexton, has often driven away those that seek to enter the church.

Public Relations for the churches means acting in a friendly manner, but two other points are of prime importance. 1. Acting in the public interest, caring for others in the community, not making the Church the selfish property of a few but always inviting in others to share what our Lord has left us. 2. Telling the truth, giving the facts, good or bad. Now some secular organizations do not tell the truth, and that makes it all the more important for the Church to uphold the Ten Commandments and say only what is so.

Recently, a bishop became ill. Instead of denying that he was going to have to be away from his state for many months, recovering in an institution, the church leaders frankly called in the press, told the city editors what was the problem, and no misleading articles or rumors resulted. When a clergyman has to leave the ministry for some reason, it is far better to tell the truth, than to say he has moved elsewhere, when knowing people in town are aware of the fact that he is beginning a new life as a layman because he found he couldn't make a good clergyman. Even when a new social change takes place, such as the change in local or regional social regulations, it is best to let people know the facts. Sometimes they cannot get them from government, industry, or labor, each of which often tries to suppress data which belongs to the public.

Wise church groups make available all financial or personnel data and problems to as wide a group of clergy and lay people as they can, for greater knowledge often means greater support and understanding. Ignorance means lack of support and action. How could one live the Ten Commandments if one had only been given five out of the ten, and the other five were thought not to be available for the average church member, but only to the chosen few church leaders.

Just as it is wise for the doctor to see any member of the family for a check-up, so it is often good for an outsider to take a look at your church. What is it doing to attract or reject new people? What is it doing to make friends, to influence more people to lead a Christian life? Public-relations workers, be they consultants, visiting professors, or guests can help bring them into your church and give the fresh approach of someone who can question, and so help improve the church.

Facts or lack of them often mean the difference between success or financial failure for a church group. Recently, two important New York church groups faced serious budget cuts, as they had not raised their full quota. One church leader called in fifty of his top laymen, told them the facts, gave a story to the papers, and had his chief aide give a broadcast report on what would happen if the funds were not raised. They came in within one week, and no work was discontinued. On the other hand, a few blocks away, another church leader rejected the advice of his public-relations men and the church's annual convention had to cut the budget because they could not see the money needed in sight anywhere. So a big New York church group had to lay off its full-time director of religious education, executive secretary of its Christian Social Relations Commission, and others. Key lay leaders felt sure that if they had been told of the facts in advance of the annual meeting, newspaper and broadcast news of this major cut at a time of unprecedented national prosperity would have brought immediate action by indignant lay people who would have made up the deficit and would not have wanted their church shamed by a major retrenchment. Basically the forward progress of one group and the backward moves of the other depended, in the final analysis, on the enlightened public-relations attitude of its top leaders.

Once your church knows that its policies are right and that it is willing to give its members and the public through the press the facts of church life, then one can turn to some of the "how it is dones" in successful press relations.

For the most part church people read the church page in the Saturday papers, so missionary and expansion-minded church men try to place articles on any day *but* Saturday. They get to know their city editors on their local papers, for, just as you have to know your doctor to get and give good service, so it is often helpful for you to have spent a few minutes with your editor to find out what he wants and can print, so that you will be giving this to him and won't waste your time and his.

Each week in your press you can read the news of the world. As you read it, think of where the Church might fit in and what local service you might be rendering that would make news.

Make your news interesting instead of routine. When a new clergyman is appointed to your church, don't just give the papers facts on what colleges and theological seminaries he has attended. You will find it of much greater interest for papers that he was a paratrooper chaplain and that he has been active in a boys' club.

Often photographs are taken at a church. Instead of always having visitors greeted by the ancient and honorable male leaders of the church, show young people welcoming the guests. Children greeting their new minister make for a much more interesting story. And it shows that your church is alive, not just the property of its leaders.

Below follows a press guide that has worked well for many churches. Tied in to your own local situation, it will fit into any American town, large or small. It was written by the author and is based on field interviews in many states, from farm churches to city parishes, from missions to wealthy brick structures on Main Street.

YOU AND YOUR PARISH
PRESS, RADIO, AND TELEVISION RELATIONS

(A guide for use of clergy and lay people in their relations with the press, radio, and television.)

The reason for and the aim of all church news is simply this: to interest others in what we believe to be supremely worth while—the Church, its message, its work, and its program.

The aim of church news is to reach two groups of people:

1. Parishioners: to inform them and to deepen their enthusiasm and loyalty.

2. Non-active and potential parishioners: to attract and to enlist their active interest and support.

Remember: News is simply the art of making things known. It is the things you do in your parish that make news. News, not notices, consists essentially of names and actions.

A good photograph is worth a half-column of words. Newspaper space is free, pleases your people, helps your work.

Amount and quality of news a parish will get in the local press, radio and television depends on:

1. Use of available news talent in the parish.

2. Degree of cooperation between clergy and lay people and press.

3. Newspaper friendships and connections.

4. Observance of newspaper ethics and mechanical rules.

HOW TO OBTAIN MORE AND BETTER NEWS
FOR YOUR PARISH

I. *Make use of available talent in your parish.* There's hardly a parish which does not have a parishioner who is qualified to help with this part of the parish work. Use this person.

If you are fortunate enough to have a trained newspaper or radio man in your parish, use him for parish news. Profit by his counsel.

If no trained helper is available, develop someone to take care of this work. This is a way to make good use of a layman who wants something to do which will help. This follows the philosophy of committees for layman's work that laymen are willing to help their church in various lay fields if they are asked.

II. *Cooperate with the Press.*

1. Be of help to your newspaper, radio, and television friends. Do what you can to satisfy all reasonable demands of the press for information. Allow them use of your library and books if need be. Assist them with names and proper titles, especially important in a church. Help them to be right in use of church terminology. Remember, reporters don't deliberately try to be wrong! See that your newspaper-radio-TV friends have a copy of the Prayer Book and the latest official year book of your Church, both locally and nationally.

2. *Anticipate the newspaperman's needs.* E.g., if an important church meeting is taking place in your parish, either personally or through a qualified deputy, aid the photographer to get any legitimate pictures he desires. Help get together persons to be photographed.

3. *Regarding important statements, speeches, sermons:* Prepare in advance mimeographed or carbon copies or summaries for the reporters. The newspaper and radio accounts will then probably bear some resemblance to what you said.

4. *Let newspapers, radio, and TV stations know they can rely on you,* as to accuracy, etc., of your stories and that you will notify them in advance of what might be news or a picture.

5. *Cooperate with newspapers, radio, and TV staffs,* as mentioned in #2, as part of their staffs. This will

work to the mutual benefit and advantage of both parties.

6. Don't be so busy that you can't spare a few minutes for a reporter. They can be useful allies and they are human beings.

III. *Establish newspaper, radio, and TV friendships.*

The main thing is to do it yourself. Make yourself known to the editor or owner of a small-town newspaper. Know the city editor or the church-news editor on a big-city newspaper. Know, as man to man, the strategic men on the local newspaper, radio, and TV staffs.

Such personal connections and friendships will prove themselves invaluable.

IV. *Observe newspaper mechanics and ethics.*

1. *Be prompt—ahead of time.* Find out the deadline on your local newspaper and local news radio station desk and get your copy in well in advance. Early copy on editor's desk naturally gets preferential treatment.

2. *Be courteous.* Don't demand service, request it. The press holds the Church and clergy in high esteem. Don't abuse this.

3. *Preparation of copy.*

Write out your copy; don't phone it.

Use one side of sheet only.

Type, if possible, and use double-space.

Legible long-hand is permissible, but busy editors will not bother to decipher illegible manuscripts.

Conform with style usages of your local newspapers.

Don't attempt to write headlines or leads for your story.

Be sure you have covered in first paragraph—who, what, where, when, how.

Paste caption for photograph on reverse of glossy print—do not write on back of print with hard pencil.

Have your story complete in every detail.

Be sure you have used correct spelling and titles.

Send addresses as well as names. Those news agencies who don't want to use addresses will eliminate them.

Carbon copies are acceptable if they are easily readable. It helps if they are on a heavier grade of paper than onion skin.

Put sender's name and phone number at top of first page so that newsmen can obtain additional information, if needed.

4. *Names.* First of all, use them—"names make news." Secondly, spell them correctly. Thirdly, use a man's name as he wishes it to be used. Everybody likes to see his name in print—correctly spelled.

5. *Timeliness.* Most events that happened more than twenty-four hours past are dead. Present and future events are of interest to newspapers, radio, and TV station.

6. *Time your stories judiciously.* Don't overwhelm the newspaper and stations with a batch of stories at one time. Spread them out.

7. *Release of stories.* Release a story of general interest to all newspapers and stations at the same time. Play no favorites. Be fair and on the up and up with all alike. Don't conceal from one newspaper or station a story given to another. Even the score as soon as you can.

8. *A few tips:*

Don't manufacture stories.

Avoid Saturday editions, if possible—they are the last read. The best time to get space is early in the week—about Tuesday or Wednesday.

Be sure to emphasize the news angle. Don't strive to write literature.

Regarding unpleasant news. Face up to it and help to get it straightened out. Don't be unavailable; don't say you won't talk. By the way you handle such a case, you will win or lose valuable newspaper and station connections.

WHAT'S NEWS IN A CHURCH?

Elections—of a new minister and church officials; officers of important organizations.

Special speakers—at a special service or meeting. Who the speaker is, etc.

Anniversaries—of the parish, minister, society.

Formation of new organization—with history and aims of group.

Gifts to parish—as bequests and legacies and memorials.

Awards and prizes—as church school awards for attendance during Lent or school year.

News about preceding minister—he has left behind him many friends in the parish eager to follow his career, new responsibilities, and honors.

Plans for new buildings, alterations, repairs and improvements.

Parishioners attending a conference or important meeting.

Appointment of minister or parishioners to state or area offices—field of wider service.

Special services

Masonic

Ordination

Confirmation—print candidates' names

Lenten—guest preachers

Corporate Communions

Saints' Days and Feast Days—not observed by other churches

Sermon or speech—if of interest to people beyond parish.

Special projects in parish.

MEDIUMS OF PARISH NEWS

Local newspapers, radio, and TV stations.

Community newspaper in big city.

Parish magazine.

Direct mail to parish list.

Weekly bulletin distributed at services.

Bulletin boards, signs.

Tract-case.

The underlying purpose of church public relations activities is to teach and disseminate information about the church and its work. This purpose was defined by the Reverend Albert A. Chambers, of the Church of the Resurrection in New York, an outstanding promotion leader on the local level, as: *"Promotion is the propagation of the Christian faith within and without the family of the church, through every available technique, and covering every area of the church's commission and life."*

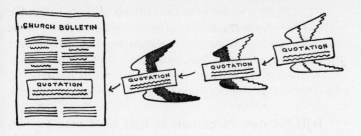

Chapter 25

QUOTATIONS FOR
CHURCH BULLETINS

Church bulletins can be one of the most influential forces of all religious publications. We should realize what an important audience they reach, and make them more than just a program of the services and a record of parish activities. To be more helpful, each bulletin should contain a religious quotation from some well-known person. This continuous testimony for faith in God will inspire the readers and make them realize that they are a part of world-wide fellowship of believers.

Those who work on church bulletins should be ever watchful for religious quotations or statements to use for this purpose. They will find them in newspapers, magazines, and books. The editorials, "Words to Live By," in *This Week* Sunday supplement, are an excellent source. To get this plan started, we give you herewith some excellent quotations for your bulletin:

"I shall need, too, the favor of that Being in whose hands we are, who led our fathers, as Israel of old, from their native land and planted them in a country flowing with all the necessaries and comforts of life; who has covered our infancy with His providence and our riper years with His wisdom and power, and to whose goodness I ask you to join in supplications with me that He will so enlighten the minds of your servants, guide their councils, and prosper their measures that whatsoever they do shall result in your good and shall secure to you the peace, friendship and approbation of all nations."

Thomas Jefferson, 1805, Second Inaugural.

"It is the duty of nations as well as of men to own their dependence upon the overruling power of God; to confess their sins and transgressions in humble sorrow, yet with assured hope that genuine repentance will lead to mercy and pardon; and to recognize the sublime truth, announced in the Holy Scriptures and proved by all history, that those nations only are blessed whose God is the Lord."

Abraham Lincoln, 1863; Preamble of Proclamation Appointing March 30, 1863, a Day of Humiliation, Fasting, and Prayer.

"Whosoever thou art that entereth this church, remember it is the House of God; be reverent, be silent, be worshipful and leave it not without a prayer for thyself, for the minister, and for all who worship with thee."

"Lord, make me an instrument of your peace. Where there is hatred, let me sow love; where there is injury, pardon; where there is doubt, faith; where there is despair, hope; where there is darkness, light; and where there is sadness, joy. O, Divine Master, grant that I may not so much seek to be consoled as to console; to be understood as to understand; to be loved as to love; for it is in giving that we receive; it is in pardoning that we are pardoned; and it is in dying that we are born to eternal life."   *St. Francis of Assisi.*

"Sometimes I pray for inspiration, sometimes for good fortune, sometimes for certain benefits, and so many times in thanksgiving. It helps me when I am feeling dispirited to remember the almost miraculous results which prayers have brought."   *Ann Blyth.*

"A man, no matter how weak, or poor, or ignorant will be exceedingly strong and rich and wise if only he has an idea for which he can die, and therefore for which he can live. Christianity is that idea."
          A Statesman from Lebanon

"One man dozed by a singing kettle. Watt dreamed an engine drawing heavy loads.

"One man dodged a falling apple in the yard. Newton discovered a natural law.

"One man closed his eyes in terror at the lightning. Franklin snared it for his own use.

"One man stumbled against a block of granite. Rodin chipped 'The Thinker' with skilled hands.

"One man passed a Carpenter on the road. Paul lived before the living Christ."   *Charles Emerson*

"I shall pass through this world but once. Any good, therefore, that I can do, or any kindness that I can show to any fellow creature, let me do it now. Let me not defer or neglect it, for I shall not pass this way again."   *Stephen Grillet*

"Have you ever heard of the disease, morbus sabbaticus—peculiar to church membership? Symptoms vary but never interfere with appetites; never last more than twenty-four hours at a time; no physician needed; contagious; always proves fatal in the end to the soul.

"It comes on suddenly every Sunday; no symptoms felt on Saturday night and patient awakens as usual feeling fine; eats hearty breakfast. About nine the attack comes on and lasts till around two. In afternoon patient is much improved. He is able to take a motor ride or go on a picnic. Patient eats hearty supper but the attack comes on again and lasts until about eight. Patient is able to go to work Monday.

"If this disease has troubled members of your family lately, may we suggest that the following exercises may prove useful: a short walk or drive to nearest church and a brief hour spent variously sitting, standing, or kneeling in company of those who successfully resisted the disease!"

Chimes of St. Paul's Cathedral, Buffalo, New York

"If nobody smiled and nobody cheered and nobody
  helped us along,
If each every minute looked after himself and good
  things all went to the strong,
If nobody cared just a little for you and nobody
  thought about me,
And we stood all alone in the battle of life, what a
  dreary old world it would be!"   *Edgar A. Guest*

"Our Creator would never have made such lovely days and have given us the deep hearts to enjoy them, above and beyond all thought, unless we were meant to be immortal."   *Nathaniel Hawthorne*

"Based on the excuses for not attending church here's 'Why I do not attend the movies':
"The manager of the theater never called on me.
"Every time I go they ask me for money.
"I did go a few times, but no one spoke to me. Those who go there aren't very friendly.
"Not all folks live up to the high moral standard of the films.
"I went so much as a child, I've decided I've had all the entertainment I need.
"The performance lasts too long; I can't sit still for an hour and three quarters.
"I don't care for some of the people I see and meet at the theater.
"I don't always agree with what I see and hear.
"I don't think they have very good music at the theater.

"The shows are held in the evenings and that's the only time that I am able to be at home with the family.
The Reverend Grant H. Elford

TEN COMMANDMENTS FOR CHURCHGOERS

"1. Thou shalt recognize that churchgoing is a fine art which demands the best preparations of which thou art capable.

"2. Thou shalt go to church regularly, for a prescription cannot do thee much good nor be effective if taken only once a year.

"3. Thou shalt get in condition for Sunday by refraining from late hours and activities that clash with the will of God during the week, especially on Saturday night.

"4. Thou shalt go to church in a relaxed state of body and mind, for the absence of tension is a primary requisite to successful worship.

"5. Thou shalt remember that worship in church is not a gloomy exercise, therefore go in a spirit of enjoyment, radiant and happy to enjoy thy religion.

"6. Thou shalt sit relaxed in thy pew, for the power of God cannot come to thy personality when thou art rigid and full of tensions.

"7. Thou shalt not bring thy problems to church, for six days are sufficient for thee to think upon thy problems, but the church service giveth thee a supreme opportunity to let peace of God bring thee insight for thy intellectual processes.

"8. Thou shalt not bring ill will to church, for the flow of spiritual power is effectively blocked by harboring a grudge against thy neighbor.

"9. Thou shalt practice the art of spiritual contemplation by the daily use of Scripture reading and prayer so that thou be not a stranger to the God whose Presence thou canst enter in the Sanctuary.

"10. Thou shalt go to church expectantly, for great

things have happened to those who worship in spirit and truth—and the spiritual miracle can happen unto thee according to thy faith."

Benjamin F. Swartz, Christian Herald

HOPE

A Message for Easter

World, O world of muddled men,
Seek the Peace of God again:
In the humble faith that kneels,
In the hallowed Word that heals;
In the courage of a tree,
In the rock's integrity;
In the hill that holds the sky,
The star you pull your heart up by;
In the laughter of a child,
Altogether undefiled;
In the hope that answers doubt,
Love that drives the darkness out . . .
Frantic, frightened, foolish men,
Take God by the hand again.

Joseph Auslander

Friend, there is a welcome in this Church for thee,
Come in and rest, and think, and kneel, and pray,
What men have builded for God's glory see;
Give thanks and so in peace go on thy way.

SUNDAY MORNING PRAYER

A Detroit newspaper recently printed the following prayer:

"Almighty God, as I lie here on this sofa this lovely Sunday morning, surrounded by the Sunday paper and half listening to one of the bog preachers over the radio, it has just come to me that I have lied to thee and to myself. I said I did not feel well enough to go to church. That was not true. I was not ambitious enough. I would have gone to my office had it been Monday morning. I would have played golf had it been Wednesday afternoon. I would have attended my luncheon club had it met this noon. I would have been able to go to a picture show if it had been a Friday night. But it is Sunday morning and Sunday illness covers a multitude of sins. God have mercy on me! I have lied to thee and myself! I was not ill—I am lazy and indifferent!"

A PRAYER FOR PEACE

Keep me quiet, Master,
Patient day by day,
When I would go faster,
Teach me Thy today.

Restless, oft I borrow
From the future care.
Teach me that tomorrow
Shall its burden bear.

From Thy full provision
Daily richly fed,
By Thy clearer vision
Ever safely led.

Let me to my brothers
Turn a face serene,
Sharing thus with others
Peace from the Unseen.
William Adams Brown

SOMETHING MORE

"I will never forget how we sat for hours on a hillside garlanded with cherry trees and fragrant with the bouquet of Alsatian vineyards. The late afternoon sun was falling over the green valley, and Dr. Schweitzer seemed to be listening to the chirping of the blackbirds, the jingling of cow bells, the buzzing of bees, and the laughter of schoolchildren playing at the riverside.

"I had asked him what the ordinary man could do in

his daily life to carry out Dr. Schweitzer's famous principle of 'Reverence for Life' and to help in some way to cure the ills that beset the world. This was his answer:

" 'Just do what you can. It's not enough merely to exist. It's not enough to say, "I'm earning enough to live and to support my family. I do my work well. I'm a good father. I'm a good husband."

" 'That's all very well. *But you must do something more*. Seek always to do some good, somewhere. Every man has to seek in his own way to make his own self more noble and to realize his own true worth.

" 'You must give some time to your fellow man. Even if it's a little thing, do something for those who have need of a man's help, something for which you get no pay but the privilege of doing it. For remember, you don't live in a world all your own. Your brothers are here, too.' "

An interview with Dr. Albert Schweitzer

WHICH POSITION DO YOU OCCUPY IN YOUR CHURCH?

A power or a problem;
An attender or an absentee;
A promoter or a provoker;
A giver or a getter;
A supporter or a worrier;
A friend or a faultfinder;
A helper or a hinderer;
A campaigner or a camper?

The Challenger

Lord, grant us so to desire the things
Which belong to our peace,
That we may accept with quietness
And with confidence the disciplines
Which are their cost. AMEN.

I'M NOT VERY WELL

It is extraordinary how many of our people are quite

well enough to do a number of things during the week. They are seen by the clergy, quite able to get about. On Sunday mornings they are suddenly not well enough to worship God. Well enough to do almost anything but that! This excuse will not stand up under the scrutiny of Almighty God.

I'M TIRED ON SUNDAYS

So is everybody else. You are not so tired but what you can come to church if you so desire. No excuse.

I HAVE TO GET DINNER

So does everybody else. Come at 8 or 9:30 and then get dinner, if you are really serious about being a practicing Christian.

I LIVE A GOOD LIFE, ANYWAY

So do Mohammedans, Jews, Ethical Culturists, and millions of others. The Christian Religion is Christ AND His Church. In the New Testament there is no such thing as a Christian who is not a church man. Nor can there be. "On this rock will I build MY CHURCH," said our Lord. If He took the trouble to build it, it must have been in order that you might be WITH it and IN it and OF it. As a Christian, you are not living a good life, the life expected of you, apart from the church.

St. Peter's, Westchester, New York City

Here are some challenging church axioms from that growing source of unusual bulletin quotations, Christ Church and St. Michael's in Germantown, Pennsylvania.

"Germantown's Liveliest Church"

"Strangers Always Expected"

"Meet Friends, Make Friends in Church"

"God's Lovely Acre"

"Parents Worship While Children Learn"

"If You Have Two Church Jobs, Train Another for One and Turn It Over to Him"

"Too Few Doing Too Much Wreck a Church"

"If There Are Five Parts to a Job Get Five People to Do the Job"

He couldn't speak before a crowd,
  He couldn't teach a class.
But when he came to church,
  He brought the folks "en masse."
He couldn't sing to save his life,
  In public couldn't pray.
But always his old "jalopy" was
  Just crammed on each Lord's day.

And though he could not sing or speak
  Nor teach nor lead in prayer,
He listened well, and had a smile,
  And he was ALWAYS THERE!
With all the others whom he brought,
  Who lived both near and far.
And God's work prospered, for he had
  A CONSECRATED CAR!

                              W. H. Aulenbach

A DIET FOR THE SPIRITUALLY FAT

Upon arising in the morning, try this spiritual fruit juice, "I WILL LIFT UP MINE EYES UNTO THE HILLS OF THE LORD, FROM WHENCE COMETH MY HELP."

At the breakfast table avoid such spiritual fats as, "I didn't sleep well last night!" "Can't you get this breakfast ready on time?" "Wish I didn't have to work." "I can't stand that man Jones." "What a mess the government has made out of the present crisis." Such comments add pounds of weight to your spiritual weight and put too great a burden on the heart—the seat of all emotions.

Try such energy-creating foods as "Thank you, Lord, for another day." "It is such a good world." "It is great to be alive."

Resolve during the day to do three things: 1. Do something beautiful. 2. Remember something beautiful. 3. See something beautiful. The familiar Douglas Molloch's "You Have to Believe" could be memorized word

for word when tempted to worry, be anxious, or hate.
Here it is:

> You have to believe in happiness,
> Or happiness never comes.
> I know that a bird chirps nonetheless,
> When all that he finds is crumbs.
> You have to believe the buds will blow,
> Believe in the grass in the days of snow.
> Ah, that's the reason a bird can sing.
> On his darkest day he believes in Spring.
>
> You have to believe in happiness.
> It isn't an outward thing.
> The Spring never made the song, I guess,
> As much as the song the Spring.
> Aye many a heart could find content,
> If it saw the joy on the road it went.
> The joy ahead when it had to grieve,
> For the joy is there,
> But you have to believe.

PRAYER

ALMIGHTY GOD, from whom all thoughts of truth
and peace proceed; kindle, we pray Thee, in the hearts
of all men the true love of peace, and guide with Thy
strong and peaceful wisdom those who take counsel for
the nations of the earth, that in tranquillity Thy Kingdom may go forward, till the earth shall be filled with
the knowledge of Thy Love; through Jesus Christ our
Lord. Amen.

> Drop thy still dews of quietness,
>   Till all our strivings cease;
> Take from our souls the strain and stress,
> And let our ordered lives confess
>   The beauty of thy peace.

Breathe through the heats of our desire
   Thy coolness and thy balm;
Let sense be dumb, let flesh retire;
Speak through the earthquake, wind, and fire,
   O still, small voice of calm!

                John Greenleaf Whittier

Wouldn't this old world be better,
   If the folks we meet would say:
"I know something good about you,"
   And then treat us just that way!

Wouldn't it be fine and dandy,
   If each handclasp warm and true,
Carried with it this assurance:
   "I know something good about you!"

Wouldn't things here be more pleasant
   If the good that's in us all
Were the only thing about us
   That folks bothered to recall!

Wouldn't life be lots more happy
   If we'd praise the good we see,
For there's such a lot of goodness
   In the worst of you and me!

Wouldn't it be nice to practice
   This fine way of thinking, too—
"You know something good about me,
   I know something good about you!"

                Author Unknown

"The one kind of pride which is wholly damnable is the pride of the man who has something to be proud of. The pride which, proportionately speaking, does not hurt the character is the pride in things which reflect no credit on the person at all. Thus it does a man no harm to be proud of his country, and comparatively little harm to be proud of his remote ancestors. It does him more harm to be proud of having made money, because in that he has a little more reason for pride. It does him more harm still to be proud of what is nobler than money—intellect. And it does him most harm of all to value himself for the most valuable thing on earth—goodness."

G. K. Chesterton

"I believe that faith is the biggest gift any parent can give a child, and it's more valuable than anything money can buy. Build your faith together—by going together to the church of your choice."

Gene Autry

"You cannot go to church and pray and expect to find the road smooth and easy when you come out. Prayer will give you a new outlook, a sense of unity with your fellow men, the courage to stand up straight on your own two feet and fight a good fight . . . it gives you the kind of confidence no lesser force can take away."

Eddie Cantor

"If I could have one wish for America . . . it would be that all of us, a hundred and fifty million strong, might attend our churches regularly and there eternally renew our faith in the qualities which make us men and brothers."

James A. Farley

"In Churches all over the world, I have made friends —people who have no use for pretense, for their faith makes them real, who don't need to escape, for they have the strength to stand fast—people, above all, whom I respect.

"These people gather in church, every Sunday because they find here, each week, fresh strength and peace of mind."

Olveta Culp Hobby

"The parents of America can strike a most effective blow against the forces which contribute to juvenile delinquency, if our mothers and fathers will take their children to Sunday school and church regularly."

J. Edgar Hoover

"John and I honestly feel that even with our strong religious backgrounds, there are still many questions of right and wrong that perplex us. And especially with moral values fluctuating as they are doing in the world today, we want our children to have the guidance and fortitude that only the Church can give them."

Maureen O'Sullivan

"We regularly take Jackie, Jr., to church with us though he's only three. For my wife, Rachel, and I want him to know, as early as possible, the faith that will guide and help him all his life, as it helps and guides us. For to be without the help of the friendly hand of God is something we cannot imagine. I know without His help I could never do my job."

Jackie Robinson

"Whenever I feel tired or discouraged it is my custom to turn my thoughts to God, if possible in a synagogue, if not, wherever I may be. Never yet have I done so without being refreshed and encouraged."

Roger W. Straus

"The value of religion, particularly at this time, is basic, and every effort must be made to strengthen and enhance the place of the Church in the community. In the face of the growing world crisis, we must multiply our strength many times; and religion can be—should be—our greatest source of united, national strength."

Charles E. Wilson

All of the above quotations are from the *Religion in American Life* campaign.

"Happiness for perplexed men came out of the first Christmas, and joy to the world hallowed simple seeking for a place to lodge. We struggle with forces that are huge these days, but the best hope to build an ampler home for man's free spirit still lies in his striving toward the tallest star."

Gabriel S. Hauge

HELPS FOR THE LAYMAN
by Lee Hastings Bristol, Jr.

1. I will pretend each day is the first of my spiritual program, because I am best at the beginning of a campaign.

2. I will use "flash-prayers" frequently throughout the day, because repeated "through-the-day" contact with God can multipy my effectiveness immeasurably.

3. I will try to be honest in my prayers, because only then do they mean anything to me and, consequently, anything to God. If my mind is wandering, I'll tell Him so and ask His help.

4. I will pray about specific problems, because such prayers will mean more to me than overly general prayers.

5. I will make a regular effort to know the Bible better, trying to see the great relevance of Christ's down-to-earth principles to life today.

6. I will try winning others to Christ, not only because it was Christ's command that I do so, but also because faith seems to grow when it is shared.

7. I will try to see the human equation in everything I do, realizing how individuals are affected by every decision I make, every letter I write, and by even the most casual encounter.

8. I will ask myself at the end of the day, as George MacDonald suggests, if I have that day done anything because God said 'Do it' or abstained from doing anything because He said 'Do not do it.'

9. I will try to have a partner in my spiritual program, because "comparing notes" with someone else can

give a program "wings" and appreciably help both of us.

10. I will accept opportunities for service, as Albert Schweitzer suggests, with sober enthusiasm, remembering the many others, willing and able, who are not in a position to do the same.

NOTE: Printed copies of these ten helps, on wallet-size cards, are available at .03 cents each from the Laymen's Movement for a Christian World, 347 Madison Avenue, New York 17, N. Y.

COPY FOR OUTDOOR BULLETINS

The hundreds or thousands of people who pass a church daily represent a valuable source of visitors and members. Therefore your church should have an outside bulletin board in front of the building. This board should carry the following essential information:

    a. Name of church
    b. Name of minister
    c. Name of sexton
    d Hours of Sunday services
    e. Subject of sermon

During the week this bulletin board should show some thought to inspire the passer-by. An excellent source of these thoughts is the *Pulpit Digest* magazine of Great Neck, Long Island, New York. Here are some typical basic themes and epigrams found in this magazine's monthly feature article entitled "Bulletin Board Barbs."

"Churchgoing Families Are Happier Families."

"Only the brave can live by faith."

"Prey less on your neighbor; pray more on your knees."

"The narrow way will straighten out twisted lives."

"Anger is slow poisoning; forgiveness is the antidote."

"Grudge-bearing is nerve-wearing."

"Crime can be stopped in the high chair better than in the electric chair."

"Kindness is never in vain."

"Peace, it's wonderful; but also expensive."

"You cannot make Christ the King of your life until you abdicate."

"Big heads offer ample room for small minds to rattle."

"Preserve your face value by having your 'no's' in the right place."

"Christ is the Lord of humanity, not a word for profanity."

Chapter 26

BETTER CHRISTIANS
THROUGH MORE
RELIGIOUS READING

"Thou shalt worship thy God
With all thy heart and all thy mind"
AND WITH THINE EYES, DAILY

As FAR AS SACRED READING is concerned, how many of us are "7th-Day Christians"?

How many of us realize we literally "turn off" our religious reading six days a week?

And which ones of us are doing anything specific to correct a situation that is either warping our lives or preventing the fullest development of our fullest Christian lives?

No, we won't dare ask our readers to answer these three questions with a showing of the hands. I'm afraid it would be too discouraging.

Yet in other walks of life, we know that continued reading is the one and only, the surest way to success, achievement, or to happiness. Take the baseball player or baseball fan. He reads about his favorite sport *daily* in the newspaper. The women who sew well, continually develop their skill with the needle, by reading the women's service magazines, the pattern books, and the fashion pages of the newspapers. The successful businessman reads his trade papers, business news magazines, special reports, and never fails to catch the business news in his favorite local or national newspaper.

So it goes with men, women, children. Yes, even the

kids keep up on what interests them by devouring comic books like gum drops. Yet with us Christians too many of us read nothing religious from Monday through Saturday. Is it because we don't want to? No! Is it because we don't care to learn more about Christ's way of life? No! Is it because we fail to realize the benefits of worshiping God daily through our eyes? No!

The plain truth in most cases is just that we never developed the habit of *daily religious reading*. Or in the press of modern life, we lost that inspirational reading habit. So let's highlight some simple easy steps which will help us to develop or redevelop the practice of daily religious reading. Because it is God's own word, we will start with Bible reading. How badly we need help here. This was reaffirmed by a survey made for Thomas Nelson & Sons, publishers of the forthcoming *Revised Standard Version of the Bible*. The study covered almost 3,000 families in the consumer panel of Batten, Barton, Durstine, & Osborn. Each family was asked about its possession and reading of the Holy Bible. The discouraging findings on Bible reading are found in the chapter on "Women's Club Projects" on page 115.

This can be corrected by all of us—clergy, lay workers, and ordinary churchgoers.

Here are just *six* suggestions or ideas for us to follow:

1. Ask your clergyman to give a talk every other month on how to read the Bible.

2. Clergymen should assign a specific Bible reading to the congregation each Sunday, for during-the-week reading. In doing this, they should explain why they assign the passage and what benefits its reading will bring members of the congregation.

3. The church office can run off mimeographed copies of the excellent Bible reading suggestions developed by the Forward Movement of Cincinnati, Ohio, the Gideons Bible Society, or the American Bible Society. These worth-while organizations have worked out a helpful list of specific readings. They cover specific purposes or sit-

uations that exist in every family's life. On a certain Sunday have the ushers pass out mimeographed copies of these suggestions.

Right now some readers may be saying how do we know these directions stimulate Bible reading? This is shown by check-ups on their use. Surveys by the Gideons have proved that the above-mentioned list actually gets travelers to read the Bibles the Gideons place in the hotel rooms. As these suggestions get busy hard-boiled businessmen and traveling salesmen to read the Bible during the week, they are certain to increase daily Bible reading among your congregation. (Note: It's unfortunate that these instructions aren't placed on the *outside front cover* of the Gideon Bibles instead of being on the inside, hidden cover. Located on the outside cover they would automatically increase reading because they would be seen immediately without the seer having to open the Good Book.)

4. A new, interesting and complete set of instructions for Bible reading is found in "Biblegraph." This easy-to-use dial was developed by the Brotherhood Press of Greene Farms, Connecticut. By simply turning the dial you can find specific Bible readings to help you solve the thirty-six most troublesome questions of modern everyday life. Best of all, the "Biblegraph" gives suggestions for readings on each problem for a full seven days of the week. Costing only $1.00 each, this useful device is a fine article to be sold at all church bazaars, or it could be sold by church organizations wishing to raise money. Some churches keep a supply at the back of the church with the other booklets on sale.

5. The writer has been praying to the good Lord for some time that the publishers who put out new Bibles would include an *adequate* section on how to read the Bible for inspiration, comfort, and happiness. The writer is convinced that those publishers who sincerely want to stimulate Bible reading, as well as Bible buying,

will have a chapter or more on suggested readings for all age groups, at the *front* of the Book.

When you purchase a car, an electric appliance, or even a chest of silverware, the manufacturers help you get more and better use out of the purchase by enclosing a book on the best way to use the product. Isn't it even more essential for every Bible publisher to do likewise? For reading the Bible during the week is far more important than using any appliance during the week.

6. Another sure way to increase your Bible reading is to place your Bible on the night table right next your bed. Then develop the habit of reading it for five to ten minutes just before you fall asleep. There is no finer way to go to rest, than to go with God's holy word in your mind and soul. If you're reading this chapter in the home, why not put your Bible on the night table *right now*. Then you're all set to carry out this suggestion *tonight*.

7. Put a pocket-size copy of the Sermon on the Mount or the New Testament in your briefcase. Then plan to read it daily to and from work.

8. Before or after the evening meal, when the family is all together and not rushing different places, read from the Bible for five or ten minutes.

9. Buy one of the several books on how to read the Bible. Some of these are as follow:

10. When a new Bible comes out get a copy for yourself and children. Its newness provides a fresh approach to Christ's way of life. For example, the new *Revised Standard Version of the Bible* was published by Thomas Nelson & Company in September, 1952. Many clergymen are increasing the Bible reading of their congregations by recommending that members get the *Revised Standard Version of the Bible* and enjoy its new way of telling the old old story.

HOW DAILY DEVOTIONALS HELP

Another excellent way to worship God "with all our eyes" is to use one of the several pocket-size daily devotional publications. These provide a Bible quotation, meditation, and prayer for every day in the week. One of the most universally used is *The Upper Room,* published in Nashville, Tennessee. This interfaith publication comes out every other month and goes to more than 3,000,000 subscribers. Thousands of copies go to the men in the armed forces through distribution by army chaplains.

The cost of this daily inspiration is very small. On an annual subscription basis you can get *The Upper Room* for only 10¢ a copy. Ten or more copies are 5¢ each. *The Forward Day by Day* is 10¢ per copy, and 6¢ per copy for ten or more copies. The annual cost of the daily meditation pamphlets of your denomination is equally low. Many churches have a special committee for securing annual subscriptions from the congregations. Other churches order a certain quantity of each issue, place them on a table in the vestibule, and have a plate or a box in which people pay for their copies. Some far-sighted churches subscribe (out of the over-all budget) for the entire congregation and have the *Forward* or *The Upper Room* sent to every member's home. They have found that this automatic mailing deepens the spiritual life of the members. Daily reading of a devotional publication turns a "7th-Day Christian" into a "Deeper Daily Christian." It makes the reader get more out of church services and attend church more frequently. So for the "treasure-type reader" who says his church budget can't afford to spend much less than $2 per year for each member to receive a daily inspirational booklet, here's a challenging thought. The resulting increased Sunday attendance from the *Forward* or *Upper Room* readers quickly pays for the cost of the small yearly subscription.

Yet no matter which way your church handles the purchase and distribution of daily devotionals, it really owes it to the congregation to make them available— and to recommend their use. The cost is a widow's mite, compared to the deep and constant inspiration they assure.

GROWTH THROUGH RELIGIOUS BOOKS

We can all grow in grace and Christian strength *faster* if we add religious books to our reading habits. And nowadays we have a wide selection of interesting and well-written books with a Christian backgound. They are being purchased and read more today than ever before. Yes, the return to religion is real in books. Join it and you'll enjoy your spare time more.

Just ask your bookstore or library to recommend some religious books to you. You'll be surprised at the number which are available. The American Booksellers' Association includes 350 titles in its basic religious book list. They are in constant demand. (Note: If you know the owner of a bookstore or library urge him to put in a window of religious books three or four times a year.)

Plan to read at least one religious book per month. Then pass it on, or recommend it to your fellow Christians.

Some churches stimulate and expand the reading of religious books by having a church-book-lending table in their vestibules. As they go out, the members can pick up books, sign their names in a little notebook, together with the title. When the book is returned, the member crosses off his or her name in the notebook. Copies of religious magazines can be added to this lending table.

To make this booksharing more successful it would be well to put one of the following signs on the wall over the table.

SHARE THE INSPIRATION
OF RELIGIOUS BOOKS

———

LEND OR BORROW ONE
EVERY OTHER SUNDAY

HOW LONG SINCE
YOU'VE READ
A RELIGIOUS BOOK?

———————

TAKE ONE HOME
THIS SUNDAY!

Massachusetts Rector Adds Parish Library with Appeal

The Reverend Albert J. Chafe of Lynn, Massachusetts, has come up with a new "tool" that may serve as an "entering wedge into the problem of dark places and blank stares."

It's a parish library.

It was built in the rear of a small apse in St. Stephen's Church. Above the books a large display was posted. To catch the eye, the shelves were painted a Chinese red. "We want people to know the books are there. Bright colors help a lot," Mr. Chafe said.

Books include many of those suggested by the National Council, and church magazines. The library is kept up to date. "Use modern books," the Rev. Chafe warned. "Don't let people put over on you their grandfather's old Bible."

To introduce the idea a series of oral book reviews was given. "This, we think, is the best type of book review because it does not substitute a reading of the book for the people but sends them to the feast by stimulating their appetite," Mr. Chafe declared.

Every clergyman can stimulate his congregation to read more religious books by recommending a new title every Sunday. It should be listed in the bulletin or included in the verbal announcements.

Some clergymen prefer to recommend four or five books, all in one list, each month. But whether he gives his recommendations weekly or monthly, the minister owes it to his members to guide and stimulate their reading of religious books.

The clergyman should also urge his listeners to read the religious sections in the weekly magazines: *Time, Newsweek, Pathfinder, Quick.* If the local papers have church papers, daily prayers, or daily devotionals, these should also be called to the attention of the congregation. And when a magazine like *The Saturday Evening Post, Ladies' Home Journal, American Magazine, Life, Cosmopolitan,* or *Coronet* publishes a fine religious story (as these publications have many times) the minister should, in his anouncements, urge its reading.

All of us should not only read the religious articles in the magazines but then we should not "sit on our hands." We should applaud those far-sighted religious-minded editors and publishers who bring us an ever increasing wealth of religious writings. Yes, we should write them a letter or postcard of appreciation. If we grateful Christians would take that one definite step of writing magazine editors, the space given to religious editorial matter would show a 25 to 50 percent increase in just one year.

The writer prays that you will make it a practice of doing this letter writing from now on. And ask your fellow Christian to do likewise.

In your plans for increasing the religious reading don't forget the boys and girls in your congregation. Two books which are popular with youth are *The Story of the Bible* and the new book *The Bible Story for Boys and Girls.* Both were written by Dr. Walter Russell Bowie, former Dean of New York's Union Theological Seminary. Your local bookstore can recommend other religious books which will interest your junior congregation.

It is now more essential that every church and every Christian family take an interest in the reading habit of youth. That is because the insidious growth of some types of 25¢ and 50¢ cardboard-covered books is poisoning the minds of boys and girls. These lurid books on sex and crime are now sold in many stores which have a big teen-age business. The semi-nude sex-stimulating or murderous covers offer terrific temptation to boys and girls with loose change in their pockets.

As Christians we should start a drive against these bad books. We should ask the store keepers to stop exposing our churches' children to this bad influence. You'll find that many of the proprietors are Christians who will gladly cooperate when the evils are explained to them.

In closing, the writer prays that you will urge the establishment of a "Religious Reading Committee" in your church. Then this committee can work out the details of carrying out the ideas discussed in this article. In fact, a wide-awake committee will develop additional ways of "worshiping God with all our eyes—*daily*."

Chapter 27

ACT IT OUT[1]

By Walter H. Rockenstein

A RECENT SURVEY of drama among some 241 churches of six major Protestant denominations, conducted by the writer, revealed these trends in religious playmaking today:

1. An increase in the use of plays in the church school.
2. An increase in the use of biblical plays and a decrease in the production of non-religious plays.
3. An increase in plays given at Christmas and Easter.
4. An increase in productions at week night services.

These facts may be encouraging to those interested in putting on a church play. However, don't allow the idea that you have to do a play "in full production" to frustrate your hopes of putting religion "on the boards." In theatrical production new and stimulating things are happening which many churches have taken up.

You might try doing a play "in walking rehearsal." You need no scenery, no stage, and a minimum of costuming. Let the actors go over their lines sufficiently to be thoroughly familiar with them, but carry the play through with script in hand. A walking rehearsal offers the opportunity of doing plays which, because of difficult production problems, might not otherwise receive consideration.

Take for example a one-act play such as *By-line for St. Luke* by Ronald Lorenzen. The setting is a modern newspaper office. A narrator can set the scene by reading the stage directions and all necessary stage business not acted out by the players. A minimum of equipment will

[1] Reprinted with permission of *Presbyterian Life*.

suffice: two tables with typewriters and possibly a telephone. The actors use scripts and walk through the action. Emphasis falls upon the lines and the basic dramatic action. Let the audience grasp all of the imaginative details through the narrator's reading.

Three-act plays may also be done in this manner. Victor Wolfson's *Excursion* or Marc Connelly's *Green Pastures* both pose difficulties for any church group attempting a full-blown production. Presented in walking rehearsal the task is simplified. In the former play an arrangement of chairs to form an imaginative ship's deck gives the illusion desired. In the latter, chairs and tables and other minor properties can create the needed effect for the scenes portrayed. One outstanding item of costuming will suffice to define a character in any play. With the proper description of the setting, the creative thought of the audience will do the rest.

Youth fellowship groups, young adult clubs, men's gatherings, choirs, and missionary societies should find a real appeal in this method of dramatizing. It lends itself to the development of group discussion, arising out of the issues posed by the play. The fact is, you need not do a whole play. Certain scenes will offer adequate meat for discussion. One caution: if the public is admitted to a walking rehearsal, even free of charge, a royalty fee must be paid.

Another type of presentation receiving wide attention today is "playing in the round," also known as "intimate playing." The players are surrounded by the audience. The stage may be no more than an open space in the midst of those present. In many college and little theater productions, audiences frequently stop the dialogue to talk with the players or argue with one of them if the actor is portraying a controversial character.

At the Religious Drama Workshop in 1950 at Green Lake, Wisconsin, a panel discussion was built around two scenes from T. S. Eliot's *The Cocktail Party*, played in the round. The panel participants were cast among those waiting to see the psychiatrist in the play; they were able to speak before and after the scenes, as if in the play and yet as part of the surrounding audience. When they took up the argument following the final scene from the play, they deliberately put the psychiatrist on the spot by pinning him down with questions before he could leave the "stage."

Still another movement gaining momentum in the drama field is "group playmaking." A number of people sit down together over a period of weeks or months and create a play. Fifteen people is about the right number. Everybody throws in his bit. This technique creates that community of spirit and labor which is an integral part of dramatic work and of church work. When the writing is completed, production is simplified because everyone knows the play by having contributed thoughts, dialogue, and action to it.

Suppose a men's group in the church or a missionary society wants to tackle a social problem within the community and give it publicity. Juvenile delinquency is an example. A group of ten to fifteen persons is asked to read and gather all available information regarding the problem, both nationally and locally. They will be called together by a person with dramatic talent and leadership ability. This group will discuss what is involved in juvenile delinquency. They will turn to the Christian solution of the problem.

Gradually the group will move into the task of putting the basic concepts and facts in terms of deeds done by characters on a stage. These dramatic incidents will come out of real life. One person might suggest using as dialogue some sentences he heard at a Rotary meeting last week. Someone else will be able to delineate a characteristic he has seen within some individual, thus personifying an aspect of the problem.

A story line will be developed—that is, a basic plot. Each person will then contribute thoughts, facts, dialogue, and action to the development of this plot so as to achieve a climax and get across the point of the story. Finally one person with literary skill will be chosen to write out the play in final form to give it the continuity of one mind. After revision, through suggestions of the group, it will be ready for production.

Akin to group playmaking is "creative dramatics for children." Here the alert teacher may find a splendid chance to apply the learning-by-doing process. Children love to act, to "be somebody." By allowing them to act out Bible stories and by setting up imaginary scenes of real-life problems, the teacher may help the pupils learn new truths about the Bible and about living with one another. The lesson will really come alive, and it will stick. Moreover, teachers gain insight into children's lives and homes never before realized because of the things youngsters say and do under the spell of acting.

The Bible lends itself beautifully to creative dramatics for children. Take the story of Joseph sold into Egypt by his brothers as an illustration. The teacher may read the story through to the children, or if they are junior or senior high students, they can read it aloud themselves. Then the teacher announces they will play-act it. Each person is asked what part he would like to take. Then he is asked to think how that character in the story would react to all that goes on. Let the children imagine what each character would say and do. After a second reading, when the children listen and think through their parts, the group will begin to act out the story.

To help the children face everyday problems, the teacher may make up incomplete stories of real-life events happening to youngsters. A group of boys, for instance, playing baseball in a vacant lot, knocks a ball through the window of a house. The teacher asks the class to "play" what happened after the ball went through the window. Relevant ethical issues can be presented to boys and girls in this way, and the problem of working out the solution rests upon their shoulders.

Finally, there has come in our own day a revival of a very old form of religious drama—"the chancel play." This type of production makes use of the natural setting of the sanctuary for the staging of the play. Installations of divided chancels in many, many churches across the nation have lent impetus to the effort to capture the beauty of the worship center for staging. We are thus returned to the early Middle Ages, when men saw fit to dramatize the Christian faith before the high altar of God as a fitting form of worship and instruction.

Though Phillip Osgood has a number of excellent chancel productions suggested in his books, which have been in print many years, it took T. S. Eliot and Christopher Fry in England to bring back the chancel play. Eliot's *Murder in the Cathedral* makes most effective use of the center of worship as the place of dramatic action, having been prepared for presentation at Canterbury Cathedral. *A Sleep of Prisoners* by Christopher Fry, also written for the Canterbury festival, has now been played by the original British cast in churches all across America; and, having seen it, church people have gained a new sense of the majesty of poetic drama set in the midst of the very elements of worship. It is the story of four prisoners of war billeted in the chancel of a church, whose dream sequences in poetry and action intermingle their own hectic experiences with those of the biblical characters which their surroundings recall to the subconscious mind.

Fry's play caused such a restoration of interest in this form of drama in Evanston, Illinois, that the Theater Department of Northwestern University's School of Speech revived a custom which had not been followed for several years: the preparation and presentation of a medieval church play at the Advent or Lenten season. The particular play used in five of the Evanston churches during the Lenten season of 1952 was the Brohm *Abraham and Isaac*.

Perhaps a good drama for you to begin with in producing chancel plays would be one of the Nativity plays found in *The Harvard Dramatic Club Miracle Plays*, edited by D. F. Robinson. Or, one of those from Osgood's *Old-Time Church Drama Adapted* might prove more exciting for some church-drama groups.

These many innovations of modern theatrical production which we have described remind us that the churches have at their fingertips a new and yet very old medium for Christian inspiration, education, and evangelism. For, as Fred Eastman has said, "Religious drama is that kind of play or pageant which . . . sends the audience away exalted in spirit and with a deeper insight into the struggle of men's souls and with a closer sense of fellowship with God and man."

Now, if you would like to get at some plays for production or for personal reading, a list follows of noteworthy pieces to be found in your public library or to be ordered from the publishers as indicated.

ONE-ACT PLAYS
From Samuel French, 25 West 45th St., N. Y. 19, N. Y.:

Dust of the Road, by K. S. Goodman (50 cents). Easter. Dramatization of the old legend of Judas returning to earth once a year to plead with some soul tempted to betray friendship.

He Came Seeing, by M. P. Hamlin (40 cents). Biblical-general. Dramatization of the loyalty to Jesus of the youth born blind.

A King Shall Reign, by M. Wefer (40 cents). Christmas. A mother, whose child has been a victim of Herod's slaughter of the innocents, bitterly nurses her sorrow until Joseph and Mary visit her briefly on their flight to Egypt.

American Saint of Democracy, by Fred Eastman (40 cents). Brotherhood. An incident in the life of John Woolman and his struggle to bring freedom to slaves.

The Separatist, by M. P. Hamlin (40 cents). Thanksgiving; Pilgrims. A brief drama about William Brewster, leader of the Pilgrims.

Spreading the News, by Lady Gregory (50 cents). A delightful satire about gossipy neighbors.

From Walter H. Baker Co., 569 Boylston St., Boston 16, Mass., or 829 15th St., Denver 2, Colo.:

A Child Is Born, by S. V. Benet (75 cents). Christmas. Half-hour poetic modern drama of the Nativity, originally written for the radio program "Cavalcade of America."

Peace I Give Unto You, by D. C. Wilson (40 cents). Christmas. Two sons, serving in opposing armies, meet at their home on the border on Christmas Eve.

The Coming of Christ, by J. Masefield ($1.75). Christmas. A poetic production, difficult, designed for the chancel.

The Lowly King, by M. B. Shannon (40 cents). Palm Sunday. An imaginary episode in a Jewish home—friends of Jesus—just before his triumphal entry into Jerusalem.

The Two Thieves, by E. W. Bates (40 cents). Good Friday; Post-Easter. A beautiful ten-minute fantasy about the thieves on Calvary with Christ.

Were You There When They Crucified My Lord?, by Willis and Ellsworth (40 cents). Good Friday. A fine dramatic service for Eastertime; in which Peter, Judas, Caiaphas, Pilate, Simon of Cyrene, the Centurion, and John the Beloved each tells of his part in the Crucifixion.

From Dramatic Publishing Co., 1706 S. Prairie Ave., Chicago, Ill.:

Uncle Jimmy Versus Christmas, by Fred Eastman (40 cents). Christmas. With humor and fantasy this play tells how a Recording Angel changed the mind of Uncle Jimmy, who had been soured on Christmas.

By-line for St. Luke, by R. Lorenzen (50 cents). Christmas. A modern play about a newspaper reporter who types out the Christmas story from St. Luke, as if it had happened today against the background of the housing shortage.

From Abingdon-Cokesbury Press, 810 Broadway, Nashville, Tenn.:

The Christmas Pageant of the Holy Grail, by W. R. Bowie (25 cents). The story of King Arthur and his knights searching for the Holy Grail at Christmas-time.

THREE-ACT PLAYS

Winterset, by M. Anderson. Samuel French, Inc. A poignant drama in blank verse about people who might have been connected with the Sacco-Vanzetti trial.

R.U.R., by J. and K. Capek. French. A fantasy about a group of scientists who create robots so lifelike that they finally turn on the men and destroy them.

Family Portrait, by Coffee and Cowan. French. In modern speech, a story built around the family of Jesus, and what his brothers and sisters thought of him.

Our Town, by Thornton Wilder. French. Beautiful and moving because of its simplicity, this play is about ordinary people living in a little New England town just after the turn of the century.

The Silver Cord, by S. Howard. French. A possessive mother, struggling to hold her older son even at the price of breaking up his marriage, finally loses the battle but envelops her younger son in her possessiveness.

Abe Lincoln in Illinois, by R. Sherwood. Scribner's. Incidents in the life of the emancipator which reveal the molding of his character before he left Springfield for the White House.

The Green Pastures, by M. Connelly. Farrar and Rinehart. A delightful presentation of an old Southern Negro's concept of the Bible, God and man, and the coming of Christ.

Death of a Salesman, by A. Miller. Harcourt, Brace & Co. The pathetic struggle of a modern man trying to find a meaning to life for himself and his sons in our commercialized, mechanistic society.

Saint Joan, by G. B. Shaw, Dodd, Mead. The late

G. B. S.'s dramatized version of the immortal story of Joan of Arc.

Street Scene, by E. Rice. French. Episodes in the lives of New York's tenement dwellers. A play fast becoming an American classic of stark realism.

Chapter 28

EXTRA IDEAS

THE GLORIOUS PART about putting this book together is the use of the proven ideas sent in by clergymen and layworkers in all faiths—all denominations. They alone have made this book possible. We thank God for His help. May He bless all of you for your cooperation.

Just as in the case of our first book, *Building Up Your Congregation*, there are many good ideas for adding power to your church which do not fall logically into any of the regular chapters. So we put them all together in this last chapter. We pray you will find several ideas or plans which can be used in your church or synagogue. If you do not consider some of them "big ideas," remember that both morale and perfection consist of a number of little things done well. Likewise these little helps can produce big results.

1. Clergymen and devout church workers have long complained that business has overcommercialized our great religious feast days and celebrations. The comparison between the ways business and the Church observe Christmas and Easter would not be so unfavorable if we churchgoers would do more new and different things to call attention to these great religious festivals. One example is the Easter Parade held in the East Harlem section of New York City. No, it wasn't a showing of fashions and fabrics. This was a true Easter parade of

about two hundred devout worshipers, led by a crucifer with a simple wooden cross. It terminated in a recently cleared, open lot. There an Easter Service was conducted before a flower-bedecked altar, led by the ministers of the East Harlem Protestant Parish.

Churches which want to put up an impressive Easter Story panorama, 19½ feet wide by 7 feet high, on the church grounds, should write to William H. Dietz, 10 South Wabash, Chicago, Illinois. This reminds all passers-by of the Resurrection promise.

2. Here is how one growing church keeps track of its lost or missing members:

A simple, inexpensive way to "Save Church Members from Being Lost" is being used at Grace Church, Utica. At the back of the church there is a bulletin board which lists the names and addresses of the people who belong to the church, but whom the minister and leading lay people have not seen in church for quite a while. Then, as the regular churchgoers file in and out after services on Sunday, they have to pass the board and can see the names on it. It is their opportunity to volunteer to look up a certain family and invite them to church the next Sunday, or to report why they have been absent. By telling the minister's lay aide, standing beside him as he is shaking hands at the church door, the volunteer lay family can let their church know that they will try to save another family from being lost.

In Toledo, Ohio, "Go to Church" signs have been placed on benches at bus stops and other locations, as part of a local drive to increase church attendance. And there is choice aplenty, not far from where a new city bus bench is located along Collingwood Boulevard. Queen of the Holy Rosary Cathedral, Collingwood Temple (Jewish), and seven Protestant churches line the boulevard. Among them, and within a little more than a block of this bus stop, are the Collingwood Presbyterian, Washington Congregational, St. Mark's

Episcopal, First Unitarian, and Second Church of Christ, Scientist, Churches.

3. Has your church many golfers or sailors? If it has, here is a proved way to increase their attendance at Sunday services:

Few young people and summer visitors ever attended Sunday services at a little Long Island summer chapel. The minister, a 6 foot 2 former New England boxing champion, was puzzled by this as he began his first summer services. Soon he learned through interviews with the young people with whom his wife and he sailed or played golf on Sunday afternoons, that they never came to church on Sundays because it took away half their day. For the many who worked on Saturdays, it was obvious that they did not want to ruin their only day off which they could use for sailing and golfing. The young clergyman knew that he also liked to sail and play golf, but he wanted these good people to join their God first at the Altar each Sunday. Therefore, he moved the ten o'clock service up to 8 A.M.

His congregation grew from 12 to 65 and stayed there. He asked one of his young parishioners why, and he said, "Formerly I had to get dressed up for church, wait until 10 A.M. for church, and finally, at 11:30, I was in my sailing clothes and ready for the water. Now I can come to church in my sailing clothes. Our minister said, God primarily wanted us to worship. God didn't care what we wore as long as we were dressed. Then the minister served doughnuts and milk in the small parish room. After that all would go sailing together. The minister joined right with us, and that was good for all. No one had to go home again as the members were encouraged to bring their golf bags and sailing gear and leave them in the church vestibule."

A nationally known business leader, who for years has served as a leader of the Long Island Church, said in the 1930's, "That young clergyman will be a Bishop some day and lead thousands of people into the Church." His prophecy came true in 1950.

4. We like the introduction to that interesting, helpful booklet "101 Things a Layman Can Do" (10 cents a copy, from Presiding Bishop's Committee on Laymen's Work, 281 Fourth Avenue, New York 10, N. Y.).

It inspires as follows:

GREETING . . .

Have you ever moved to a new community, knowing no one, feeling utterly lonely? It can be a dark day, indeed. Or, have you ever been stranded in a strange community on a week-end? There is nothing very uplifting about the four walls of a hotel room or a table for one in the corner of the hotel dining room. Or again, remember some of those homesick week-ends at school or college when a touch of home life would have lifted the pall of loneliness?

People are having just such experiences constantly. They crave fellowship. And they should be able to find it in the Christian Church, if anywhere. Sometimes they do. Sometimes they don't. Whether they find friendly people or not in a church may be the basis upon which they will judge the Church. A friendly church attracts. A cold church drives people away.

One way to carry out this Christian advice is to be on the alert for new families moving into your neighborhood. Do not wait to make a formal call, drop in right away, even when the moving van is still disgorging its precious load. After you introduce yourself, ask if you can run any errands for the newcomers, or answer any questions about local sources of food, drugs, schools, etc. Better still, take the new family something to eat and drink. A plate of sandwiches and a bottle of milk shows your Christian friendliness—it does it better than just a verbal expression of interest.

After you have given the new neighbors information about the neighborhood—shopping, medical care, schools—*then* say, "If you have no other plans for church *this Sunday* we would like to have you worship with us at (name of church)." Should you find that the new people are of another faith or denomination tell them where the nearest church of the choice is located. And then be a helpful Christian by phoning the clergyman of their church, telling him about his new prospective parishioners. When we cooperate in this way with other churches and synagogues in our city, we prove the Brotherhood of Man.

Some influential churches organize this greeting of new neighbors on a basis of assigning neighborhoods and sections of the city to appointed lay greeters. This is a sure way to make certain that the calls are made as soon as possible. It is the way to help the clergy in this vital activity.

Experience shows that moving to a new city or neighborhood is one of the chief causes why people get out of the habit of attending church regularly. Let's all prevent this from happening by greeting new families just as soon as possible. Remember every unloading moving van is an opportunity for you to show your "love for your neighbor."

5. Here is how a minister extends the right hand of fellowship to newcomers:

When Mr. and Mrs. Milton M. Schneiderman and their son Laurence, 6, arrived in Saginaw, Michigan, from Arlington, Virginia, their furniture was hardly in place before the Rev. Howard B. Spaan, pastor of the Community Christian Reformed Church, rang the Schneidermans' doorbell. He welcomed them to Saginaw on behalf of the city's seventy-seven Protestant, Anglican, Orthodox, and Jewish houses of worship.

Spaan gave the newcomers a church directory, got in return a card stating their religious preference. He sent the card to Rabbi Harry A. Cohen of Saginaw's Temple B'nai Israel, who took over from there. The call on the Schneidermans was part of a new and unique interfaith visitation program sponsored by the Saginaw Ministerial Association. Twenty-four denominations and two local synagogues are cooperating.

Saginaw has been divided into eleven zones with a pastor assigned to each. The Ministerial Association receives a list of all newcomers from the local credit bureau, passes the information to the appropriate zone clergyman, who makes the first call. Dr. Don A. Morris, pastor of Saginaw's First Methodist Church, and Ministerial Association president, says ten to fifteen families a week are guided to the church or synagogue of their choosing.

Surprised and pleased, new Saginawan Schneiderman summed up his impression of the program in words which Dr. Morris said were typical:

"Sometimes you put off finding out about a new church in the bustle of moving. This makes it easier for us to join in the community."

6. *Pathfinder* magazine ran the following news story about an Oklahoma minister who finds sermons in comic strips and trains children to discover religion in funnies.

"When Charlie Shedd was a kid, he often sneaked out behind the barn and read the comics there—to escape the wrath of his strict minister father.

"By last week, memories of those juvenile escapades had led to a novel idea in young people's religious training: the 'God in the Funnies' program of the thriving First Presbyterian Church of Ponca City, Oklahoma.

"Now thirty-four, and the First Presbyterian's pastor, Charlie Shedd periodically sets aside one of his regular Sunday young peoples' vesper services for a discussion of who found what signs of God's work in the funnies the previous week.

"Sample discoveries:

"Rusty Manning, eleven, was impressed by a sequence in 'Terry and the Pirates' showing soldiers radioing for help. 'They just barely got their signal through,' he reported, 'so God must have been with them.'

". . . Nancy Ramsey, seventeen, noted that L'il Abner fell in love with ugly Nancy O., 'which proves that real beauty is on the inside, and everybody is beautiful to someone.'

". . . One small girl, an 'Orphan Annie' fan, pointed out that 'if Gramp had told God instead of Bancroft he'd committed a crime, he would have gotten it off his chest earlier.' "

7. The First Presbyterian Church of Sebring, Florida, opens its 11 o'clock Service with chimes. This musical opening provides an ideal background for the start of one's worship.

8. The Western Massachusetts churches have a special service the Fourth Sunday in January, which other congregations could adopt with real benefit. It is for the reaffirmation of marriage vows. Standing before God in the churches, husbands and wives repeat in unison:

"I have often failed to do my part in our life together," and chorused, in separate groups:

"I have taken you . . . to have and to hold, for better, for worse, for richer, for poorer, in sickness and in health, to love and to cherish, till death do us part, according to God's Holy Ordinance, and today I gladly reaffirm that vow."

In many churches, as in St. Luke's, Springfield, the couples married the shortest and the longest time stood before the priest at the altar, while others repeated the vows in pews.

9. The Reverend Charles Allen of Christ's Church, Atlanta, Georgia, writes a Sunday newspaper column for the *Journal Constitution*. To find out if people were reading his column he offered to send a color reproduction of Christ, billfold size, to anyone who wrote in. More than ten thousand requests came in for nearly

60,000 copies of the picture. This is an idea which can be adopted by religious broadcasters, other religious columnists, and churches whose services are on the air.

10. A growing number of churches celebrate Family Week. This is built around the basic idea that "Faith is a Family Affair." Family Week develops rich dividends for the coming years. Here are a few simple things which help form a program for Family Week:

a. Attend church as a family, and sit together in a "family pew."

b. Read helpful literature on the family, provided by the Church and its organizations.

c. Listen to the good regular family radio programs and to special broadcasts, like "The Upper Room Family Week Series."

d. Develop some family recreation or hobby.

e. Establish daily family devotions, using a devotional guide.

All these help carry out the following truth: "The Family That Prays Together Stays Together." This is a slogan or truism that deserves a frequent place in your church bulletins.

11. Bass Hawkins of Lake Ronkonkoma, New York, likes to carry God's message to the hundreds of thousands who read the fine Saturday church page of the *New York Herald Tribune*; so he runs, and pays for, two column by five inch ads on this page. Each features a list of Bible readings which have to do with world events.

Mr. P. L. Norton is another devout Christian who is using a large share of his income to bring the Sermon on the Mount to the readers of newspapers. His full-page ad, "Can You Spare 9 Minutes to Read a Message 19 Centuries Old?" has appeared in the *New York Herald Tribune* and Washington newspapers. His Sermon on the Mount Project offers free reprints of the page and free mats which other Christians can use to publish the Sermon in their local newspapers. All you have to do is write Mr. P. L. Norton, Room 706, at 1790 Broadway, New York 19, N. Y. He sums up his objective for this project as follows:

"WE BELIEVE there is no problem of any kind, concerning the individual or family, the community or commonwealth, or of any 'ism,' or among the nations, which would not yield to the intelligence, the courage, and the faith of free human beings, *if those who seek solution* approach the problem in the spirit of the Sermon on the Mount."

We who try to follow Christ's divine guidance in *The Sermon on the Mount* are glad to know that this secret of inspired living is now recorded. Yes, the record is available for use in the home, school, hospital, prison, and other institutions. Write H. C. Burke at 306 Southway, Baltimore 18, Maryland, for complete details.

12. Stamp collector Arthur R. Von Wertheim decided to collect stamps which illustrated the Lord's Prayer. The April 17, 1952, issue of the *New York Herald Tribune* illustrated his collection. Each stamp depicts a section of the prayer as follows:

(Portuguese stamp) "Our Father who are in heaven . . . (Vatican City) Hallowed be thy name . . . (French Somaliland) Thy kingdom come . . . (Brazil) Thy will be done, on earth as it is in heaven . . . (Romania) Give us this day our daily bread . . . (Croatia) And forgive us our debts, as we forgive our debtors . . . (Monaco) And lead us not into temptation . . . (France) But deliver us from evil . . . (Austria) For thine is the kingdom and the power, and the glory, for ever and ever. Amen."

A stamp collector in your church could develop an interesting exhibit for your Sunday school and vestibule by duplicating Mr. Von Wertheim's collection:

Portuguese—2½ Reis
Vatican City—3 lire MCMXLIV
French Somaliland—10c postes

Cote Française Des Somalis
Brazil—3.00 of 1934—Franchieta
Romania—3700-5300 Posta Lei
Croatia—16 + 8 kn. N.D.Hrvatska
Monaco—50
France—Postes 2,50.50
Austria—IS 40

13. Jack Garvin, of New York City, has an excellent idea for increasing church attendance. He points out that around 10 percent of the public is hard of hearing. Too many of these people dig up all kinds of excuses to play "hookey" from church services. They figure that if they cannot hear the sermon why bother going to church. One way to solve this problem is to install hearing aids in some pews. Then advertise this helpful service in your newspaper announcement and outside bulletin board. Another solution is for the clergyman to urge in his weekly announcement that the congregation tell their hard-of-hearing friends—their absentee friends—that they can enjoy the sermon, the same as everyone, by wearing a hearing aid in church.

14. If you have a dance instructor in your congregation she might be interested in duplicating the interesting project staged by the Oneonta Congregational Church of South Pasadena, California. This group took literally that part of the 149th Psalm which reads: "Let them praise His name in the dance." They interpreted the Lord's Prayer in a liturgical dance. This is quite proper, as dancing was probably one of man's earliest ways of worshiping his maker.

15. Herbert N. Morford, Superintendent of the Hospital of the Good Shepherd in Syracuse, New York, is a Christian who takes his religion into his everyday life. He helped re-establish the Huntington Chapel in this fine hospital.

Just after a patient is admitted he or she receives an

attractive card inviting the use of the chapel. This invitation reads:

"The Chapel, open every hour of the day and night, is for the hospital family, workers, patients, and friends. A place of spiritual refreshment, beautiful, intimate, restful, the Chapel seems to say:

" 'Whoever will, may enter here, of any creed or no creed. Whatever your care, your problems, your sorrow, your hope, yield your best self, make of me what you will, I am at your service.'

"In silence, in thought, in prayer, in search for fresh light and faith, in a few moments of reading, or of music, we gain courage and hope: we go out refreshed, strong, serene, confident."

This is a Christian service which should be available in more hospitals, for there we are often very close to our Maker.

16. The Reverend Harold J. Quigley has used most unusual methods for his unusual success in tripling the membership and attendance at the Central Presbyterian Church in Haverstraw, New York. The objective was to dramatize the pastor's search for a congregation—the search for *real* churchgoing Protestants among the passive stay-at-home Christians.

Pastor Quigley took a kerosene lantern in hand and went looking through the homes, stores, and banks of this conservative community of 8,000. He told people he was searching for the lost membership and vigor of his faith; not exactly lost, perhaps, but definitely mislaid.

He took a picture of a typical small Sunday congregation . . . enlarged the picture . . . and lettered over the empty pews: "Where are the others?" This homemade sign was publicly shown in the midtown window of the People's Bank. Because of no money for advertising, he made over large hair-tonic posters to carry challenges to the stay-at-homes and backsliders. To increase Sunday school attendance and interest youth in

Central Presbyterian, the Reverend Mr. Quigley turned the church's little basement into a roller-skating rink. Realizing that Rockland County is the home of many famous artists, this progressive pastor organized a three-day art exhibit at the church.

Yes, one would say that all of the Reverend Mr. Quigley's method's are dramatic. A few might say they are too "undignified." But these same people might say that some of Christ's miracles were also "undignified." We do know that conservative Haverstraw said they liked this search for a congregation. They said it with increased membership and attendance.

17. Rabbi Jacob K. Shankman has a service at Temple Israel in New Rochele, New York, once a month, called "Family Worship." Parents bring their children with them to worship. The service is abbreviated (easier on the squirmers) and the sermon is directed to the children, but planned to be of equal interest to the parents.

18. In another part of this book we have referred to the advantages of sending out blotters to members. The Reverend Frederick R. Ludwig, Pastor of St. Paul's Evangelical Lutheran Church, Postville, Iowa, uses these long-lived reminders in a most logical way. He sends them out a Lenten blotter containing the subjects of the sermons at his mid-week services. We like his basic theme (or slogan) used on his printed literature: "You Are Always Welcome At St. Paul's." We all applaud the Reverend Mr. Ludwig's use of the truism: "Christians Attend Church, Others Find Excuses."

19. Here is an ideal way to assimilate new members: When a new member joins the Men's Club of First Presbyterian Church, Bay City, Michigan, he is given a card listing all phases of the group's program. He chooses the activities in which he is interested and for which he is fitted before some enthusiast tries to influ-

ence him in the wrong direction. Youth groups and women's societies use this device in other cities.

This plan is used by Christ Church in Tacoma, Washington, with equal effectiveness.

20. Has your church considered this growing means of getting more people into a church service?

Last summer many churches experimented with outdoor Sunday services in drive-in theaters and parking areas. All can hear and see while seated comfortably in their cars. Some have called early services 'picnic specials' because they give picnickers opportunity to worship in their picnic outfits at an early hour.

Among churches which reported drawing up to four times average church attendance last year were St. John's Lutheran in Buffalo, Zion's Lutheran in Utica, New York, and First Christian, Virginia, Illinois. All plan to repeat. Early preparations and publicity are recommended.

The Reverend George A. Rustad, State Director of Arizona's Seventh-Day Adventists, and Elder Lawrence E. Davidson have both pioneered in drive-in church services.

A typical drive-in service begins at 8 P.M. after a half-hour prelude of organ music. Elder Davidson opens with a story for the children, then runs off a thirty-minute religious movie, or a "family problem" movie with such titles as *Love Thy Neighbor* and *Honor Thy Family*. After a brief prayer, Davidson (or a guest speaker) begins the half-hour illustrated sermon. Since May, both drive-ins have been drawing steady crowds. (Top attendance so far, for a visiting minister: 2,000.) Says Adventist Rustad: "We live in a new age, and the churches should keep moving with the times."

21. The influences that are desirous of destroying Christianity are hard at work at home and abroad. The challenge must be answered. The Heifer Program was originated so that important groups of Christians, *the*

farmers, could help in the fight without leaving their farms.

Each farmer is asked to raise a heifer; the church will buy the calf and deliver it or will buy the calf direct from the farmer.

The farmer raises the calf until it is ready for breeding; then the Church breeds and sells the heifer.

If a farmer prefers to raise a steer, we will be grateful. If he prefers to donate a calf or older animal, we welcome and are thankful for his cooperation.

Most farmers take care of vaccination themselves in the course of having their own stock treated. The Laymen's Committee, however, agree to do this if the farmer doesn't wish to have it done.

If a farmer for any reason moves, loses his farm, retires, or any unforeseen contingency arises, the Laymen's Committee will remove the animal from his farm upon notice.

A directory of cooperating farmers is maintained at the Bishop's office. The Bishop will visit each farmer and give his personal thanks.

All placements should be reported to the undersigned so ear tags may be arranged for.

> Carl O. Hoffman, *Chairman*
> Bishop's Committee of
> Episcopal Laymen.
> "Broadfields"
> Chestertown, Maryland.

If you have a rural church, this project is one which is well worth considering.

22. The Community Synagogue of Rye, New York, believes in worshiping God outdoors during the summertime. Rabbi Samuel H. Gord places the Ark between the outside pillars at the front of the building. The service is held on the lawn in front of the Ark. There's a church down in Greenwich Village that holds Sunday night services outside. Worshiping out of doors is a change of pace that congregations appreciate and

that has many precedents in the Bible. Has your church the grounds and the chairs to do this?

23. Minnesota has made at least two experiments in using drive-in theaters for church services.

Reverend Morris C. Robinson of Grace Presbyterian Church, Minneapolis, writes the City Church:

"Our Church sponsored a drive-in church service at an outdoor theater some eight miles from the city and just a few miles from Lake Minnetonka, which is a heavily populated summer resort area. We had guest ministers for three of the services and I conducted the other four. Since we expected the congregation to be made up of people of all denominations, we felt the offering should go to the work of Cooperative Christianity and we are sending checks very soon to the local Church Federation, Federal, and World Councils of Churches.

"Our attendance varied from a high of two hundred cars to a low of seventy cars. Our ushers estimated that the number of people per car averaged three and one-half to four. We had many expressions of appreciation from people who, because of a physical handicap, could not attend regular services. One elderly woman who attended every service had not been able to attend church for five years. A woman who suffered a stroke two years previously and who had been unable to be in crowds since, attended every service. Many young parents attended with children in arms or children of younger years who played on the theater's playground equipment.

Our session is planning on services again next year, the first Sunday in July through the first Sunday in September."

Advance reports that on July 2 Dr. Howard A. Vernon of the Congregational Church of Brainerd, where the local theaters had carried a trailer for several weeks announcing the "Church of the Open Air," found himself facing a congregation of 639 at a drive-in theater six miles north of town. Some of these were local towns-people, old folks, and shut-ins, and vacationers. Later attendance passed the one thousand mark. "Come as you are and remain in your car," ran the invitation—and they did, "in cool, comfortable clothing." Local newsmen pointed out that this sort of service seems to throw the members of a family unit into much closer relationship to each other. When some youngsters "acted up" a bit in the back, others were not annoyed. A church previously closed for the summer discovered new family-as-a-unit values along with large attendance.

Is this a modern equivalent of the old camp meeting? Could your church organize and conduct an open-air church? It would bring Christ's message to those who might otherwise be unable to reach or be reached frequently.

24. *The Gold In Your Backyard.*

"What we need is a talent committee in every parish that can explore and find out what people can do or what they would like to do."

These words are from a fine pamphlet written by Bertram Parker, entitled, "I Am a Layman." (Available at 3 cents each or $2.25 per hundred from Presiding Bishop's Committee on Laymen's Work, 281 Fourth Avenue, New York 10, New York.)

Check your congregation thoroughly; list the people with skills and talents. Ask them, invite them, and use them. They will be pleased and the church will prosper.

Form a committee and call the members "Talent Scouts for Christ." They could send out and process a questionnaire to be tied in with announcements from the pulpit and in the church bulletins as to its intent.

25. *The Flying Deacon.*

Looking for a new and profitable idea for your church fair or bazaar? Here is one that was fun for all, those who worked in it and those who patronized it.

At a meeting of the college group in a Syracuse, New

York, church, their role in a forthcoming "fair" was brought up for discussion. With sighs and moans the young people said that the fair was the same every year and was a matter of Christian duty rather than a looked-forward-to event. Why couldn't it be both? The ministers called for ideas, new and workable ones.

A young man who was a professional photographer suggested that a photo booth with different backdrops could be worked out. The big thing was to deliver pictures on the spot and at reasonable prices.

Young college art students volunteered to paint several comic backdrops, and amateur carpenters offered to construct the booth. A retired wooden horse from an old carousel was offered; others agreed to repaint and mount it. There would also be plain backdrops for "glamour" pictures. A polaroid Land camera was made available. This camera produces a 3 x 5 finished print sixty seconds after the picture is taken. Film and flashbulbs were obtained at cost helping to make low charge possible. By this time, every member of the young peoples group had a job to do and the group as a whole accepted other duties at the fair as well.

The photo booth was advertised in the church bulletins and programs. Displays were put up in the vestibule and Sunday school hallways. Parishioners were urged to bring entire families and friends to have their "picture took."

The booth was the hit of the fair and drew the largest crowds. Young cowboys had their pictures taken on the wooden horse, and the comic backdrops caused much amusement. A favorite picture was to have the church elders seated on the small horse with their coat tails trailing behind, hence "the flying deacon." It was fun, good public relations, because everyone, young and old, entered into the spirit of it. And the group raised more money than ever before.

26. *An Effective Hospital Ministry*

We all remember that well-known statement of

Christ's in St. Matthew's gospel, "I was sick and ye visited me, in prison and ye came unto me." Yet how few of us ever take on a planned Christian project of visiting people in hospitals or prisons. An inspiring example of service to hospitalized people is the dynamic program developed by the Los Angeles Baptist City Mission Society. Here is how it is described by Arnold S. Boal, Assistant to the Executive Secretary, in an issue of *The City Church Bulletin*.

"Many newcomers to the Los Angeles area apparently packed their church membership in mothballs when they moved West. In an effort to minister to the patients in the Los Angeles County General Hospital, one of the largest in the world, the Baptist City Society found that eighty percent of the patients who registered Baptist preference had no local church relationship. Consequently, a chaplaincy was instituted to provide double service. Patients are visited and aided while in the hospital. Then, in cooperation with local churches, there is a well-organized follow-up of dismissed patients.

"When patients are contacted in the hospital, they are provided with spiritual help, counsel, literature, and other services. Worship is conducted in the hospital auditorium, to which patients are brought in beds, wheelchairs, etc. Young people from churches in the area are enlisted to bring the patients from their wards to the auditorium. Those who cannot be moved are able to listen to the broadcast of the service by using earphones provided by the chaplain.

"A friendly call in the home following an experience in the hospital has produced amazing results in spiritual restoration. One staff member provided by the Woman's American Baptist Home Mission Society gives full time to this follow-up ministry and has the assistance of volunteer visitors in almost every Baptist church in the area.

"The magnitude of the work is indicated by the fact that over 1,600 Baptist-preference patients pass through the hospital each month. Scores of these patients are finding the joy of new or restored Christian fellowship in local churches.

"Baptists, with a burning sense of mission and foresight which anticipated this phenomenal growth, formed the Los Angeles Baptist City Mission Society in 1906. The Society has been the missionary arm of existing churches and the fostering agency for scores of new churches during the intervening years. For the past fifteen years Dr. Ralph L. Mayberry has been Executive Secretary of the Society and is largely responsible for its present program, which is outstanding in scope and effectiveness."

Most of our churches should have some organized program for calling on the sick at neighborhood or city hospitals. In addition to leaving inspirational literature, it might be possible to loan some of the patients a radio so they could listen to early-morning and Sunday religious programs. Some families in most churches have spare portable radios which can be fixed up at low cost for hospital loaning. In summertime, members with gardens could supply flowers for the "hospital visitors" to give out on their calls. A bouquet is one of the ways to remind us all of God's love for us, and the beautiful world of nature which he provides for his children.

Calling on Prisons

One group of inspired Christians who remember to call on hospitals *and* prisons is the Gideons. These businessmen have given hundreds of thousands of Bibles to hospitals and prisons. In the case of the prisons, their work just begins with the distribution of Bibles. The Gideons arrange and conduct religious services for the prisoners. As a result, hundreds who were lost in hopelessness are finding new hope in Christ. The prisoners join in singing their favorite hymn from the Gideon hymnal. Hundreds openly profess their faith . . . ask to be forgiven . . . and rededicate their lives to the Saviour. Some of the hardest and toughest prisoners have responded to these services arranged for both male and female institutions. God bless the Gideons! May they be given more strength and means to give out more Bibles . . . more hymnals. And may we fellow Christian follow the Gideons in calling on the unfortunate people in prisons. If we cannot arrange or participate in religious services, we can do some of the following:

a. Read the Bible to individuals or to groups of prisoners.

b. Pray with and for prisoners.

c. Take magazines and books to prisoners and to prison libraries.

d. Take flowers to prisoners, or for use on prison dining tables.

e. Help ex-inmates get work on release from prisons. This is vital to the rehabilitation of ex-prisoners.

f. Send Christmas cards to five or ten prisoners.

g. Arrange to send prisoners birthday greeting cards on their natal day.

h. Give games to prisons, such as playing cards, chess, checkers, backgammon.

i. Shut-ins or bed-ridden Christians can write letters to individual prisoners.

In working with prisoners and prisons, an excellent guide for us all is the experienced advice of Lt. General John C. H. Lee of York, Pennsylvania. He is now executive secretary of the Brotherhood of St. Andrew. From years of helping men in prisons, he can give you the right procedure. Why not write him this week?

Calling on prisoners is a most needed project for men's clubs, and Women's Auxiliaries. Let us all plan our spare-time activities, so that it can be said of us, "I was in prison and ye came to me."

27. *A Pastor's Anniversary Plus Wedding Anniversaries*

Special events are always newsworthy and create a great deal of interest. The Reverend Morris Robinson, pastor of the Grace Presbyterian Church, Minneapolis, Minnesota, observed his twentieth anniversary of serv-

ce in the parish by underlining the place of the Church
n the sanctity of the home. As part of the anniversary
program, he read the marriage service, as fifty-five
couples whom he had married renewed their vows. This
drew the interest of the press, his congregation, and his
community.

In a time of many divorces he dramatically showed
that "Churchgoing Families Are Happier Families."

28. Don't drive to church with an empty rear seat.
If you do, your conscience should bother you unless you
have made an honest effort to take some friend or neighbor with you. To say, "Why don't you go to church?"
is good. To say, "I hope to see you in church," is better.
To do the right thing and say, "I'll pick you up on
Sunday morning," is best. Try it!

29. Ushering. This is a man's job, sometimes done
continuously by a few; often distributed among the
manpower of a parish. Training is essential. An usher
must have a broader concept of his task than merely
showing people to their seats. Friendliness (refuting the
charge that we are God's frozen people), cordiality,
graciousness, and a host of other Christian qualities
make up a good usher. Noting the absent, procuring
the names and addresses of newcomers, meeting emergencies with confidence and dignity, all this and more
is expected of a good usher. And don't forget that others
also must be trained to do the job.

30. In this book you will find a chapter on "Activities
for Active Old-Timers." Naturally few readers under
the glorious sixties will read it, except those who have
to do with organizing their projects. Yet eventually the
present members of the men's and women's clubs will
find themselves so-called old-timers. Even the young
adults end up in this useful group.

So the $64 question is: "What are we doing now to
prepare our lives to be interesting, fun, and useful,

when thanks to geriatrics we will cross the sixty-yea line?" Will we have useful hobbies we can carry o which will help others? Will we have developed talent which will then be perfected so we can entertain, and or instruct younger members of the church? How ca you answer those questions?

Ada Simpson Sherwood gives the answer in a recen issue of *Christian Herald*. She tells how active old-timer accumulate interests, hobbies and skills through th years, just like a savings account. Then, when they ar 60-plussers, these helpful older people can do one o more of the following:

Teach others to knit and mend.

Teach others to make minor repairs to the church redecorate, etc.

Make patchwork quilts or comforters.

Take Sunday school classes on nature trips.

Teach kids wood carving with jack knives.

Show the young people how to make pictures.

Keep the church grounds and garden in good shape.

Right now is the time for us younger people to tak up and develop hobbies which will help us live wit ourselves and help others in the autumn of life.

31. Mrs. Nell H. Snyder writes us about the succes of the Young Married Couples' Sunday school at he Methodist Church in New York City. Although ther is a wide range in ages, their tastes are congenial as t sacred music, recreation and open-minded discussions Good speakers of different religious faiths help keep up the good attendance. This group plans a year ahead for guest speakers and projects.

32. The Reverend Frederick R. Ludwig, pastor of St. Paul's Lutheran Church, follows the proved method of increasing church attendance by announcing, *in printed matter*, the subject for *a series of sermons*; yet he doesn't stop there. He gets out handy cards (3"x6") which tie up the services with a "Church Loyalty

Pledge for Loyalty Month." The paragraph before the sermon series reads:

"I appreciate my Church, the Message it seeks to bring, and the Christ it desires to serve. I will help to give testimony to the community of my love for the Church by attending, God willing, the following services at St. Paul's."

This series leads up to Loyalty Sunday. This is explained below the service series listing, as follows:

"The Annual Every-Member Visitation for greater loyalty, for good will, and for our immediate financial objectives will be conducted throughout the congregation by the men of St. Paul's Sunday afternoon, November 30."

At the bottom is a place for the recipient to sign his or her name. Then comes this challenge:

Signed ....

"The best excuse for absence from church is not as good as actual attendance. Attendance may save your soul but it is not likely that the excuse will. Place your signed card on the offering plate or hand it to the ushers Sunday."

33. Gracie Pugh, the illustrator for this book, was asked to draw a "before and after" illustration for a canvass letter to be used by her church in Mamaroneck, New York. The following drawings speak for themselves, even without including the contents of this successful mailing.

He passed on the other side!

He came across!

These are two attention-getting, moral-proving drawings which you may want to use in one of your next letters or mailings. You can trace them on your multigraph sheet or have a local engraver make a cut of them. Remember you can make the same *handy* local use of Gracie Pugh's other illustrations in this book. It isn't necessary to write for permission. Gracie Pugh, the other collaborators, and the author want you to use the material in this book in every possible way. This is a book for stimulating action. It is to be used, not just read. So use anything and everything you want for your church. But magazines and newspapers must contact Farrar, Straus and Young, 101 Fifth Avenue, New York, N. Y., about any use of this copyright material.

Dear reader, you may get a little confused and upset reading all about the hundreds of ways to add power and people to your church. Don't let that bother you. Any conscientious church worker is, at times, overwhelmed with the many things to do, and with the urgent need for carrying on the good work. Just to visualize this great need for extending God's work we quote from a news story in the *New York Herald Tribune*: "A new church is needed somewhere in the United States every nine hours to care for the nation's increasing population." This challenging statistic was given to the delegates to the Evangelical Lutheran Church Convention. So, dear reader, "be strong and of good courage," and be sure to read the chapter on getting the best results from this book starting on page xxiii.

34. This past June I was attending a baccalaureate service of a junior college with my good friend and fellow churchgoer, Charles Hahn. It took place in a well-known, successful church. The weather was "melting" to put it mildly, and not one fan in the church. After suffering through the service and getting outside my friend asked these logical questions: "Why is it that churches turn their backs on most forms of air con-

ditioning when they know that they have proved their ability to increase "attendance" at business, theaters, restaurants, etc? And why is it so many churches have uncomfortable seats and show no effort to tell visitors where a rest room is to be found?"

I couldn't answer my friend because lack of funds is not the full answer to these matters of good public relations. Most churches cannot afford expensive air-conditioning equipment. Yet many could get window air-conditioning units like those made so popular by many manufacturers. And most houses of worship can at least put in fans. We should not forget that cool, comfortable pews are likely to have *more people* in them, during the summer, and cool worshipers can be more worshipful. Yes, I know that comfort shouldn't be any determining factor in going to church in hot weather. Yet people are still basically people, even on Sunday, and successful merchants are educating them to expect some form of air conditioning and other comfort facilities. It's another proved way to avoid that "summer slump" in attendance.

35. Just before this book was finally closed for any more editorial material, we learned of a new group providing a badly needed service which can be duplicated by any faith or denomination. This was a small group of advertising men being organized to help individual churches prepare the printed matter for the annual church canvass or for a special appeal. Other objectives were: to help congregations, committees, and boards use material available through headquarters *more effectively*, to be of assistance to those preparing headquarters material, and to maintain active, up-to-date files of printed material used by various churches. This is such a sound plan. The authors hope it will work out and be adopted by others. There are plenty of sales and advertising men in every denomination to man the groups.

36. You, who are looking for new ways of raising money, should read *Lifetime Living* magazine. According to Ray D. Buras of the Wertheim Advertising Associates, nearly every issue contains a money-raising idea which can be adapted to church work.

37. The other day a prominent and successful minister in Kentucky told me how much he missed the usual companionship of a man his age. It seems most clergymen naturally attend a lot of meetings where women and children predominate. So why not ask your parson or rabbi on your next fishing trip or golf date? If you don't fish or play golf, have him over to dinner (with wife) twice a year. You'll both get a great deal out of it.

38. How many churches recognize the birth of babies? Does your church send the proud parents a card? If not, you may want to adopt the excellent one used by Covenant-Central Presbyterian Church in Williamsport, Pennsylvania.

> *Our congratulations to you on the arrival of a new child in your family. To rear a child is both an opportunity and a responsibility, with which your church is ready to help you.*
>
> *Attend the church of your choice; take advantage of the program offered there for your whole family. If you have no church affiliation in Williamsport, you and your family are invited to attend Covenant-Central, to acquaint yourselves with its program, and to make it your church home.*

39. To restore the church and religion to its rightful place of importance, the Reverend Russell J. Olson, pastor of St. Mark's English Evangelical Lutheran Church of Chicago, starts with the children. He has developed special services which deepen the child's religious feelings and build churchmanship for their future leadership.

In the children's services, the Reverend Mr. Olson teaches an appreciation of their church, the symbolism of the altar and the stained glass windows, etc. Mimeographed outlines of these windows are run off for the children to color and keep after the explanation has been given. Slide films show religious pictures which are used as subjects for sermonettes. Miniature reproductions with text are mounted in the child's book.

This children's program includes junior sermons in adult church services, special worship services for children in Lent and Advent, participation of children in prayers and responses, offering envelopes and encouragement of tithing.

40. Just before this book went to press a friend of mine asked me: "Why are most church bulletins printed in black? Why cannot churches use live, attractive colors which attract attention and invite readership? Why don't more churches increase the interest in their bulletins by printing them in dark blue, green, or brown? And at Eastertime, or once a month, why not use the Church's own color, purple?"

Perhaps the only answer is that this use of color costs a little more money to print the bulletin. And there are still some church board members who do not realize that it is worth far more than the few extra dollars to obtain a far greater readership of the bulletins.

41. Another friend of mine takes his glasses off in church. This gives everything an out-of-this-world aura, or those undefined outlines which can lift some minds away from the details of everyday life.

42. Of course your church doesn't have a "summer slump" in attendance. Yet if you know of some congregation which sags badly in hot weather, tell them about Dr. Harold M. Mallett of the First Presbyterian Church in Hutchinson, Kansas. He has specialized in activities which increase summer attendance and avoid a "summer slump." Here is how he describes them:

"With the coming of hot weather, the vacation period and the general slack in active community interests, churches experience a noticeable decline in attendance, interest, contributions and service during the months of June, July, and August. For that reason fall is a little slow in picking up because the people have gotten out of the habit. May I offer the following suggestions as to how this slump may be prevented from ever occurring:

"In the first place, I believe it is well not even to mention the word summer slump or in any way suggest the negative possibilities that people will lose interest. After five years of attempts in this direction I have found that slogans like "Watch the summer slump" only call attention to the fact that summer is here and that a slump is somewhat anticipated.

"Secondly, many churches that publish a folder, paper, or bulletin stop its publication some time in June. This is the poorest psychology because it means that the church staff and the minister themselves are entering into a summer slump and that the congregation will take the hint from them. Moreover, it prevents the people from being informed and inspired as they are during the other nine months of the year. In our church we publish our *First Church Chimes* the year round; although in the summer the material is somewhat lighter and there is less to announce than at other times. However, in the year-round publication of *The Chimes*, we indicate that we do not expect to let up our effort for the Kingdom.

"In the third place, there are such splendid opportunities for special services. It has been the custom of

First Presbyterian Church for a number of years to announce these special services over the radio, in the newspapers, and through our church publication, as well as from the pulpit, well in advance. This may be done without any particular effort. The following is a sample arrangement of services during the summer.

"First Sunday in June, usually Pentecost—a time to emphasize the place of the Holy Spirit in the doctrine, worship, and life of the Church. A special sermon on the Holy Spirit or the Holy Trinity, plus outstanding music, together with publicity concerning the service.

"Second Sunday in June is generally Children's Day —a time for the children's or youth choirs to sing and for the minister to deliver a sermon especially for children but announced "for all children four to ninety-four." One year we had a small boutonniere of daisies or some cut flowers from the garden to give each child present. Parents were urged to come with their children.

"The third Sunday in June, usually Father's Day. We urge families to come and sit with their fathers and we give boutonnieres to the fathers who do come. The Minister of Music arranges for a men's chorus for that Sunday instead of the usual choir, and the sermon is on a subject of particular interest, such as "To Busy Men in a Busy Time" or "A Man's Highest Good." Attendance at this service has generally been very strong.

"The fourth Sunday in June. Since June is a month for many weddings, we have had the practice now for five years of observing "Annual Marriage Sunday." For this service the altar is decorated as though there was to be a wedding, the music by the organist and the choir is wedding music, although we take care to avoid the traditional "Here Comes the Bride" theme. This gives us opportunity to use the splendid hymns that are in most of our hymnals, especially upon the subject of marriage. The sermon that Sunday is generally on a subject such as 'Your Key to Married Happiness' or 'The Art of Marriage.' This service is generally of a

unique nature, but we try to avoid any suggestion of
ballyhoo or cheapness.

"The First Sunday in July—generally mid-summer
Communion with an emphasis on the flowers and
beauty and an appropriate message.

"Second, third, and fourth Sundays in July—generally a series of three sermons on Bible subjects, such as
'Great Psalms of the Bible,' 'The Gardens of the Bible,'
'Questions Jesus Asked.' We generally announce that,
if there is sufficient request, printed copies of these
sermons will be available.

"For the month of August, in a previous parish, we
followed the custom of having laymen from the congregation take turns in conducting the worship service.
This was a unique experience because it gave the people an opportunity to hear some of their own men
giving interesting interpretations on the subjects of religion and the Bible. One year we had a lawyer one
Sunday, a doctor another, a director of the State Agri-
cultural Experimental Station another, and a young
salesmen for the fourth. We gave these sermons wide
publicity and announced the subjects in advance. The
attendance held up well.

"In my present parish, the associate minister announces a series of special sermons and these are announced in advance and encouragement given to solicit
the interest of the people.

"The sum-total impression is that we have a summer
in which the attendance has greatly increased without
our saying anything about how many people do not
come or do come. We simply keep up our publicity and
our sense of novelty so that there is as much interest kin-
dled as possible. In my first parish when I followed this
program, the attendance went from an average of about
125 per Sunday, through the summer, to more than 275
average per Sunday. In my present parish, where I have
just come, this type of program for the summer has
shown an increase of an average Sunday attendance for

1951 of around 275 to a little more than an average of 360 per Sunday this year thus far."

Congratulations on this sound planning, Dr. Mallett. We are sure that other churches can adopt and benefit from your summer attendance methods.

43. *A Back-to-Church Campaign Idea*

If you have something good and you wish to make it available to all, you must let people know about it. What finer thing is available to men than religion and the comfort and happiness it can bring? Good advertising should be used by all churches to let people know where they are and what they have to offer.

The Reverend Harold J. Quigley, pastor of Central Presbyterian Church in Haverstraw, New York, built up the attendance at Sunday worship services from seventy-five to two hundred fifty with a back-to-church campaign. He set up an advertising program that included an art exhibit, featuring local artists; a skating rink in the church basement for young people; a booth with a phonograph that played hymns to passers-by in the street; and by personal appearance. He let people know about his church and where it was and the time of services. Old-time members and new ones now fill the pews on Sunday. His church is growing and many are added to the service of the Lord.

Perhaps some women in the parish collect buttons. Did you know this is the third-largest hobby in America? Only stamp and coin collecting precede it in popularity. An exhibit would bring many to your church, afford an opportunity for newspaper stories, and give your parishioner a chance to serve her church through her hobby.

A surprising number of people are amateur artists and photographers and are always interested in displaying their works and viewing the works of others. You will attract housewives, doctors, mechanics, and others by exhibits of this type. Many an unchurched individual who comes to see the paintings will see the church for the first time and decide to attend services.

Plan a back-to-church campaign that will feature exhibits and other events of general interest, advertise it well, and use good salesmanship. This will enable you to show, as can be done in many ways, that the church is not merely a building but a living entity composed of humans who seek God in their everyday living and gather together to worship Him on Sunday.

44. Practical Community Relations for Your Church

Ministers and their families should have a deep and personal understanding of the problems people face when moving from one community to another. The youngsters are uprooted from familiar surroundings and chums; the entire family must go through a trying period of acclimatization. What do you do to welcome new residents in your community?

Many church councils and ministerial associations use the services of Welcome Wagon, Inc. to greet new neighbors. A trained and gracious hostess visits them with gifts from local merchants and with information about their new community. Schools, libraries, and churches are located for them and religious preference data in turn is collected for follow-up by the indicated denominations. The service is paid for by merchants and there is no charge for the churches. For information write to Welcome Wagon, 2 Park Avenue, New York 16, N. Y.

While walking one day, the Reverend Howard E. Mumma, of the Broad Street Methodist Church in Columbus, Ohio, made an observation, reflected on what he saw, and came up with a good idea. He noticed how business women clustered about their places of business during noontime. Gaining the support of ten firms near his church, he started a weekly luncheon fellowship club, prepared and served by the church's Women's Society of Christian Service. The price is sixty cents and a twenty-five minute program follows.

This is a good idea and is a practical implementation of religious principles. The women are provided with a pleasant change and the minister has an extra two hundred people a week to tell of His message.

Take a stroll through your community and make a check list as to whether or not your church can provide a needed function. Is there delinquency about? Boys will be big shots, as noted by James Farley, and seek to express their individuality. City life does not always provide an opportunity. Enter into a conspiracy with these budding men; you provide the idea and let them provide the responsibility. Within a few blocks of your church, in any direction, there may be a need to be met with a soul-satisfying and soul-saving solution. How are your community relations?

45. The tape recorder can be put to many uses, all of them highly practical public-relations aids within the church and without. They can be used to record trustee meetings, choir rehearsals, sermons, sermonettes, ceremonies, special services, guest speakers, and activities such as church conventions that only a few could attend. The Reverend J. Wesly Prince, of the Plymouth-Union Congregational Church in Providence, Rhode Island, records services for the ill and aged who are unable to attend. A layman, Oscar Lemke, of the Kingsley Methodist Church in Milwaukee, has a regular "circuit" of calls for the aged and ill church members with tape recordings of previous Sunday services. Wedding ceremonies can be taped to be replayed in later years. Radio programs can be taped in their entirety and repeated and edited till you get just what you want. With a tape recorder and a little ingenuity the minister has a valuable public-relations tool at his disposal that adds many arrows to his bow and can figuratively place him in several places at the same time. An "assistant to the pastor" that can cost $200 or less and is inexpensive to operate.

46. Successful companies conduct field trips for stock-holders, suppliers, employees' families, and newcomers. Colleges and schools also sponsor trips. That's all because people learn faster and get deeper impressions by seeing things and projections in action; in their natural setting, instead of just on paper. That's why we were encouraged to learn of Dr. Clifford Morehouse's (of Morehouse & Gorham) plan for religious field trips in New York City. There are many local and regional religious groups which can arrange field trips to visit missions, church hospitals, and homes, jails, camps, etc. This is the best way to develop sincere interest, constructive help, and adequate support.

The Church Club of New York recently conducted an open house for visitors passing through New York City on their way to the General Convention. Dr. Clifford Morehouse, President, organized a trip to include a visit to St. Barnabas' House, temporary shelter for children; the Seamen's Church Institution; the General Theological Seminary; and the Cathedral of Saint John the Divine. Giving the visitors a chance to see two church institutions working among persons in need, a school teaching future clergy, and ending the day's trip with inspection and worship at a centrally located house of worship, the New York Church Club covered all transportation and food charges for $3.00 a person. This reasonable charge made it possible for many visitors to participate who would not otherwise have done so. The Club President thought that these were the very people who would obtain the most benefit from such a field trip.

47. Down in Dallas, Texas, the Reverend Boyd E. DeVore developed a simple yet effective visitation campaign which nearly every church can adopt successfully. It sells the church services without asking for money. The latter usually follows the former automatically. Read how the Reverend Mr. DeVore describes his pro-

gram for the Wesley Methodist Church. These fine people certainly cooperated.

"As a new wrinkle on church-wide visitation we mimeographed a five-page folder on colored paper (with a very attractive drawing of our church at the top and with the first page $8\frac{1}{2}$ x 9 and the next $8\frac{1}{2}$ x $9\frac{1}{2}$, then $8\frac{1}{2}$ x 10, the fourth $8\frac{1}{2}$ x $10\frac{1}{2}$, and the last a different color and a full $8\frac{1}{2}$ x 11). This folder contained detailed information about the program of our church. No appeal for money, attendance, evangelism, etc., but explaining the work of each organization. We made a thousand copies and got 109 people. We asked each to take ten or less to assigned homes of our membership or prospects. The idea was to get into the house, deliver the folder, and make a brief visit. It was a most successful period. Our people were happy that they had been able to do an assigned job well.

"The secret was to make a friendly visit and the folder was the entree. Even the very timid people were able to do a good job by this method. Some of the by-products were to find who had moved, who was no longer a prospect, and where there was sickness or other special need. It did much to draw our people closer to one another and to the new people. Each person had his assignment on individual cards that were filled out and returned, so we knew exactly who was contacted. About thirty of the folders were finally mailed out to complete the distribution."

48. The Second Presbyterian Church of Bloomington, Illinois, has grown from a membership of 800 to more than 2,000. The church attendance average has increased from 175 to more than 700. Several methods have been used to interest the congregation in their own services. Here are the highlights as described by the Reverend Harold R. Martin:

"Each year, usually just before Lent begins, an organization is perfected whereby some two hundred to two hundred fifty lay people call upon the rest of the congregation on a Sunday afternoon (people not at home are followed up in calls during the week). The object of the calls is to make a friendly visit, invite them to church, and ask them to pledge their faithfulness to attend one of the morning worship services each Sunday for seven weeks. There is plenty of printed material used. There are two Sunday morning services now, to accommodate the worshipers. Goals are set for attendance for Sunday school adult classes and for the school as a whole. Also attendance goals are set for youth meetings, women's meetings, and all other organizations that will be together during that period. We do not include Palm Sunday or Easter in the seven Sundays. They do not need to be promoted.

"Some fifteen years ago we organized our youth choirs. We now have six such choirs. Last year there were 272 young people from pre-school to college age who were in these choirs. This now takes the full time of a minister of music. These choirs do not sing each Sunday, though the one comprised of the oldest youths does. Two rehearsals a week are scheduled for the choirs. The youth choirs have brought parents and relatives to church who before were not interested.

"We also have some twelve prayer groups that meet each week, mostly in homes. One of the major interests for prayer is the morning worship services. When people pray for these services, they take new interest in them.

"Each year we try to bring in one or more special speakers to bring spiritual messages to our people. This constant presentation of the spiritual life keeps alive a strong undercurrent of vital spirituality in the church. This may be a small group but it has its wide influence on all."

49. Just before this book went to press we discovered a new and different way of using our faith to meet life's everyday problems. It was so helpful we could not delay announcing it until the second or third edition of *More*

Power for Your Church. So we persuaded our Farrar, Straus & Young friends (our most cooperative publishers) to add this last-minute description of a brand-new religious recording which will bring inspiration and comfort to you and many thousands. It is entitled, "How to Face the Future Unafraid."

This 45-minute record brings real inspiration through the constructive religious counsel from: Bishop G. Bromley Oxnam, Dr. Norman Vincent Peale, Dr. Ralph Sockman, and Dr. Truman B. Douglas. Lowell Thomas is the narrator, with its outstanding music by the famous Westminster Choir. The recording was directed by the radio producer George Kondolf. Every church with a record player that uses long-playing 33⅓ records should get "How to Face the Future Unafraid." It's ideal for all groups, shut-ins, sick people, etc. Your music store can get it from "Special Records Corporation."

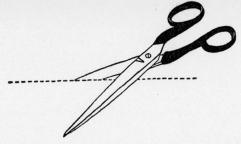

Handy Coupons For Requesting Material Described in This Book and Offered By Various Sources

....

Abingdon-Cokesbury Press, 150 Fifth Avenue, New York 11, N. Y.

Please send me a copy of "A Handbook for Evangelism" by Mr. Byron for 50¢.

Name _____

Address _____ City_____

....

American Bible Society, 450 Park Avenue, New York 22, N. Y.

Please send me copies of the material checked: Stories of the Bible ( ), Men and Women of the Bible ( ), Poetry of the Bible ( ), Wisdom From the Bible ( ), Forty Favorite Chapters ( ), Month of Devotional Readings ( ), Bible Alphabet ( ), Daily Bible Readings for Year ( )

Name _____

Address _____ City_____

....

American Booksellers Association, 724 Fifth Avenue, New
York 19, N. Y.

Please send me a copy of your basic list of religious books.

Name _____

Address _____ City_____

. . . .

Bishop Richard S. Emrich, Diocese of Detroit, 63 East
Hancock Ave., Detroit 1, Michigan.

Please send me a complete copy of "1952 Reinecker Lectures" at $1.00.

Name _____

Address _____ City_____

. . . .

Brotherhood Press, Green Farms, Connecticut

Please send me _____ copies of your Biblegraph at _____¢
each.

Name _____

Address _____ City_____

. . . .

Guideposts, Pawling, New York

Please send me _____ subscriptions to Guideposts at $1.33
per year.

Name _____

Address _____ City_____

. . . .

The Judson Press, 703 Chestnut Street, Philadelphia 3, Pa.

Please send me _____ of your Cards for Volunteering for church activities at $1.25 per hundred.

Name _____

Address _____ City_____

. . . .

Muhlenberg Press, 1228 Spruce Street, Philadelphia 7, Pa.

Please send me _____ copies of "Whatever You Do" @ 60¢ each.

Name _____

Address _____ City_____

. . . .

Religion in American Life, 287 Fourth Avenue, New York, New York

Please send me the following material specified on this coupon at costs listed on page _____.

Name _____

Address _____ City_____

. . . .

Presiding Bishop's Committee on Laymen's Work, 281 Fourth Avenue, New York 10, N. Y.

Please send me _____ copies of "I Am A Layman" at 3¢ each or $2.25 per 100.

Name _____

Address _____ City_____

. . . .

Upper Room, 1908 Grand Avenue, Nashville, Tennessee

Please send me a year's subscription to The Upper Room
at 50¢.

Name _____

Address _____ City_____

. . . .

Forward Movement Publications, 412 Sycamore Street,
Cincinnati 2, Ohio.

Please send me one year's subscription of "Forward Day by
Day" at 50¢ (five issues).

Name _____

Address _____ City_____

. . . .

To_____ Address_____

We have secured so many good ideas and usable plans from
the book MORE POWER FOR YOUR CHURCH that we
recommend it to you. It is published by Farrar, Straus &
Young, 101 Fifth Avenue, New York 3, N. Y.

Name _____

Address _____ City_____

LIST OF BOOKS ON PUBLICITY
AND RELATED SUBJECTS

Courtesy of the Public Relations Department
National Council of the Churches of Christ in the U.S.A.
297 Fourth Avenue, New York 10, New York
DONALD C. BOLLES, *Executive Director*

CHURCH PUBLIC RELATIONS
General

PUBLIC RELATIONS FOR CHURCHES—By Stewart Harral. Abing-don-Cokesbury, New York, 1945, 135 pages. These "tested methods of winning goodwill for your church" include relations with the press, church printing and other advertising media, as well as direct mail.

SUCCESSFUL CHURCH PUBLICITY—By Carl F. H. Henry. Zondervan Publishing House, Grand Rapids, Michigan, 1943. 246 pages. Traces history of religious journalism and describes techniques.

PUBLIC RELATIONS MANUAL—By Stanley Stuber. Doubleday, New York, 1951. 284 pages. A handy "how to do it" guide on all phases of church public relations by a former pastor who became a public relations director for the churches.

PUBLIC RELATONS HANDBOOK—By Philip Lesly. Prentice Hall. New York, 1950. 990 pages.

INTERPRETING THE CHURCH THROUGH PRESS AND RADIO—By R. E. Wolseley. Muhlenberg Press, Pa., 1951. 350 pages.

PUBLIC RELATIONS AND THEIR ASSOCIATION ACTIVITIES—By Clark Belden. Privately printed by the New England Gas Association, 41 Mt. Vernon St., Boston 8, Mass. Written by a noted churchman, with many trade association activities bearing directly on problems faced by churches.

YOUR PUBLIC RELATIONS—By Glenn and Denny Griswold.

395

Funk & Wagnalls, N. Y., 1948. The editors of the *Public Relations News,* America's only weekly public relations newsletter, have written a textbook on the foundations of this profession.

PRACTICAL PUBLIC RELATIONS, ITS FOUNDATIONS, DIVISIONS TOOLS AND PRACTICES—By Rex Harlow and Marvin Black. Harper & Bros., N. Y., 1947.

PUBLIC RELATIONS FOR HIGHER EDUCATION—By Stewart Harral. University of Oklahoma Press, Norman, Oklahoma, 1942.

HOW TO INTERPRET SOCIAL WELFARE—By Helen Cody and Mary Routzahn. Russell Sage Foundation, N. Y., 1947. Because social welfare organizations in many communities face the same problems as church groups, many ideas in this book can easily be transferred to church use.

HOW TO MAKE FRIENDS FOR YOUR CHURCH—By John Fortson. Association Press, 1943. The former Public Relations Director of the Federal Council of Churches gives a down-to-earth, local example, series of case studies.

KEEPING YOUR CHURCH INFORMED—By W. A. Brodie. Fleming H. Revell, Westwood, N. J., 1944.

PATTERNS OF PUBLICITY COPY—By Stewart Harral. University of Oklahoma Press, Norman, Oklahoma, 1950.

Church and Press

CHURCH AND NEWSPAPER—By William B. Norton. The Macmillan Co., 1930. 260 pages. Not new, but an admirable treatise by the former religion editor of *Chicago Tribune.* Because the author was a minister, the book is written with understanding both of church life and requirements of the newsroom.

KEEPING YOUR CHURCH IN THE NEWS—By W. Austin Brodie. Fleming H. Revell Co., New York. 125 pages. A Handbook on methods of securing publicity through numerous media, written by a newspaper man.

Church Promotional Plans

A CROWDED CHURCH—Through Modern Methods—By Eugene Dinsmore Dolloff. Fleming H. Revell Co., New York, 1946. 147 pages.

WINNING WAYS FOR WORKING CHURCHES—By Roy L. Smith. The Abingdon Press, 1932. 240 pages.

JOURNALISM IN GENERAL

THE ART OF PLAIN TALK—By Rudolf Flesch. Harper & Bros., New York, 1946. 210 pages. Tells you how to speak and write so that people understand what you mean. A popularization of Dr. Flesch's doctoral dissertation on readability.

FUNDAMENTALS OF JOURNALISM—By Ivan Benson. Prentice Hall, New York, 1937. 329 pages. A good journalism textbook.

NEWS GATHERING AND NEWS WRITING—By Robert M. Neal. Prentice Hall, New York, 1940. 566 pages. As fascinating a journalistic textbook as has ever been written and as unlike a textbook as one could imagine. The author teaches by narrative method.

NEWSPAPER EDITING, MAKE-UP AND HEADLINE—By Norman J. Radder and John E. Stempel. McGraw-Hill Book Co., New York, 1942. 398 pages. Technical and professional.

AN OUTLINE SURVEY OF JOURNALISM—By J. F. Mott and others. Barnes & Noble, Inc., New York, 1940. 381 pages (paper-bound). A valuable course in journalism, closely packed, written by professors from several schools.

PUBLICITY IN GENERAL

HOW TO GET PUBLICITY—By Milton Wright. McGraw-Hill Book Co., Inc., New York, 1935. 220 pages. Deals largely with newspapers and periodicals.

PRESS AGENTRY—By Charles Washburn, well-known press agent. National Library Press, New York, 1937. 153 pages. Experiences related center largely in promotion of theatrical productions and personalities. Includes chapter containing valuable suggestions from editors.

PRINCIPLES OF PUBLICITY—By Quiett and Casey. Appleton & Co., 1926. 400 pages. A modern and comprehensive publicity textbook. Contains a chapter on church publicity.

PUBLICITY—HOW TO PLAN, PRODUCE AND PLACE IT—By Herbert M. Baus. Harper & Bros., New York, 1942. 245 pages. A book of practical help to those who handle publicity and are interested in its technique, and for those also whose lives or business are influenced by public opinion and who wish to know more about the forces behind it.

PUBLIC RELATIONS

BLUEPRINT FOR PUBLIC RELATIONS—By Dwight Hillis Plackard & Clifton Blackmon. McGraw-Hill Book Co., Inc., New York, 1947. 355 pages. Expert public relations counsel.

PUBLIC RELATIONS—By Sills and Lesly. Richard D. Irwin, Inc., 1945. 321 pages. A thoroughly practical book containing many valuable suggestions.

YOU AND YOUR PUBLIC—By Verne Burnett. Harper & Bros., New York, 1943. 194 pages. A highly human and personal discussion of how to deal with the various publics.

RADIO AND TELEVISION

RELIGIOUS RADIO—What to do and how—By Everett C. Parker, Elinor Inman and Ross Snyder. Harper & Bros., New York, 1948. 272 pages. It is doubtful if any three people know more about religious radio than these authors. Programming motivation, script writing and production.

PROFESSIONAL RADIO WRITING—By Albert Crews. Houghton, Mifflin Co., New York, 1946. Designated primarily as a textbook for the beginner, by the program director of the Broadcasting and Film Commission of the National Council of Churches.

BROADCASTING RELIGION—Compiled by Clayton Griswold and Charles Schmitz. Published by the Broadcasting and Film Commission, National Council of Churches, 220 Fifth Ave., N. Y. 1, N. Y.

MANUAL OF GOSPEL BROADCASTING—By Wendell Loveless. Moody Press, Chicago, 1946.

RELIGIOUS BROADCASTING—By Jerry Walker. National Association of Broadcasters, Washington D. C., 1945. Pamphlet.

WINDOWS TOWARD GOD—By Charles F. Schmitz. Abingdon-Cokesbury, New York, 1950. The abc's of how to make a good devotional talk on the air.

THE TELEVISION PROGRAM—By Ed Stasheff and Rudy Bretz. A. A. Wyn, New York, 1951. 355 pages. Provides a thorough insight into developing acceptable programs for this new medium.

MISCELLANEOUS

FUNDAMENTALS OF MIMEOGRAPH STENCIL DUPLICATION—edited by Dr. Peter L. Agnew. A. B. Dick Co., Chicago, 1947. A practical manual on stencil preparation, machine operation and the uses of mimeographing.

HOW TO WRITE SIGNS, TICKETS AND POSTERS—By Hasluck. David McKay Company, Phila., Pa. 160 pages. Just what its name implies. (paper-bound)

SUCCESSFUL LETTERS FOR CHURCHES—By Stewart Harral. Abingdon-Cokesbury, 1946. 247 pages.

YOUR CREATIVE POWER, How to Use Imagination—By Alex F. Osborn. Charles Scribner's Sons, New York, 1948. 375 pages. Gives specific ways to develop your creative and imaginative powers. The various techniques explained and documented will enable you to discover, adapt and create ways of exposing more people to the influence of Christ and the services of His church. The author of "Building Up Your Congregation" is a product of Mr. Osborn's creative training.

HOW TO INCREASE CHURCH MEMBERSHIP—By W. F. Crosland. Abingdon-Cokesbury, 1950.

FLOWER ARRANGEMENTS IN THE CHURCH—By Katherine M. McClinton. Morehouse & Gorham, 1944. 105 pages.

HOW TO RAISE FUNDS BY MAIL—By Margaret M. Fellows and Stella Akulin Koenig. McGraw-Hill Book Co., Inc., New York, 1950. 342 pages. Tells you how to raise funds by effective use of letters. Contains numerous suggestions which are particularly applicable to church fund-raising.

HOW TO MAKE MORE MONEY WITH YOUR DIRECT MAIL—By Edward N. Mayer, Jr. Funk & Wagnalls Co., New York,

1950. An expert on the use of direct mail here lists tested rules for getting best results.

GO TELL THE PEOPLE—By Theodore P. Ferris. Charles Scribner's Son, New York, 1908. 116 pages. This is written by one of America's leading preachers. A helpful book for clergy and laymen alike. It is specific and thorough.

GUIDEPOSTS FOR THE CHURCH MUSICIAN—By Paul Swarm. Church Music Foundation, 1949, Decatur, Ill. An exhaustive loose-leaf manual work-book with all the information the average organist-choirmaster would want to have at his fingertips.

THE TECHNIQUE TO WIN IN FUND RAISING—By John Price Jones. Inter River Press, N. Y., 1934.

THE ART OF READABLE WRITING—By Rudolf Flesch. Harper & Bros., N. Y., 1949.

Closing Prayer

OUR DEAR HEAVENLY FATHER, bless and strengthen the hundreds of helpers who have made this book possible. Bless and strengthen the readers, each and every one of them. May each reader find new ways of serving Thee personally, and of using group plans for giving More Power to Thy Church. So may the light of our faith shine lovelier and attract more people into Thy way of life.

AMEN

Dr. Louis Finkelstein